Mud, Malaria, Guns

& Miracles

by

Graeme Robert Bell

MUD, MALARIA, GUNS AND MIRACLES
Copyright © 2020 Graeme R Bell

ISBN number 978-1-990937-68-2

Written by Graeme Robert Bell

Edited by Luisa Bell
Cover design by Luisa Bell
Photos by Luisa, Graeme and Keelan Bell

Disclaimer: The material in this book contains content/language of a mature nature.

MORE TITLES BY GRAEME BELL
We Will Be Free
Travel The Planet Overland
Overlanding the Americas "La Lucha"
Europe Overland - Seeking the Unique
www.a2aexpedition.com

FOREWORD

If it is our goal to seek an adventure and experience that which very few do, we are certainly successful. Our faith in humanity and our own capabilities only grows with each challenge we face and submit ourselves to.

If the title of this book seems dramatic, I assure you, it is not. If there are three elements of the West African overland journey which combine to create a true adventure; it is the abundance of mud, malaria and automatic weapons. Each of these elements individually presents significant challenges but combined, they represent some of the greatest challenges a modern traveller can face. The overland route from Morocco to South Africa is, arguably, the last great overland route. Yes, there are routes which are more remote, wilder, more extreme in terms of terrain, temperature and location, the Canning Stock Route in Australia and the Asian Silk Road are good examples of great overland routes, which pale in comparison to the Western Africa route where extreme elements are compounded. Morocco and Namibia (and Angola) are the delightful bookends of this journey - relatively modern, prosperous countries which suffer far less from the lack of infrastructure and resources which inhibit those countries between them. Western Africa is very, very hard work. As if the physical demands of the journey are not enough, there is the maze of bureaucracy which has to be negotiated; from expensive visas to customs regulations to the countless police and military checkpoints. There are no significant customs unions or regional visas or concessions to tourism; each country presents its own challenges in terms of bureaucracy (admittedly, some countries are worse than others). When you are exhausted and overheating, ill with a tropical virus or malaria and just trying to make it through the day, the sight of yet another roadblock can bring you to tears. But, as they say, back home in South Africa, Africa is not for sissies. You have to fight through the fog of illness, the stifling heat and occasional chaos and meet the challenge with strength, patience, respect and resilience. If you are able to achieve this, you will learn to love the journey and the people you meet along the way. If you are not able to rise to the challenge, you will be swallowed whole and spat out, defeated.

Why does the title of this book include the word "Miracles"? We encountered much along the way which impressed upon us the wonderful magic of Africa. We met hundreds of people who welcomed us with great hospitality and friendship; we encountered ancient culture and saw signs of welcome progress despite often terrible leadership, we hardly ever felt imperilled (but when we did we truly were in danger). We have a renewed sense of gratitude and wonder and a certainty that one day, in the not too distant future, West Africa will rise from the destructive legacy of colonialism and fight its way into the future - all the ingredients are there, waiting to be stirred into the pot of sustainable progress, delivering the wonderful, humble, hard-working people to a modern but purely African state of education, health and appropriate prosperity. Aside from telling our story, we study each country (as we always have) looking to connect the dots of the new Africa, experiencing that which very few have and doing so through the eyes of a family who has had the privilege of being born in Africa and having travelled, through our own resourcefulness and mostly by land, from (and returning to) the developing world to the most wealthy, industrialized nations on the planet, learning and observing and always trying to understand what separates the prosperous from the impoverished with often startling insights. We travel to learn, and Western Africa taught us more about the world we live in and about ourselves than we ever would have imagined. The word "Miracles" in the title is also a homage to the book Africa: Altered States, Ordinary Miracles by Richard Dowden. This book first read in the shadow of Kilimanjaro in 2010, has done more to educate us about the reality of modern Africa than any other book and has answered a lot of questions which we had. South Africa is not "Africa" in the true sense, though it seems that the prosperous yet tumultuous southern nation is resembling its neighbours more every day, and our upbringing was more culturally Australian than African. If you have not yet read Altered States, I suggest you do.

This book continues where the narrative of our fourth book Europe Overland - Seeking the Unique ends.

GLOSSARY

Afrikaans and Other South Africanisms (words used randomly throughout our books)

Bakkie: "pick-up", a Blue Bulls player who likes to head-butt
Banky: A measure of dagga, one plastic Standard Bank bag full
Bloody: to make the word more appealing, angry, or exaggerated, 'Bloody hell Frikkie!'
Braai: BBQ, to grill meat on a fire, usually accompanied by a cold beverage or three
Dagga: Marijuana
DHA: Department of Home Affairs in South Africa, full to the brim with poephols
Eita: A casual greeting
Frikken: A classy South African way of saying the F word
Frikkie: an unfortunately common Afrikaans name
Ja Nee: "Yes No", sarcastic 'Sure'!
Jislaaik: "Yis-like" – To express astonishment
Knobkerries: A club with a large knob one end and used to hunt or clubbing an enemy's head
Koeksisters: A plaited deep-fried doughnut, Luisa makes lekker koeksisters
Lekker: Nice, cool, the Afrikaans word for a 'sweet'
Poephol: "asshole"
Rondavel: A westernised version of the round African style hut
Rooineck: "red-neck", English speaking South African.   The name literally comes from the sunburnt necks of the British Army soldiers who wore pith helmets during the Boer Wars in South Africa and should not be confused with the American Redneck
Skrik: "Fright"
Sokkie: "sock", Social ballroom style dance with a partner
Soutpiel/soutie: "Salt-penis", British oriented person in South Africa, whose feet are grounded in both England and South Africa with his penis hanging into the salty ocean below. A great compliment.

ACKNOWLEDGEMENTS

This book is dedicated to my children, Keelan and Jessica.

You make us proud every day, you fill our hearts with joy and our lives with love and laughter. Thank you both for being such wonderful human beings and thank you for never giving up even when the road is hell.

Thank you to the many friends who have become such an essential part of our journey and who have been the greatest friends a family could wish for. Thank you all!

Thank you especially to Paul Couzis, Billy Creech, Ray Hayland, Jeff Wilner, The Overland Journal team, Bill and Kate Soucess, Morgan Kinney, Hein van der Vyver and family, John Miller, David Priddis, Mitchell Ponton, Gaffyn Price, Guy Salmon, John Chen and Sam Kirby-Fahey.

Luisa's dedication - Thank you to Christina, my mother, a woman of strength, tenacity and determination. She taught me to work hard and persevere through difficult times.

GENERAL FACTS

African travel and border crossing

- Don't pay for fixers. You will find it easier and the officials less officious when dealing with your own paperwork. Feigning stupidity and lack of understanding of the language will work in your favour.
- Try and bring along the undermentioned items. It will be requested at some point or other, if not in your possession, a bribe will be requested or a fine issued:
    - First aid kit
    - Two triangles
    - Two safety vests
    - Fire extinguisher with a valid expiry date
    - Fiche for Morocco, also used in Mauritania and the remainder of West Africa
- Apart from Morocco and Namibia, try not to drink the local water directly from the faucet alternatively use a Lifesaver jerry can or a similar filtration system
- Use iOverlander for camping spots and more useful information
- Wikiloc for trails
- You can also try Maps4Africa, but this only comes in handy when closer to Southern Africa
- Wild-camping can be done throughout most of West Africa (with caution), but we found that it's cheaper to camp in the parking lot of a motel, restaurant or compound than to drive around aimlessly searching for a clearing away from populated areas
- The ECO, a common currency to be merged with the West African CFA Franc is to be introduced to ECOWAS and is proposed to be distributed by July 2020 to the following countries:
  Benin, Burkina Faso, Guinea-Bissau, Cote d'Ivoire, Mali, Niger, Senegal and Togo, Gambia, Ghana
- Please note: All data provided in the infographic page per country is subject to change, due to country policies and/or fluctuations of the currency

TRAVEL TRIVIA

"Hodophobia" is the fear of travelling or road travelling. The word "hodo" is Greek for "travel" or "road," and "phobia" is Greek for "fear"

A "xenophobe" is someone who fears travellers from a foreign land

The word "siderodromophobia" is the fear of trains, railroads or travelling on trains. "Sidero" is Greek for "iron" or "things made of iron," and "dromo" is Greek for "racecourse"

Ever heard of the DRD4-7R gene or "the wanderlust gene"? You may have inherited this gene which gives you the desire to travel with increased levels of curiosity and restlessness

Its always been said that travel will test a relationship and couples who travel together generally have a stronger bond when they need to trust each other in new environments with difficult circumstances

The German word "fernweh" means "far sickness," or an intense urge to travel

"Travel is fatal to prejudice, bigotry, and narrow mindedness, and many of our people need it sorely on these accounts" *Mark Twain*

MOROCCO

Morocco is located in the Northwest of the African continent with an area of 710,850km². It is slightly larger than the State of California. The Moroccan coastline reaches from the Atlantic Ocean, past the Strait of Gibraltar and into the Mediterranean Sea. It is bordered by Spain and Algeria is situated to the east and the disputed Western Sahara to the south. Since Morocco controls Western Sahara, its *de facto* southern boundary is with Mauritania.

1 DIRHAM (MAD) = EU0.092 / USD0.10
The Euro and Dollar can be traded at banks or the border at the time of arrival. "Cash is King" in Africa

American, British, Canadians and most European citizens do not require a visa to enter for a period of three months. All other nationalities are to apply abroad at their nearest Consulate and pay the visa fee of approximately 30EU/35USD.
If you intend on staying for a full period of six months, your visa can be extended by attending the local police station. Just ensure that you purchase six-months insurance at the time of entry, as this may be more problematic to obtain than the visa extension

Unleaded = 1EU/1.13USD per litre
Diesel = EU0.92/USD1.06 per litre
It is 30% cheaper in Western Sahara but also more difficult to source further South, fill up when you can

Maroc Telecom
Orange
Both telecom service providers have surprisingly great reception   across the whole country

Morocco is a country with rich culture and civilisation. Throughout Moroccan history, it has become home to people of the East (Phoenicians, Jews and Arabs), South (Sub-Saharan Africans) and North (Romans, Andalusians). These civilisations have each contributed to Moroccan culture, population, architecture and society. 99% of Moroccans practice Islam (majority Sunni).

Your left-hand should not be used for eating or greeting (bums are wiped with the left hand) / Friday is a Holy Day / Woman are to wear modest clothing / Do not show the soles of your feet

You should purchase insurance when you arrive at the border. It will be an approximate EU90 for three months cover for a 4x4/camper van

Police = 190
Ambulance = 150
Tourist Police = 0524384601

Passport with visa (if required)
Vehicle title papers

Arabic, Berber and French
Labass – How are you?
As-salaam Alaykum – Hello
Respond with - Wa Alaykum As-salaam

Shukran – Thank you	Beslama – Good bye
Afek – Please	Iyah – Yes
Lla – No	Kayen – Do you have?

Couscous - Steamed balls of crushed durum wheat semolina that is traditionally served with a stew spooned on top
Tagine - Is a cone-shaped cooking vessel traditionally used in Morocco. Most tagine recipes layer aromatics, meat, and vegetables, along with spices, oil, and water
Bissara or Harira - Thick Pava /Lentil soup served with a generous dollop of Olive Oil
Morocco is not dry, but liquor is only available at certain stores, and the liquor store is usually underground
Mint tea - Traditional mint tea poured from above, served with copious amounts of sugar

Zagora - A town in the South East of Morocco which follows the Draa river valley with twists and turns
Chefchaouen, "The Blue City", nestled in foothills of Rif Mountains and 20miles from the Med coast
Fes - A historical medina and world-famous tannery
Ifrane - a little Switzerland

Marrakesh - A city with sandstone buildings, minarets, also known as the Red City with famous souks and the Jemaa El-Fnaa square

Casablanca - A city with a blend of European deco art and Moorish style. The famous Hassan II Mosque stands partly over the ocean

Meknes - A former Imperial City with a classic Medina and the shrine of Moulay Ismail with Roman ruins, Volubilis nearby

Merzouga - Lies on the edge of Erg Chebbi dunes that reach 160 metres and just 30 km from the Algerian border

Ouarzazate - A town where famous movies are made but also close to Todra Gorge

Summer - June to August - Low 16C/64F and a High of 28C/82F

Winter - Dec to February - Low 8C/46F and a High of 20C/68F

The weather in Morocco is pleasant all year round however the desert can get hot during the day and freezing cold at night

The Arabic name for Morocco, al-Magrib al-Aqsa, means "the extreme west" which attests to Morocco being the westernmost country in the Arab world

Morocco is one of the largest producers of hashish in the world

A widow in Morocco will wear white for 40 days after the death of her husband

The liver is considered the symbol of love in Morocco

Merieme Chadid, born in Casablanca in 1969 was the first Moroccan woman to travel to the South Pole

GRAEME BELL

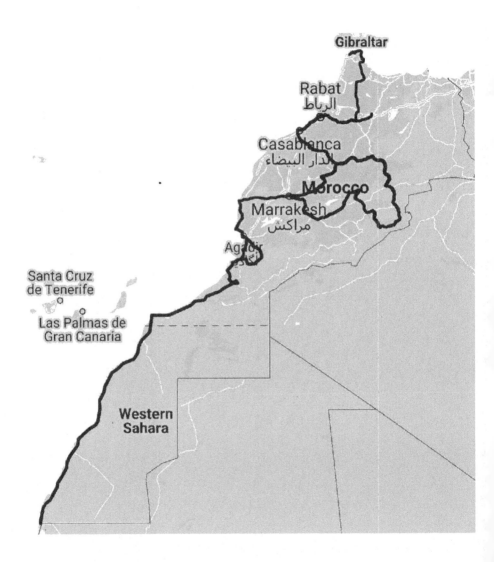

1

Morocco and our return to Africa!

There is something unique about Morocco, something magical and ancient. Turkey is similar, and both countries offer an experience so enchanting, and at times intoxicating, a traveller is drawn back, long after they have left. My dreams are often Moroccan.

On a sparkling morning, we left the campsite above Chefchaouen. This enchanting blue city had captivated us entirely and made our way towards the Rif mountain trail after filling the gas tank and buying supplies. Rain began to fall as we climbed, the trail deteriorating rapidly and offering no opportunity for return. But, together with our children, Keelan and Jessica, we had circumnavigated South America and driven to Alaska and lived in the remote San Pedro de Martir mountains in Mexico, we have experience. And we were not alone. Back in the camp, we had made friends with a couple of Austrians, one driving a Land Rover Defender and the other a Toyota Hilux. We had told them that we were going to attempt the trail and they decided to tackle it as well. The next day, after filling up with fuel in the city, we by chance caught up with them as they started the trail and followed them, even though Luisa's navigator showed that we should take another route.

After a few hours on the trail, our Land Rover crested the summit of the Rif mountains trail through the Parc National Talassemtane, and we drew a gasp of surprise and relief. The clouds parted and below us lay a valley as beautiful as any we had seen during our six-years travelling the globe. For four hours we had driven hard up the side of the mountain, negotiating endless switchbacks, relying on the power and grip of the Defender to ascend tracks which are more suited to goats and donkeys than man-made machines. We had taken a wrong turn and the trail which was supposed to be a moderate 80 km ramble, had become a test of will and ability - reaching the summit was half the battle fought, now we needed only to return to civilisation.

The Rif mountain range is home to splendid peaks, pine forest and sparkling clear spring water. It is also the origin of the vast majority of Moroccan hashish, known locally as Keif. Shortly after the summit, we experienced a debilitating mechanical failure and four days after beginning the trail; we were still deep within the bowels of the mountain. Sometimes not all goes to plan; even the most experienced travellers can make terrible mistakes.

But first, let's start the story where the last book left off...

A few short weeks before our adventure in the Rif mountains, we had left beloved Portugal and travelled to Spain where we would spend an evening with my wonderful step-sister, Nadine and her husband Jannie before boarding the ferry to Morocco. They live in the shadow of Gibraltar and over a delicious Indian dinner, explained that their beachfront apartment not only offered great views but also provided a unique vantage point over the daily battle between Moroccan drug dealers and Spanish police. The Moroccans use small, fast speed boats to cross the Strait of Gibraltar, carrying a precious cargo of sweet hashish and marijuana and sometimes deadly heroin or cocaine. That night we witnessed Moroccan speed boats approaching the shore, looking to dump their valuable cargo on the beach where men dressed in black waited in the shadows to retrieve the boxes and disappear into the dark, crumbling city on motorcycles. A Guardia Civil or coast guard gunboat patrols the shore, like an elephant chasing a rabbit, a whale after a dolphin, large spotlights illuminating the dark water and the beach. Nadine and Jannie often heard gunshots and observed the Spanish police chasing smugglers along the beachfront.

That night was cool and wet. Luisa and I slept in the Land Rover while the children enjoyed the warm comfort of my sisters home. We had not seen Nadine and Jannie since a traumatic night in 1998 when my father had left South Africa to start a new life in the United Kingdom with Nadine's Zimbabwean mother. It had been an emotional evening as I tried in vain to close a chapter of my life and finally confront my father who had essentially abandoned my brother, sister and I when he had divorced my mother fifteen years earlier. My father was a stubborn man, egotistical and fragile. He refused any responsibility for his actions and the effects those actions had had on our lives, he dismissed my reality, and that was to be the last meal we ever shared. I had always liked Nadine, despite the inherent rivalry of step-siblings and that evening together in La Linea de la Concepcion was bitter-sweet. I regretted not being a better brother and lamented the 20 years of friendship which could have been. Nadine offered me a gift as we sat in her lounge, catching up. From a corner, she produced my fathers old, coveted guitar, the neck worn from many hours of service, his scent on the body, the pick-guard lined with a million slips. I asked kind, sweet Nadine if she would hold onto the guitar for me, Western Africa was no place for a large, fragile family heirloom.

That fresh, wet morning, we rushed to the port of Algeciras, stopping to buy wine and beer as we had heard that alcohol is expensive and rare in Morocco. Boarding the ferry was a slightly complicated affair, and after negotiating a confusing maze of one-way streets, we found ourselves in a queue of vehicles waiting to be processed out of Europe. I drove the Defender onto the ferry while Luisa and the kids embarked on foot, meeting me in the cargo area before locking up the camper and joining the majority Moroccan passengers to climb the stairs to the seating area where we queued to have our passports processed by the friendly Moroccan immigration authorities. We were the only "Europeans" on the ferry and two men, tall and dressed in immaculate black and white tawb robes and long beards glared at us. These men were not Moroccan, they seemed quite different from the other passengers and had to have their green passports processed, a process which seemed to take longer than ours and which included many more questions. Luisa and I walked onto the deck and watched Europe slip away. We had the opportunity to travel, work and live in Europe, we had made many friends, and we had had wonderful adventures, while so many were giving everything they had to get into Europe, we were sailing away; away from security and safety, away from prosperity and opportunity, away from our ancestral home, away and into the unknown. We both shed a tear; my tears were invisible and incredibly manly, muscular tears. Luisa blubbed like a baby.

We arrived in Tangier Med port late on a Sunday afternoon in late November 2018 and set foot, once again, on African soil. After so many years (six), we eventually returned to the continent of our birth, excited, nervous, relieved. The sun shone warmly as we drove out of the ferry, the last vehicle to disembark. The port was enjoying a Sunday afternoon lull, and we asked an amicable, meticulously dressed policeman where to find the exit, customs and immigration. He directed us, and we arrived at the white, modern immigration booths where a grumpy woman barked a cough into Luisa's questioning face. "Park there, wait". Only two other vehicles were being processed - a black Audi with Gibraltar plates, an impatient driver and stoic blonde passenger, and a white Toyota Corolla driven by the glaring, bearded, tawb wearing men who were engaged in a screaming match with the border officials, who were insisting on a complete strip search of the vehicle. The larger of the two men, dressed in shining white with an ink-black beard swaying a foot beneath his screaming chin, regarded the border officials with contempt, how dare they search him, how *dare* they? The louder he protested, the more aggressive and suspicious the border guards became. The immigration official assisting us, politely asked for our immigration forms, if we had a drone (which are illegal in Morocco) and for us to wait a few moments. We waited quietly and watched the tall, bearded, tawb'd man perform an impressive fit of anger. How *DARE* they? I could imagine him, the firstborn of a relatively wealthy family, wedged in the shopping cart of an air-conditioned supermarket staffed by foreigners, screaming at his nanny for another Kinder Joy, slapping his bare, chubby cheeks and pulling his hair, "I will make myself *bleed*, Kiiiiiinnnnder Joy!".

Within fifteen minutes, our documents were processed, no they did not need to search the vehicle, and we drove out of the impressive harbour leaving behind the ongoing strip search and the new port. Luisa followed our iOverlander app to a small parking area opposite the port and above Ksar es-Seghir beach.

Men, many dressed in the traditional hooded djellaba, wandered the road leading to a small fishing port, the harbour controlled by a man and a boom. The man dressed in an immaculate and impressive uniform, the boom itself not worth mentioning. The policeman assured us that we could spend the night in the parking area overlooking the beach, and we found a level area to park, watched the sunset and admired the lights of Tangier Med port. The next morning, Keelan and I took a walk to the market to buy bread, intoxicated by the sights and sounds of a world within view of modern Europe but so different as to be on another planet. We had a handful of Dirham with which to purchase food but no real idea how much we should pay for a bag of oranges, a loaf of bread or a bottle of cold drink. Our large, pale bodies stood out against the backdrop of bustling locals, some of whom called to us in German or

French. I have a trick to establish prices when first buying commodities in a new country - I pay what I think the product is worth. At a bread stall, one of many selling the same bread, I asked a woman deep in conversation for six-round khubz bread. I paid the equivalent of one Euro in coins which the woman accepted, and without counting, threw into a basket full of change. She knew the weight of the transaction. We bought a bag of oranges using the same method but received change, a two-litre bottle of Coca-Cola cost the equivalent of two bags of oranges or 24 loaves of khubz bread. We returned to Luisa and Jessica parked above the littered beach and had lunch before attending to some small repairs on the Land Rover. We felt incredibly safe, the local fishermen interested but, mostly, keeping a respectful distance from us. I usually would not leave the girls alone, but the boom operating policeman was nearby, and we had a good instinct. We decided to stay another night while Luisa took advantage of the European data reaching across from Spain, and we prepared our route. A trucker working on his vehicle made an omelette and invited Keelan and me to eat with him from a large wok and to drink hot tea. We sat together with five men in a circle around the wok, scooping bread with our hands, having a conversation in Spanish. We would soon learn that many Moroccans speak a variety of languages and many in the tourist areas will speak English, French, Spanish, Dutch, German and perhaps Italian.

An hour before sunset, a large blue Ford Transit van entered the parking area and parked facing us, parallel to the sea. Dot Bekker is a Zimbabwean who had spent many years living in Europe, and she was preparing to drive the West Coast of Africa back to her native land. We joined her for a glass of wine (Dot had suffered a six-hour process at Tangier Med port as opposed to our fifteen minutes), to watch the sunset and hear her story. Dot is one of a group of women who have set off into the world to break down boundaries and misconceptions, a woman in every sense but determined to prove to herself and the world that she can achieve the seemingly impossible. In 2018/2019 she was one of a trio of women independently crossing Africa. Blanca, 62, Spanish born, British resident, cycling across West Africa and Julia Albu, a South African octogenarian who drove the relatively "easy" route from Cape Town to Cairo in a 20-year old Toyota Conquest. These women are pioneers and proof that Africa is inhabited mostly by wonderful people, people who respect the courage and their elders, and evidence perhaps that Africa itself has turned a corner after years of turmoil and conflict. But, it is still Africa and must be approached with respect. We shared with Dot, our experiences and knowledge learned on four continents, reiterating the golden rules of the road and made plans to meet up as we travelled South independently. There would be times on the West African journey when travellers would need to the convoy and work together through the logistical maze of red tape and the most dangerous countries along the route. Perhaps we might need each other in future.

We went our separate ways the next morning, Dot heading South and us heading along the coast to the Spanish enclave of Ceuta, pronounced "soota" (remind the Spanish of Ceuta next time they tell you that the UK should hand over Gibraltar) and down towards Tetouan where we enjoyed a few days in a campsite celebrating Luisa's birthday. It seemed like a decade since she had enjoyed her 40th birthday in that campsite on the Mexican / US border and I like to joke that every year I take her to a new country as a present. The climate was cool and wet, and Keelan and I would take frequent walks to the store, or the beach to photograph the wide promenade, the impressive white apartment blocks and the people who idly enjoyed an afternoon walk along the paved promenade despite the dark skies and cool wind.

Luisa located a Carrefour supermarket in Tetouan, and after stocking up we made our way inland to the Blue City of Chefchaouen, driving two hours to a city which clings to the slopes of the Rif mountain range, surrounded by clear blue skies. The navigator app chose the most complicated route up to the campsite Azilan which is perched above the city, bordered by empty municipal swimming pools, a soccer field, a large pond and the mountain forest. The clutch slipped as we drove up winding steep roads through the city until I engaged low range and we arrived at the blue gates of the campsite and checked in. Some people love Azilan campsite; some people loathe it. We loved it. Yes, the camp area is essentially either a large untarred, uneven parking lot or slim sites between trees; yes the showers are cold except for the one hot shower which you have to pay for and is always occupied. And yes, there are men in leather jackets who stand outside the camp and try and sell you hashish, and yes, it is a long walk down to the city and back up. No, the toilets are not pristine, and you often have to use a squat toilet. But. The view over the town and valley is fantastic, the cold water is fresh and clean from a mountain spring, the staff are friendly if you are and the sky is deep blue, there is a lot of timber lying around to be cut and used for campfires, there is usually a fantastic mix of campers - old French and German Tupperware tourists, hardcore overlanders and young hippies and punks living in ancient vans and trucks, getting stoned all day and out-cooling each other.

We explored the city, did the tourist thing for a few days and then set off onto that trail with which I began this story. Little did we know what adventures lay ahead.

It was the 29th of November 2018, and with the worst of the trail behind us, we relaxed, here and there we spotted small settlements, usually a cluster of homes and barns. We were now traversing the valley, the clouds began to drift away, the track improved and occasionally we would encounter other 4x4's and trucks, dark men in dark jackets behind the wheel. Luisa suggested that we look for a level place to camp, the Rif is notorious, but we still had many kilometres to travel before we would return to Camping Azilan above Chefchaouen. I steered the Defender around a switchback, down into a drift and gently accelerated to climb yet another hill. A loud BANG erupted from the front of the engine, and the vehicle lost all drive. "Damn, the clutch has gone!". This was my first thought, but there might have been another, less dramatic fault. With no other option available, I rolled the Land Rover back down the hill and steered her onto a track beside the road. I engaged the gears and accelerated. Nothing. Tried to reverse further. No drive. The Austrians we had been convoying with, were mere seconds ahead of us when we suffered the breakdown and, if I know anything about Defender drivers, it is that we don't leave each other behind. Ever. Especially not in the remote mountains in a foreign country. We waited for five minutes. "I don't think they are going to come back for us". They did not return.

It is at times like this that a man has to remain calm for his composure prevents panic if I panic we all panic, and that helps no-one. A dark invisible force twisted my stomach and clenched my heart, but I turned to Luisa, composed, "Relax, we will be fine, let's just sort this out". By some miracle, the vehicle had traversed intense terrain but had chosen to break down near a loggers camp (a ramshackle collection of plastic tents), a level section of track and a clear spring which burbled out of the side of the mountain in the shadow of the forest. We could only imagine the cave system which existed beneath our feet. With our initial mechanical diagnosis providing no solution, we had no option but to set up camp for the evening; the sun was setting; we needed to feed the kids and prepare for a bush repair. A truck pulled up next to the Land Rover, the driver opening his window to allow a billow of

21

sweet-scented smoke to escape. He smiled at me crookedly. "OK?" "Yes, no problem, shukran". We are self-reliant after all, we try to take care of our own problems, and we were not comfortable with engaging in an interaction which had no clear outcome. The sunset and a pick-up pulled up; a young, weathered man stepped out. He spoke English and offered assistance, perhaps he could have a mechanic come to us from the nearby large village of Bab Taza? He was surprised when we declined the offer but reassured us that we were safe, "No problem here, but there", he pointed back to the mountain we had earlier crossed, "There, there are problems". We were unsure if he was referring to the landscape, the drug trade, or both.

Over the following days, we worked tirelessly to diagnose and repair our four-wheeled home. To our great surprise, we found that if we trekked four kilometres to the edge of a deep and vast valley, we could find an intermittent mobile internet connection and reached out to our international friends for advice. We then returned to the truck, removed prop shafts and inspection plates, gear selectors, switches - we no longer carry a spare clutch, and it was likely that there may be another, a simpler fault which we could bush repair, or at least get the Land Rover moving again. All we needed was one working gear (preferably third, low range) and we could drive back to Chefchaouen.

Our convoy friends did not return over the next few days, and the only other foreigners we encountered were a couple on dirt bikes who were exploring the mountains. They passed us, and Luisa and Keelan ran out into the road to wave them down, too late as they had already turned the corner at the top of our hill. Damn. A few minutes later we heard the rumble of motorbike engines, and the two returned. A man and a woman. She removed her helmet to reveal a lovely brunette, her companion, a man with a tiny Beetlejuice head, was not her partner, she quickly informed us. We spoke for a while and told them our story, and after a while they set off, after I took them on a tour of our surroundings, showing off my burbling spring and describing the beauty of the stars at night. Jurga, the lady, took our details and we asked her to contact us and possibly ask around for a tow-truck when she returned to town when we eventually admitted defeat.

Something incredible happened while we were stranded - we fell in love with the mountains and her people. Every day a small group of women would climb up the mountain to collect wood. We were an endless source of amusement and fascination for them. They politely refused to be photographed but produced old smartphones to take selfies with Luisa who handed them snacks, women's hygiene products, body cream, toothpaste and fruit until I begged her to stop handing out our supplies. The women (who dressed in traditional clothing and other than the smartphones, lived like their people had for centuries), were humble and discreet when a male appeared but became cheerful and chatty when alone with us. My tall blonde son reduced the group to giggles and my daughter, with her modern clothing and long blonde hair, inspired awe. The women ranged in age from teenage to ancient and seemed completely at ease with each other and their environment, which itself was awesome in the true sense of the word. Above us stood a peak bearing a forest of Atlas cedar and Moroccan fir which shimmered in the morning sun, below us the spring gushed from the network of caves deep below, providing us with an endless supply of delicious water for drinking, cooking and cleaning. The nights were cool, a billion stars sparkling in the crisp sky as we sat around the fire ring, warming our bodies, cooking our food and discussing our plans and options to get the Landy moving again.

During the day we kept Jessica inside the vehicle, unwilling to attract attention to her, the small group of loggers camped nearby paid little attention to us, and we wanted to keep it that way. By the third evening we were known throughout the region, every pick-up and truck which passed (one every few hours) would hoot a greeting. As we slept, our dreams were filled with mythical creatures and vivid encounters, as if visited by ancient spirits. I was visited by nymphs who seduced me in high definition, the kind of dream which I had not had since I was fourteen. The morning sun warmed us slowly.

Eventually, I admitted defeat. We had always been able to recover ourselves and the vehicle but, without the necessary parts, the vehicle was crippled. I asked Mohamed, the head logger if he could tow us the thirty kilometres down the mountain to Bab Taza and offered him all the money in my wallet. He accepted 1000 Dirham (approximately $120.00), and we strapped the stricken Land Rover to the tractor. It took four hours to descend the Route de Tisemlale to the town. The Defenders engine started and ran perfectly which meant, at least, that we had power steering and brakes, but no engine breaking. I did my best to ensure that the tow strap remained taut because as soon as it was allowed to go slack, the Defender ran out of momentum, the tractor would amble forward and the tow line would snap-tight, yanking on the chassis with such force that our heads snapped back. The Rif mountains are spectacular and the forests thick, tall, old and beautiful. Had the situation not been so stressful we would have enjoyed the drive, often stopping to enjoy the breeze brushing through the forest, the burble of creeks and bird song filling the air, the skies a deep, vibrant blue, the creamy soil caramel, the stone grey. This is a paradise known by very few, and we encourage you to drive the trail, you may find your own adventure, but hopefully not as adventurous as our experience had been.

We were forced to stop beside a river to let the brakes cool. A recovery truck approached us and stopped, the driver looking perplexed and disappointed. He chatted to Mohamed for a few moments, and we established that the truck was heading up the mountain to recover us - they had no doubt heard of the family stuck at the top of the mountain and had come to rescue us. Had we not already found a way back to the valley, I would have been very grateful for their effort and my wallet would have baulked, no doubt. Looking back, it might have been Jurga, the girl on the motorbike who had found us in the mountains, who had sent the tow truck, but the driver did not mention her at all. Perhaps it would have been wise to load the Land Rover onto that recovery truck then but we had already paid for the tow, and we were hoping to find a place to repair the Landy in Bab Taza, which was not too far away. It is also very difficult to make on the spot decisions when you have a limited budget and knowledge of what awaits you, and we often struggle with indecisiveness. The last few kilometres into Bab Taza were nerve-racking as we were dragged down the side of a beautiful mountain and eventually through crowded streets, we recognised some of the men who passed us daily up in the mountains, and they waved, smiling, happy that we were back in the real world. Mohamed hauled the Land Rover onto the N2 and stopped at a crowded gas station; the attendants waved him on, they had no doubt had experiences with stricken overlanders in the past and found them to be unprofitable. Back on the N2, surrounded by fast-moving traffic, Mohammed dragged us around a traffic circle and deposited us at a large gas station on the R419, a back road which eventually led to Fez.

The gas station was large with a forecourt of twelve pumps, a restaurant, general dealer, mechanic and spare parts store. I realised, however, that we were not in a good situation for a repair. There are hundreds of Land Rover Defenders in the Rif area, but they are mostly Tdi's which have a different clutch to our Td5 motor. We would need to get a clutch from

Casablanca or Marrakesh. Our friends Bearmach told us that they could have a new clutch for us in a couple of days (we were able to communicate via email once in Bab Taza, and Luisa had been working on a solution as soon as the bars appeared on her phone). The area where we parked was uneven, and there was a lot of traffic and interest in us. I had to make a call. We had not had a shower in a week; we were low on provisions and morale, I knew that the replacement clutch would need at least a week to source, arrive and install and I knew that the family would be miserable, stuck in a bustling gas station. We needed to get back to Camping Azilan in Chefchaouen; we needed to be comfortable, with access to ablutions, electricity, wifi and privacy. My family had worked hard to recover us and not once had we become despondent or disgruntled, we had worked together perfectly as a team, and I owed them the best circumstances we could afford. It would not do to use every ounce of patience or strength for the sake of a low-cost repair; morale is incredibly important in a family who travels like we do, I had to do my best to ensure that their strength was rewarded and that they trusted that I would always find the best situation for them.

A kind and friendly gas station attendant came over to us to offer assistance. Luisa asked him whether he knew of a truck which could tow or carry our Defender back to Chefchaouen. "Sure", he said and made a few phone calls. An hour later, a flatbed tow truck arrived. The driver and assistant both had the look of men who had hashish for breakfast, lunch and dinner. The truck seemed too small to carry the large Defender.

"Are you sure that truck is big enough?"
"Yes, sure, no problem"
I was not so sure.

We negotiated the fee and settled on the equivalent of Euro 50 for the 26 km drive, a price which we considered very reasonable. While I sat in the driver's seat with Jessica behind me in the camper, the truck began to winch the Land Rover onto the platform. Luisa, who does not do well in high pressure "life or death" situations, began shouting instructions. I could see very little from my perch, but she told me later that the front of the little tow truck had begun to lift off the ground. After much shouting and direction giving and performance, the Land Rover eventually reached the winch bulkhead of the truck and the driver set about levelling the load and then strapping the Defender onto the platform. We were anxious, tired, dirty, hungry, thirsty and mentally sapped by the entire experience of the last days. Keelan climbed into the cab of the tow truck, Luisa hoisted herself into the passenger seat beside me, and the tow truck set off, back to the traffic circle which led onto the N2 and our destination, Chefchoauen. The Land Rover rocked on the back of the truck; instinctively I tried to steer, I tried to brake but, of course, had no control. The road to Chefchaouen is winding and narrow, at every curve the Land Rover would tip to the side, sending Luisa into a spasm of screams, which made Jessica laugh her wicked little laugh reserved for people falling downstairs, or bumping their heads.

The louder Luisa screamed, the more Jessica laughed while I sat there, mouth as dry as the Sahara, pleading with Luisa to get a grip because her screams were causing me to stress and sweat. The driver stopped on the side of the road; we were shouting at him, "take it easy, man!". The co-driver tightened the straps, and I evicted Luisa, sending her to sit up front in the tow truck, my nerves couldn't take much more of her panic, Jessie was still laughing as Luisa nervously climbed out of the Landy, trembling. (For those of you who would like to witness this farce, have a look at the video on our YouTube channel - A2A Expedition). Jessica and I travelled in silence and the truck swayed along the route, 26 km feeling like 100. To further complicate our mission, we had to stop in Chefchaouen to draw cash to pay for the recovery truck and *then* had still to make it up the steep hills and narrow streets to our eventual destination above the city.

Some of you may wonder why I am grey at the age of 44; well, it is days like these which age a man prematurely. If the Land Rover fell off the truck, or the truck toppled, lost its brakes or fell off a cliff... All of these scenarios were rotating through my mind, spinning like a tornado of doubt. We made it to Chefchaouen! The first ATM was out of order, unblocking the busy road we drove further, the second ATM refused to dispense cash, we drove to a third which eventually dispensed a handful of Dirham. Now to negotiate the narrow city streets and climb up, up, up to the campsite. The driver took a wrong turn, and we found ourselves in a narrow alley. Reverse, try again, listen to Luisa, dammit. Luisa knew the best route up, but some men find it difficult to listen to a woman, our driver was one of these men. Eventually, our driver listened and followed the longer, but gentler route around and up. We arrived at the camp, the truck drove in and reversed to deposit us next to stairs leading to the forest camp area, the recovery men set about lowering the Landy, the French and German campers paused lunch and drinking wine to watch the fiasco unfold. Staggering, the Land Rover rolled backwards off the flatbed ramp and came to rest, at a slight angle on the unlevel unpaved surface which was 50 m wide and 400m long, bordered by a grass bank facing the city and a whitewashed retaining wall and beyond that a cool forest. The family stopped shouting at each other and exhaled a communal sigh of relief. We had made it! That morning we had been high up in the mountains dreading the day ahead but thanks to good decision making, we had made it back to the camp above the blue city, safe, secure, elevated and very, very thirsty.

We celebrated our victory with hot showers and a cold beer. A Swiss traveller told us that we were fortunate, that a Moroccan friend had told him that the Rif takes lives and the drug traders have been known to murder entire families. I shuddered, but we had treated the people of the mountains with great respect, and I believe that they had learned to respect us and they protected us. We had made a mistake, but we also had an incredible adventure!

The next morning a German gentleman came over to have a look at the Defender, I explained to him the symptoms of the failure, he had a feel around and delivered a diagnosis. Kupplung. Clutch. He handed me a business card, he ran three immaculate workshops in Germany, specialising in kupplung. That sealed it. We spoke to our friends Bearmach, and they dispatched a clutch for us, it arrived in Casablanca two days later, and we settled in to wait for it to clear customs, Luisa hassling DHL daily and receiving a perpetually non-committal response - maybe tomorrow.

The first week the weather was cold and wet, but every day after that we awoke to blue skies and warm sun. We settled into a routine - Keelan and I would walk down to the city along a steep, rocky path which delivered us directly into the market place and an arched entrance to the medina, above the Kasbah. We would enjoy a fruit smoothie and walked through the winding pale blue alleys of the medina to emerge in the centre of town. Turning left we would buy supplies from a stall which consistently charged us local prices. We would backtrack and head past the fish market near Plaza Ronda and down to Avenue Hassan II where we had found a butchery serving lamb and spicy sausage, a bakery and a wholesaler. Besides the fish market, a grocer called Hassan would sell us bags of the most delicious oranges and vegetables. The locals soon learned our names and attempted to teach us Darija, Moroccan Arabic. After buying a few packets of crispy hot chips at Chez Aziz, we would catch a taxi back up to the camp. Sometimes Keelan refused to take the taxi, choosing instead to climb the hill back to the camp, carrying the heaviest shopping bags, dressed in his uniform of billowing hippy pants and Expedition Portal T-Shirt. He had lost a large amount of weight since his stay at the commune in Germany and was determined to keep the weight off. I also suspect that he enjoyed a bit of solitude, time to himself away from the ever-present family. Upon returning to the camp, Luisa would rifle through the shopping bags, and I would take my Granfors Bruks axe, Brazilian Tramontina machete and a thick canvas tow strap to the steep bank across the paved parking area and chop firewood from felled trees. Keelan would join me, and we chopped wood and kindling for the campfire which we had established behind the Land Rover, above the whitewashed retaining wall. Wrapping the wood with the tow strap, Keelan would haul the wood up the steep bank while I collected pine cones to start the fire. Our neighbours those first weeks were mostly German, young, rough around the edge travellers who smoked hashish all day long, strummed guitars and cooked vegetables. One young couple, punks with dreadlocks, had set up a camp in their ancient Fiat camper. Their adult bitch had nine puppies which Jessica would play with and the punks swapped with locals for food and hashish. I asked them why they had not sterilised the bitch, and their response was that she had the *right* to experience the joys of motherhood. And the puppies had the right to grow old chained in a vegetable garden or marijuana field if they were lucky?

A French couple arrived and befriended the German punks. Mr French had thinning hair and deadlocks to his waist, his partner petite - no larger than an average ten-year-old girl. They had a large dog which they struggled to control, and Mr French would lose his cool whenever the dog disobeyed. Hey, take it for a walk. Another Frenchman, who looked like Jesus and would not be out of place in a Wes Anderson movie, wandered from hippy vehicle to hippy vehicle, dressed in a thobe robe and smoking endless joints. He had the most wonderful sense of humour and no doubt came from a good family. Whenever French Jesus walked behind the Land Rover, he would open and close an imaginary gate, his mischievous eyes sparkling. Behind our vehicle, on the raised grassy camp area lived Sabine - a small French woman permanently shrouded in a haze of sweet smoke, her camp area was littered with the knick-knacks of someone who lives in a small green tent for five months of the year - a small fire, bottles, plastic bags, an old rug, coat hangers, a blackened kettle and pot, clothing drying on plastic chairs, shoes, a comb, twigs and pine cones. She wore curly black hair and oversized sunglasses, vaguely bohemian clothing and a skew smile. Her Moroccan husband had been murdered by the right-wing in France, and she chose to spend her winters in Camping Azilan, smoking hash, eating bread and oranges and talking to herself and her poodle who befriended our family and no-one else. A New Age "hand" tattoo artist arrived in a large brown Mercedes truck. He was Welsh, dread-locked, charming and accompanied by a slim, beautiful French girl. An Australian surfer couple arrived in a white van and set up camp next to the punks; a cloud hung over that section of the camp. Hashish is ridiculously cheap in Chefchouen; Euro 10 will buy you a small, clumpy block and no desire to move. A tall, thin, black-clad German family arrived two weeks in. They must have been direct descendants of count Dracula himself and the three of them (the son was twenty and 6'8") hotboxed in their van all day and all night. A balding guitarist parked his white van at the edge of the grass bank and moved it to follow the sun. He sat on the van sill all day, playing the guitar quietly, speaking to no-one, smiling. Young French driving articulated trucks with containers fashioned into homes with wood-burning stoves, fold-out windows and patios, motorbikes, packs of dogs and wild women arrived sporadically. They camped far from everyone else and encouraged no interaction at all. They were the free French, and they cared only for their tribe. Single Swiss and German girls travelled together in their vans, hiding their natural beauty behind piercings and bad, dyed haircuts and baggy clothing. They all dreamed of travelling forever.

But, the New Age Hippy Punks and vampires were in the minority. Daily convoys of Tupperware tourists would arrive. French and German mostly. They parked their Fiat campers in a row and set up long white-clothed tables in the sunshine. Occasionally some would sneak off to try the local hashish, but mostly they sat in groups enjoying the sun (no matter how hot the day was they would sit in direct sunlight) eating food brought from home and quietly drinking beer, wine, gin, whisky, bedtime. Usually, these convoys stayed only a night or two, long enough to visit the blue city below, purchase some curios and suffer sunburn. Some days there were no white convoys, and other days the camp was packed. They made sure to park far from the New Age Hippy Punks, and our vehicle formed a barrier between the high unwashed and the pickled pensioners. Oh, and if a convoy of young

Italians park beside you, expect drama. Mama yells at her children all day; papa wanders off with his friend to smoke pot, mama screams at papa for smoking pot, papa yells back and pours wine, mama drinks wine and yells that papa shouldn't drink the wine, the wine kicks in and mama laughs, shouts at the children how much she loves them, eat your pasta, go to sleep, the kids brawl over a smartphone, mama shrieks melodically, "why are you so stupid?". They wash dishes over your camping chairs, hang their washing over your camp and spend an hour in the only hot shower until all the gas is finished. Yes, they are rowdy, but also wonderful, curious people if you take the time to say hello. Yes, they may look at people like bugs, but it is a facade, learned from years living among fellow competitive Italians in competitive cities and crowded streets.

And then there were the overlanders. Please do not ask me how I differentiate the groups, surely they all travelled over borders by vehicles, overland and by definition are all overlanders. I suppose the distinction is the capability of the vehicle. While the New Age Hippy Punks might associate more with #Vanlife and the pensioners don't care what you call them as long as they have safety in numbers, sunshine and rivers of Prosecco and gin, I tend to see vehicles equipped for off-piste travelling as overland vehicles. Morocco has an incredible array of terrain to explore, and it is possible to go almost wherever you wish. The mountains, beaches, desert all offer challenging terrain and the promise of solitude, a unique experience and a sky full of stars. Morocco is to European overlanders what Namibia used to be for South Africans and what Central America offers Americans. Liberated from European rule books, Europeans are free to explore and relax. The only occasion when we have witnessed a greater variety of overland vehicles was at the Abenteuer & Allrad event in Germany. Daily new overland vehicles would arrive - massive Swiss and German registered 4x4 trucks either professionally designed and equipped or well home built. There were every shape of Mercedes van, ex fire trucks, ambulances and military vehicles, Land Rover Defenders and Toyota Land Cruisers, Unimogs, ancient Mercedes trucks, Pinzgauers and Iveco 4x4's. The overlanders usually only stayed put for a few days before heading to those mountains, deserts and beaches. Most knew Morocco intimately and had the best advice for routes, free camps and secret spots.

Our campfire was the meeting point for all the different types of travellers. Europeans see a campfire as an invitation. If you are going to make a fire on a cool night, expect company. Every other night we would make a large fire, and fellow campers would trickle in to join the circle which grew ever larger. The New Age Hippy Punks would perhaps grill some vegetables or sausage on the coals, the overlanders would bring beer and wine and song, the elderly Fiat campers would escape their wives to join the festivities, and invariably a few joints were lit and handed around. Luisa and I do not generally smoke weed or hashish. Just saying. Some nights would end in the early hours, but I knew how to control the crowd. If I wanted an early night, I would burn the wood quickly, and the revellers would leave slowly but surely as the fire died. If we like the crowd and wanted the night to continue, we would burn the wood slowly, conserving the ambience and gentle heat. One quiet night it was just the New Agers and us, there were no overlanders in the camp and no convoys. The New Agers were hiii-iigh and listening to Mumford and Sons or some French Anarcho rap. My friend Chris Ratay (more about him soon) had visited us a week before and had brought us wine, beer and a few party tricks. One of those party tricks was an American campfire amusement, a block of chemicals which, when burned, created a rainbow of colours and slow sparks in the flames. I waited until my New Age friends had finished a huge spliff and, while they were not looking, I slipped the magical cube into the fire. Slowly the chemicals released and purple, yellow, orange and blue flames began to play in the flames. I watched innocently as the New Agers noticed the colours and became completely entranced. "Look at the fire, whoa". "It must be the fungus on the wood". "Or a mushroom". "The wood is magical here".

Two weeks after we returned to Camping Azilan (after our four-day breakdown in the Rif Mountains) news broke that two Scandinavian tourists had been murdered in the Atlas Mountains, just south of our location. Louisa Vesterager Jespersen, 24 and Maren Ueland, 28 had been camping near a hiking trail to the summit of Mount Toubkal. Their attackers had stabbed them repeatedly before decapitating both girls while filming the act with smartphones. Let's be clear, anyone who has spent any decent amount of time in Morocco, and who sees photos of the murderers, will recognise immediately that these men represent the very lowest rungs of the social ladder. They are not representative of the people of Morocco who, we observed, reacted with as much horror and revulsion as we did. We were furious and concerned for the safety of the lovely young solo travellers who we had just recently befriended and reminded how very vulnerable we had been up in the Rif Mountains, alone. It would have only taken a small shift in circumstances for those cowardly murderers to encounter us alone in the mountains, but we take solace in the knowledge that they were looking for a soft target and we are not a soft target, we sleep behind solid walls and carry our own blades. That Christmas eve we ventured down into Chefchaouen and observed a vigil for the murdered girls held outside the Kasbah. An Imam chanted, and the crowd responded passionately, candles glowed across the flagstones where people drew messages of love and peace with coloured chalk. It was a moving, sad, but uplifting ceremony. A young man on a bicycle rode absent-mindedly between the vigil candles and was quickly evicted by the mourners; we could feel the tension in the air, groups of men in black jackets stood together talking, heads low, while children lit yet more candles. Before the murders, there had been few police officers visible on the streets, but after that, they were everywhere, mostly observing but sometimes searching vehicles and conducting roadblocks.

Morocco practices and promotes the moderate Islam of Maliki madhab and tourism is essential to the economy. A terrorist attack costs the country untold millions in revenue and takes food from the table of everyone even remotely involved in the tourism industry. It is safe to assume that the safest time to be in a country like Morocco is when the country is in a state of high alert. But, the government forces do operate with a heavy hand, unrestricted as modern democracies are by civil rights obligations, checks and balances. In total, 24 people were arrested in connection with the attacks, and you can rest assured that the Moroccan intelligence service was taking the opportunity to round up other known jihadists and Islamic extremists, enemies of the state. The presence of the police on the streets made us feel safe, but sometimes we felt intimidated by the authorities. On New Year's Eve, we sat around the fire, enjoying a quiet evening. Close to midnight two men, dressed in suits and wearing long, thick and expensive trench coats approached our campfire. I stood up to greet them with a handshake, and they stood there for a while asking the small group questions after introducing themselves as being local government officials, whatever that means. We were relaxed until I noticed the look on Anouar, the camp managers, face. He was terrified. South Africans my age were raised in an authoritarian country, and we have a healthy respect for our policeman, Europeans do not share the same fear of authority. A group of young men had joined the campfire, some of whom I had never met before and an eccentric young Polish man plopped down on the feet of one of the trenchcoats and threw a large joint at a Portuguese man sitting next to me. The Germans continued chatting with the Swiss and eventually only Luisa, I and Anouar were paying attention to the trenchcoats, who had lost a bit of their menace in the face of European indifference though the larger and more senior of the two men stood throughout the entire interaction with one hand on his left breast inside his coat, as if holding a handgun. Eventually, they moved on, and Anouar visibly breathed a large sigh of relief. The camp guard, a Syrian refugee who would routinely visit our campfire and warm his hands *in* the fire, was nowhere to be seen for the next few hours but he emerged eventually. I do not know if there was a connection between the appearance of the intimidating officials and the temporary disappearance of our Syrian friend, but I believe there was.

Life continued almost as it had before the attack on the Scandinavian girls, and we were relieved that there were no further reports of attacks on tourists.

One morning soon after we returned to the camp from the Rif Mountains, Luisa discovered mouse droppings in the food storage area under the sink. A mouse can be very destructive, and as much as we did not want to kill it, the little bugger had begun to chew our electrical wires and gnaw a passageway through the thin wooden walls of our kitchen unit. Luisa would lie awake at night and listen to our unwelcome guest gnawing at the wooden panel a foot from her head. It drove her crazy. Twice she emptied the vehicle entirely and twice she found no mouse. I searched the internet and found a few humane traps, the one involved a plastic bottle cut in half, the top half inverted and taped to the bottom half with bait, preferably peanut butter, along the inside of the bottle which should be placed in an accessible area. The mouse should fall into the bottom half while eating the sticky peanut butter, and you could then release it into a noisy Italian's camper. This trap did not work. The second trap was a shoebox with a hole cut in the top and a sheet of paper taped above the hole with a clean cut across the middle and peanut butter smeared on the paper. The sheet must be sturdy enough to support the weight of the mouse until it ventures close to the slice, following the bait trail, and then fall in, to be released. This did not work either. We then bought poison from the market which was not eaten and set traps with cheese, the cheese eaten, but the traps did not spring. We were outsmarted.

Meanwhile, Jessica had befriended two camp cats. The one, a ginger, was semi-wild and would claw you violently if you touched its paws. I touched its paws. She called this cat Gingie. The second cat was black and white and chubby and fought an ongoing feud with a wild black cat who was trying to mate with Gingie. He was tough as nails and always dusty - Jessica named him Tyson. Without revealing my plans to catch the mouse, I allowed the cats to enter the camper on the condition that if they became a nuisance, they would be evicted. Both cats would sneak into the camper (the lower half of the rear door left open in camp) and would sleep on Luisa's feet. Now, with my blessing, they were allowed to sleep in Jessica's bunk with her, and the three of them purred happily all night long. There is a reason why Jessica's nickname is Jessicat. The mouse naturally sensed that there were predators in her adopted home and became a recluse. We began to see less evidence of the mouse until we realised that the mouse was indeed gone, the cats must have done their job. But, I had swopped one pesky mouse for two large cats who became accustomed to a can of sardines twice a day, and that little bitch Gingie would make me bleed if I tried to evict her.

With the cats moving in, Keelan moved out, he took our small green tent, a duvet, pillow and a mattress and set up his own little camp just behind the Land Rover and a few meters from our campfire ring of stones. Each morning he would wait until the smell of coffee, eggs or pancakes wafted out of the camper, signalling that we were awake and preparing his breakfast. That tent bought in Spain and often used while we travelled as a date night "love tent" is now walking around South Africa with Luisa's cousin, Ronnie who is raising awareness about mental health issues.

Our friends from Colorado, Chris and Erin Ratay visited before Christmas. The Ratay's have travelled the world extensively (they hold a long-standing Guinness Record for RTW on motorbikes) and bought a Defender in South Africa which they drove up to Europe. They were joined by their friend Stefan and were about to head down to Senegal before returning to Europe to have the Defender converted to left-hand drive and installing a Globe Camper on the back. Stefan drove an immaculate Land Cruiser made by Tom's in Germany, and we were jealous of the quality of the materials and workmanship of his camper. We enjoyed a fire (well, Erin did not, the wood-smoked heavily and the wind always seemed to find her), we grilled some local sausage and lamb and discussed our plans for the future. Chris has a tremendous amount of energy and is always overflowing with ideas; we could certainly use some of that energy sometimes. We had first met in

Colorado in 2015, and it was wonderful to be reunited on the African continent three years later.

Other visitors included Alfonso and Carla who lived in northern Spain and were setting off to drive across West Africa to Cape Town in two months. Thank you for the drinks and fuet (excellent dry sausage pronounced "whip") and chorizo! Other visitors included the giant Adrian (almost taller than me and bulging with muscles which Luisa appreciated quietly) and his beautiful girlfriend Hortensia (Hortensia is a type of flower, so we nicknamed her Flor (flower in Spanish). They joined us and a group of German Defender owners for a night of Spanish wine and terrible jokes.

Over six weeks we watched all these wonderful people come and go. Our clutch was still sitting at customs in Casablanca, and while we were eager to get back on the road, I was as happy as a man can be, under the circumstances. It was a wonderful holiday for us. There were none of the pressures of life on the road, the climate was cool, bright and comfortable, we had pets, friends, great food (including the most delicious oranges you have ever tasted) and we had the city of Chefchaouen itself.

The city was founded in 1471 but was only painted blue in the mid 20th century. Some say the blue painted walls were inspired by Jewish refugees fleeing Hitler during the 2nd World War, some say the colour wards off mosquitoes, others say the colour creates a spiritual connection. Others insist that the pale blue was introduced to generate tourism in the 1970s. Whatever the reason, the blue is simply enchanting. In the colder winter months, the sky is crisp and clear and ever visible above the stone walls upon which grass grows in the gutters, and stray cats perch and observe the world below. The people of Chefchouen are relaxed and friendly; there is none of the hardcore bartering and sales tactics which we would later experience in other parts of Morocco. The hash sellers stop offering when you do not buy, and the vendors try and guess where you are from "Australia?" No. "Germany?" No. "America, then?" No. "You are too big to be from France". "You will never guess. We are from South Africa". "Aah, dumela, Madiba, Bafana Bafana!" The cobbled streets and alleys are entirely enchanting; you find yourself happily lost in a maze of sensory delights, the sounds and smells matching the visual feast. We could spend hours just watching the world go by before heading to a restaurant where we would order a large fava bean soup and six khubz round bread, a meal which cost

Euro 5 and fed us all, sitting in the shadow of the Kasbah, watching the world go by. Or we would head to a restaurant hidden within the medina and climb to the rooftop tables from where we could eat beef and prune tagine with a superb view over the city and valley, all the while surrounded by stray cats.

Young Moroccan men wear a uniform it seems -light blue skinny jeans, a red shirt (probably a football teams colours) covered with a black hooded jacket, sometimes with fur edging, and white, red or blue trainers. The older men may wear a hooded djellaba, long sleeve and flowing to the feet, usually striped and mythical in appearance. Moroccan girls dress modestly, usually in a pair of slacks or jeans with a loose-fitting shirt and a hijab scarf. The manufacturing, marketing and sale of the Burqa (the garment which covers a woman from head to foot with a mesh about the eyes for visibility) is banned in Morocco. Older women wear the feminine version of the djellaba, while others may dress in a western style. There are almost as many tourists as there are locals in Chefchaoen and the majority seems to be Asian girls labouring beneath large, colourful backpacks. Then you have the stoners who have travelled to Chefchaouen to sample the local delights; families, usually Spanish, looking slightly flustered and trying to cram in every site and attraction; retirees checking off the bucket list; brave young Americans; 4x4 clubs in matching shirts drift through the city on their way to the desert (we met our Portuguese friend Sergio and his family for lunch one day as they travelled with one such group), and the Instagrammers are everywhere. Overlanders are easily recognisable to the trained eye, and the vendors seem to know how to identify us as well - overlanders tend to buy very few curios.

We became local "experts" and could advise other travellers where they could find the best food, soaps and perfumes, smoothies, clothing, carpets, car parts, mouse traps, shoe repair, Tupperware, car rental, wine, beer, white cheese, decent yoghurt, tyre repair, charcoal, currency. Of course, we were new to the scene, and there were locals and visitors to the region who knew that we did not yet know the real secrets of the area. One gravelly old German shared his life between Germany and the Rif Mountain region. He would spend the summer months in Germany where he collected clothing, shoes, toys, etc. and would return to the Rif with gifts for the remote communities into which he would embed.

Another "expert" was a tall, voluminous northern European with proportions twice that of a normal man - tombstone teeth, thick sausage fingers, a curly grey-haired head the size of a North American pumpkin, tree trunks for arms, legs and neck, a large potbelly and enormous, filthy, disfigured bare feet, toenails as thick as bark, curling, rippled, grey and chipped. He laughed at his own jokes and lived in a caravan towed by an equally ancient Mitsubishi pick up, overflowing with bicycles and buckets, wooden beams, garden ornaments, dog food, spades, toys and various oddities which had been collected over a summer spent harassing the good people of Denmark (he was certainly not Danish). Not only was he a voracious collector, but he was also equally a persistent salesman. He sold (or at least was attempting to sell) cases of beer, a roof rack, an old bicycle, polished turds. His chained dogs barked as much as he talked and he dealt with them as all bullies deal with their victims. He parked opposite us and would wander over and begin a monologue interrupted only by his own howling laughter; he was, without any doubt, the most fascinating man he had ever met. "No, thank you, we do not need anything at all, we have everything we need". But, I had not considered his old bicycle or roof rack, or old bucket, all were of the finest quality, with intelligent improvements made by him and I would be a fool not to take this opportunity. His breath stank of the plague, his body of stale sweat and a hint of urine, tales of his ancestors scared little children at bedtime. I had made the mistake of buying beer from the man, and once he had seen the inside of my wallet the seal was broken, I was now a customer who owed something even though I paid in full, so good was the deal of paying a 300% mark up for Bulgarian beer. Unfortunately, the beer reminded me of the man, and I could not drink it in peace.

The garrulous, loquacious (these words seem too polite to describe someone who simply does not know how to shut up) is a time-waster, a life drainer. They abuse a polite persons nature and wedge themselves into your life and time and dominate you entirely if you allow them to. After the first half an hour of a one-way conversation, I realised the type of man I was facing and excused myself. Thanks, no thanks. Three times a day the troll would lumber over to our vehicle, a new scheme cooked in the pressure cooker. Thanks, no thanks. I secretly asked Luisa and Keelan to interrupt the man whenever he lumbered over to monologue, to call me to ask for help with dinner or with a chore. They both agreed, and I knew that this cunning plan would free me to excuse myself and escape. The block of flesh with mouth cornered me as I fixed a chair in the warm sunlight, the radio playing, a perfect day. He had a roof box to sell; he had "bought it in Germany from a silly man who could have charged double if he had only given them a spray of paint and changed the nuts and bolts to stainless steel. Those load bars would be perfect on the top of the Land Rover, space to carry more stuff, of course, being a family you must need a lot more carrying capacity than most, and there are other things you could buy to put up there like a table or some nice carpets. Really, what is the point of travelling if you can't have the things you need. I notice that you don't have a table or proper chairs and what if you wanted to buy a kayak or a surfboard, I have a really nice bicycle which you could buy, great condition, not new but what they call retro, I have just oiled the chain. It has a nice paint scheme; you want to see it, I know you do, do you want to see it"? I waited for Luisa or Keelan to call out to me, I waited and looked back at the camper often, what the hell was keeping them? They did not call me, but I could hear them laughing. Betrayal! Thanks, no thanks. I excused myself and walked to the back of the Landy and popped my head through the back door. "What the hell, guys?!". The family laughed and laughed and laughed.

When eventually, he hitched up his mobile madness, we felt relieved that he was leaving but sad for those towards who he was heading, and a hint of sadness for the man himself.

After a month waiting for our new clutch to arrive, we received a message from a Polish South African by the name of Robert who offered to help. He had some friends in Casablanca and offered to reach out to them; perhaps they could assist us in dealing with customs. The broker had told us that we needed to go to Casablanca to handle the release of the parcel and asked for payments to facilitate the process. Essentially he, the broker, was asking for a bribe, the infamous baksheesh. We don't play that game. However, shortly after Robert's involvement, we received an email declaring that the parcel was cleared for delivery! I don't know if it was your intervention which liberated our replacement parts, but if it was, I thank you, Robert!

The courier delivered the long-awaited and well-sealed box on a crisp Tuesday morning. It was finally time to get the Landy running again! A German overlander who a few weeks earlier had repairs done to his old Mercedes truck, gave us the particulars of a mechanic who had a workshop in town. He said they were good workers, but worked "the African way", meaning that they did not use modern best-practice tools like lifts, workshop manuals, torque settings, specialised tools and European workshop etiquette and had to be supervised. Keelan and I had walked the route to the workshop and had determined that, if we had to, we could roll the Land Rover there hindered only by one short, level stretch of road where we would have to push the vehicle. At the workshop, and without the stricken Land Rover, we spoke to the owner Anwar, asking for a price for the repair and whether it would be possible to replace the clutch in camp. The owner of the camp had assured us that he had no problem at all with us taking the engine out in the middle of the campsite and the mechanic agreed that he would come to the campsite with an engine hoist, replace the clutch, and charge us the equivalent of Euro 100 for the labour. That seemed a very good price, indeed. Thursday morning, Anwar arrived at the camp on yet another wonderfully clear day with two mechanics and set about removing the engine. We had done a lot of the preparation work for them - removing the bonnet, laying down cardboard boxes, chocking the wheels, arranging our tools for them to use, having the workshop manual available and open on the correct page, disconnecting the batteries and providing buckets and containers to collect any coolant or oil. Working quickly and efficiently Aziz, the senior mechanic, removed the cooling hoses, switches, turbo, exhaust, radiator, fan belt, engine mounts, etc. and within two hours they had the motor removed from the engine bay. After lunch, they returned and set about replacing the clutch. The friction plate (aka friction disc) on the original clutch had sheared completely, and we were relieved that the diagnosis had been correct, could you imagine after all of that time and effort that the clutch was in perfect condition? We would have been back to the drawing board and could look forward to another month in camp while we repaired or replaced the gearbox. Hell no, Luisa would kill me. Luisa was hard at work that day, filming and photographing the entire repair process. I was very careful to be as hands-on as possible and to keep an eye on all of the work; there is a reason why we do all of our own repairs but, considering how affordable it was to pay for the repair, it made sense to let someone else do all the hard work while we supervised. But, I dropped the ball. While Aziz worked to install the new flywheel and friction disc, Anwar called me over to show me the extent of the failure on the failed friction disc and the difference between the new pressure plate and old. While I had my back turned, Aziz installed the flywheel and friction disc and before I had time to think they bolted in the new pressure plate. They then re-installed the motor, connected all that which was disconnected and by late afternoon were ready to pack up and go home. Excellent. Now for a test drive. Anwar climbed in behind the steering wheel, and started the Landy, so far so good. He tried to engage first gear, nothing. He then worked through the gears, again the gears would not select. After a heated discussion, Aziz made some adjustments, and they tried again. As before the discussion, the vehicle would start in gear and would drive, but changing gears was very difficult. Anwar blamed the new parts, which he said were faulty. We did not agree. As evening approached, it was agreed that we would do some research and talk it over in the morning. Anwar and Aziz packed up and left, Luisa and I had a shower and then sat down to look at the workshop manual, transfer and watch the footage which Luisa had taken during the day. As per the manual everything had been done correctly but there was that one diagram which depicted the direction which the friction disc must face, which we returned to as the most likely problem. Fast forward through the mornings work, return from lunch, old clutch out. OK, now watch carefully. Luisa captured everything. While I am off in the background dropping balls and picking my nose, Aziz prepares to install the disc (which has "This side to flywheel" printed on one face), Aziz does not speak or read English but begins to install the disc in the correct orientation. As we watch, Anwar walks over and shouts at Aziz to flip the friction disc the other way, Aziz says no, this is the right way. Anwar pulls rank, Aziz shrugs and installs the friction disc, incorrectly, while I am standing vaguely in the background thinking about the distance to the moon and why some girls are bigger than others and why some girls mothers are bigger than other girls mothers.

The next morning Aziz returned to the camp, and we showed him the footage. He would not admit fault but suggested that we should drive the Landy down to his ice-cold workshop where Aziz would work all day to flip that one disc, buried backwards deep within the bell housing. This time I paid full attention. The test drive revealed no problems at all except for a small grind into second gear, I assumed that the friction disc might be a bit greasy but, then again, what do I know? We paid Anwar the Euro 100 plus an extra Euro 20 for miscellaneous expenses and Luisa and I climbed into the Landy and drove the steep hills back to the camp, triumphant. The last stretch to the campsite climbs a particularly long, steep hill before reaching a roundabout and a small climb to the camp gates. We arrived, the Landy misfired slightly once or twice, and we pulled up to the gate with huge grins. Youness, the camp owner ran over, shouting and pointing at the bottom of the Defender. "Diesel, diesel!" he shouted. Alarmed I switched the Landy off and jumped out of the driver's seat. Diesel was pouring out of the engine bay, and a long line of slick trailed the route we had just driven. We threw open the bonnet, and I discovered that the fuel line to the fuel cooler had not been reconnected properly. Using my Leatherman, I reconnected the hose, and the leak stopped. A gasoline engine might have caught fire as the engine heated up the steep climbs and the fuel sprayed across to the exhaust manifold. That would have been a disaster, as you can well imagine. The moral of the story is that while the labour may be ridiculously cheap in Morocco, you need to be fully engaged, never distracted and double-checked all the work which is done, even if the boss has all the confidence in the world and you are tempted just to let them get on with it.

The next day we packed and prepared to leave after one last trip into the city to say goodbye to our new friends and a campfire to symbolically end our long, wonderful, stressful holiday.

2

On the Road Again. Heading for "Real" Africa

Following that extended and unplanned stay in Chefchaouen, we pointed the Defender towards Meknes, Casablanca, the Atlas Mountains and Western Sahara.

There is a strange emotion which overcomes us when we leave a port of safety such as the camp in Chefchouen; it is almost as if we are on the road again for the first time. We are grumpy and slightly nervous, but as the day wears on and the new experiences distract us, we relax and recover our nomadic selves.

Luisa had plotted a course to Fes, and we were astounded by the beauty of the land as we drove towards the ancient ruin of Volubilis which is located in a fertile valley guarded by the Zerhoun mountain. The fields reminded us of southern Brazil or the Natal province in South Africa. The road to the ruins looped over the hills, and we could imagine the Carthaginians and Romans marching across this land, establishing the fringe of their empires. The deep blue sky and vibrant green crops dominated the colour spectrum as far as the eye could see, grey-brown mountains in the distance. We parked our camper outside the gate to the ruins and explored accessible parts of the ancient city. The Berber people established the city in the 3rd century BCE and over the centuries fell under the rule of the Carthaginians and Romans before falling to local tribes in 285 CE, and over the next 700 years, housing Latinised Christians and then becoming an Islamic settlement. In the late 8th century, the state of Morocco was established here under the rule of Idris Ibn Abdallah (founder of the Idrisid dynasty) and in the 11th century was abandoned as the seat of power moved to nearby Fes. Today the ruins are a highly valued UNESCO World Heritage Site and rightly so. Busloads of tourists arrived every half hour and crammed massive Volubilis with old feet.

As the sunset, a portly security guard approached us accompanied by two friendly policemen; they asked us if we intended to stay the night and responded that we were not permitted to overnight there, that there was a hotel up the road where we could camp. We had heard from other travellers that the recent murder of the Scandinavian girls in the Atlas mountains had prompted the police to restrict free camping severely. With no other choice, we drove up to the Hotel de Oualili, which in its heyday must have been quite impressive. The Hotel seemed to be accommodated only by staff members who had long since lost any passion which they might have once had for hospitality. We paid 300 Dirham to park in the parking lot and the next morning admired a large neighbouring house, an impressive grove of olive trees and the view before driving to and through Meknes the next day.

We are not conventional tourists, we seek a unique experience, and we found exactly that in the Rif mountains and, to a degree, in Chefchaouen. Meknes and Fes were to be disappointing by our standards, the standards of travellers who enjoy the serenity and peace which the great outdoors affords, as opposed to the bustle and hustle of a city, no matter how beautiful or historic that city may be, with a few exceptions. Luisa loves cities only for their supermarkets, and we tend to avoid these urban centres as fastidiously as others flock to them. We chose to explore the Pyrenese and skipped Paris, crossed the Taurus mountains and transited through Istanbul, relaxed with friends in Bavaria and avoided Berlin and only visited London briefly to apply for visas. A Norwegian reader sent me an email lamenting the fact that we do not search out the "urban culture" of the countries which we visit and that we had missed a significant opportunity. He has a very good point, but we are not city people, we have been and chose not to be. City culture is a melting pot, a mish-mash, and a modern city is a place of industry almost exclusively, with distractions and amenities designed to make life comfortable. Yes, theatre, malls, fashion and restaurants and promenades and convenience are incredibly important to many people, they are simply not incredibly important to us.

When we are in a city we make eye contact, we hold hands, we laugh and have conversations with people we encounter, and we walk with a rural disposition. In modern cities (I am talking about you San Francisco, New York, London, Rio, Tel Aviv) we are like aliens beamed down from above. We are oddities of old fashioned conversation and politeness, the city folk can't place us, but they know that we are alien. No, we don't have an apartment in a nice neighbourhood, but we go where we please, no we do not eat at the finest restaurants or wear the latest fashions or have a routine which revolves around the five blocks closest to our expensive, cramped accommodation and a weekly visit to where we would rather live. In San Francisco, we wore flip flops and truck t-shirts - the fashionistas and homeless stopped harassing themselves to watch us walk by, and we could not have left that beautiful city soon enough. We find a country's culture through the people who are not wringing themselves out, the land feeds the soul and the wide-open spaces are where your mind can soar and be free, away from a pair of shoes and sunglasses selling a personality, the culture of greed, extremes of having and have not. In the country, people share food and conversation, time and space or they leave you alone, you can choose to be who you are. The best people are usually those who have escaped the cities; we can relate to them; they know the best of both worlds. Songs for the Deaf.

But, with all that said, I think we could live happily in either Cape Town or Buenos Aires, for a year, maximum.

Rhymes of a Rolling Stone, by Robert W. Service

I'm scared of it all, God's truth! so I am
It's too big and brutal for me.
My nerve's on the raw, and I don't give a damn
For all the "hoorah" that I see.
I'm pinned between subway and overhead train,
Where automobillies sweep down:
Oh, I want to go back to the timber again . . .
I'm scared of the terrible town.

I want to go back to my lean, ashen plains;
My rivers that flash into foam;
My ultimate valleys where solitude reigns;
My trail from Fort Churchill to Nome.
My forests packed full of mysterious gloom,
My ice fields agrind and aglare:
The city is deadfalled with danger and doom . . .
I know that I'm safer up there.

I watch the wan faces that flash in the street;
All kinds and all classes I see.
Yet never a one in the million I meet,
Has the smile of a comrade to me.
Just jaded and panting like dogs in a pack;
Just tensed and intent on the goal:

O God! but I'm lonesome . . . I wish I was back,
Up there in the land of the Pole.
I feel it's all wrong, but I can't tell you why . . .
The palace, the hovel next door;
The insolent towers that sprawl to the sky,
The crush and the rush and the roar.
I'm trapped like a fox and I fear for my pelt;
I cower in the crash and the glare;
Oh, I want to be back in the avalanche belt,
For I know that it's safer up there!
I'm scared of it all: Oh, afar I can hear
The voice of the solitudes call!
We're nothing but brute with a little veneer,
And nature is best after all.
There's tumult and terror abroad in the street;
There's menace and doom in the air;
I've got to get back to my thousand mile beat;
The trail where the cougar and silvertip meet;
The snows and the campfire, with wolves at my feet . . .
Goodbye, for it's safer up there.

True to form, we skipped through Meknes (after visiting a supermarket) and arrived in Fes to endure a city experience as, apparently, the city deserves a visit. We followed the Park4 Night app directions and found ourselves in a large parking lot just outside the walls of the massive medina. The parking area was where we would spend the night, and we parked the Landy in a cigarette butt strewn but quiet area before visiting the city and the (in) famous tanneries. The ancient city is cool and relatively quiet in late January, Luisa led us along a maze of high, pitted walls parallel to Boulevard Ben Mohamed El Alaoui until we emerged out into a square where families sat and chatted and then through the gates of the city and a large square where traders sold snacks and curios, scarves and shoes, children's toys, carpets, carvings, beads, nuts and coffee. Every so often, a breeze would blow in our direction, and the smell of a soapy death would assault us. Following Luisa, we walked through the narrow streets past many closed stores (it was a Sunday afternoon, thankfully) and attracted a skeletal tout wearing a large black leather jacket and blue toothpick legs. He trailed us and then took the lead, we told him thanks, but no thanks and in response, he took off ahead to wait for us at the next junction where Luisa would stop to consult her map. No thanks. The narrow alleys were crowded with locals and very few tourists, again and again, the sewerage reek hit us, but no-one else seemed to notice. We could hear water gushing and were surprised to find a large construction project taking place in the middle of the crowded medina where the Oued Wisslane river crashed along its new angular concrete bed. The tout followed us still, and we found ourselves climbing narrow stairs to a leather store with a view of the tanneries where young, angry salesman sat smouldering as they would for eternity. We peered down upon the stinking tanneries and large numerous clay concrete vats where the hides are soaked to soften in white liquid or dyed various colours - the process of converting a natural hide into an ugly jacket. The smell wafted up towards us and, after the obligatory tip to the demanding touts and salesman, followed us down back through the medina, along the boulevard, past a coffee shop and to the Land Rover waiting, unmolested.

The evening was beautiful in a bizarre way. The parking lot is sandwiched between a highway, a field and the city. In the field goats and cows graze, a herdsman lives in a shack, and young men take a short cut across his land to sit on the walls of the freeway and spend time alone, together for whatever reason. A dog ran atop the roof of the ancient apartment block to our right, en-route to the medina, the Azaan called the faithful to prayer as the moon rose behind the large castle on the hill and the mosque below it. We watched people go about their business, watched the goats and cows graze, picked up litter around the Land Rover, ate a simple dinner and headed out the next morning, happy to leave the city behind us.

Unfortunately, we were headed to another city, the most famous of all Moroccan cities - Casablanca. We stayed in an expensive campsite for a night and enjoyed the pleasures of a city mall before heading into the city to have a look at the sights and decide that we had not the energy for the tourist traps, instead choosing to leave the city and head to the Sahara. I am sorry to disappoint you, dear reader, if you were expecting a tour of the city but you will have to accept that our passion lies in nature. A few hours spent in traffic watching touts feed on tourists was enough for us to promise each other that one day we would return when we had more money and patience.

Luisa set a course to the Ouzoud Falls, and we were happy to be cruising along through rural areas. The falls are said to be the tallest in

North Africa, and we arrived at the Zebra camp, not expecting much, but finding one of the most beautiful and comfortable camps in Morocco. Owned by locals and a European couple the campsite has everything you need to get sucked in for a few days of relaxation and work. The sunsets were beautiful across the crags and hills surrounding the camp, and the nights were cold and crisp. Luisa and I made a small fire and relaxed while the kids soaked up all the wifi, and we all enjoyed one of the best showers in the northern hemisphere. Yes, it really is that good. I took a walk into town but found that the locals were tourist-driven to the point of insanity and I was not left alone to walk the streets, everyone with something to sell, was selling it with enthusiasm. The walk was pleasant despite the attention, the climb back up to the camp was steep and got the pulse racing, I met a few friendly locals and befriended a stray dog who shadowed me as I walked beside the wide, well-paved road. The falls were spectacular before restaurants and hotels were built, and curios stores lined the streets. Plunging deep into a canyon, and with little regard for the safety of silly tourists, plumes of mist rose from the depths, where boats shuttled tourists to the base of the falls, a restaurant sat moist, surrounded by mist and green and while we walked along the paths admiring the view an old lady banged clothing on rocks, meters away from the 110m drop. We brushed aside touts and "official" persistent tour guides, hid Jessica from groups of young men wandering along the rim and waited for Luisa to take some photos, struggling with the light and moisture and angles. I enjoyed the beautiful drive to the falls more than the falls experience (the waterfalls were quite amazing, it must be said) and I was looking forward to the road out of the mountains and across to the Sahara.

Just past the town of Ouarzazate, we stopped at the lake, Barrage El Mansour Edahhbi and parked a decent distance from a couple of campers vans who were having a whale of a time, bustling about as the sunset and then cranking up the music and stoking a bonfire as the moon rose among the glistening stars. The lake reached out around us and offered the opportunity for agriculture in a region which reminded us of the high altitude Turkish plains - olive trees and interesting towns, conservative people and old tractors, a bird in every tree and stray dogs scouring the land, nose to the ground. During the night, a sedan drove close to the Land Rover and had a good look at us before moving along to park in a secluded area, lovers perhaps, or bored young men. The morning was chilly, and we took turns sitting on the porta-potty inside the camper with the rear door wide open, a beautiful view from the throne, while the other family members stood around the front of the Land Rover washing faces and brushing teeth before heading out to hike around the banks of the lake where yellow melons grew rough on the ground connected by a network of creepers, one huge organism bearing bitter fruit. An abandoned building stood at the peak of the hill, overlooking the lake and the forest on the horizon and could have been centuries old. The sky was blue with wispy clouds; the day looked to be long and calm and beautiful.

The destination was La Source Bleue, an oasis just beyond the city of Errachidia where dusty, charming streets led to large roundabouts and a long drive past a military complex. We arrived at the oasis, which is quite well hidden beside a dusty neighbourhood and drove down a tight circular driveway and along a beautiful road into the oasis. There were a few stalls and a boom which controlled our entry. The water had been channelled into a large swimming pool, and through a concrete causeway, palm trees swayed idyllically, we spotted a good place to camp, we were eager to make a fire and have a cold drink. Once through the boom, we drove to a grove of palms and chose our spot for the night and settled in. What an excellent place, really quite beautiful, and peaceful. Unfortunately, the peace did not last long. A man showed up selling dates, no thanks, another man selling melons, no thanks. The young camp administrator arrived and offered us tea, thanks, but no thanks. "Firewood?" "Yes, that would be great". A man jumped over a wall and retrieved stumps which would not burn, we paid him $5 for the wood and thought we would settle in for the night. No luck.

The young camp guy lingered. "Tea?" "No, thanks". I made a fire and opened a beer. The young man licked his lips, and I offered him a beer. He took that as a sign that we would be feeding him and supplying him with drinks all night long. He took a seat, and a friend joined him. I struggled with the fire which would not stay lit, and I struggled with the young man who told me the story of his life and how many languages he spoke and how most of his Facebook friends were German and French and how he planned to go to Europe and all he needed was enough money. You get the picture. He sat, very comfortable, for two hours and waited for me to offer another beer through the uncomfortable silences. Instead, I asked him to leave and let us cook dinner. With a broken heart, he and his friends reluctantly stood up and left only to return in the morning to extract money from us, to offer tea and to invite us to the curio shop. He would not leave us alone and what could have been a wonderful camp for a few days was left in a cloud of dust, not even the beautiful oasis could compensate for the humans which had seized ownership of a communal resource.

We soon discovered that it was Morocco's furthest solitary reaches which impressed us the most, not the markets of Marrakesh or the colours and scents of Fes - the desert and the Atlas Mountains drew us in with an authentic charm and beauty. The road to Merzouga dips out of the Atlas mountains and into the verges of the Sahara. The new road follows the ancient trail along the river which has eroded sandstone into beautiful formations and carved oasis where palm trees grow in abundance, and people live as they have for centuries, with the addition of technology.

Merzouga lies on the edge of the Sahara where the creamy soil of the Atlas meets red dune. The town is weathered by the sun and beaten by the wind, the streets narrow and scarred, the homes ancient with walls of thick soil. We drove past the vendors and the tourist office, the curio stalls and the eager children. We bought a bag of coal and filled our tanks with water, before driving out into the desert. Desert driving is difficult and fraught with danger. A vehicle must be equipped with sufficient provisions but cannot be too heavy as the deep, soft sand waits patiently to trap. Experienced 4x4 drivers know that momentum is everything and grip provides momentum. Using a valve key, I deflated the Defenders large mud-terrain tyres until the side walls bulged, a deflated tyre has a larger "footprint" thus more grip. We did not have to venture too far into the desert to find a quiet, beautiful hollow to call our own for the night. While our teenage children explored the dunes, Luisa and I prepared the camp - a simple affair really, a few chairs sat in the shade of our camper, the BBQ ready to be lit and grill our lamb dinner. A caravan of camels meandered past us, silhouetted against a pure blue sky, led by a Bedouin, followed by a calf. The sunset, the temperature dropped, and we lit the fire while the universe did what it could to impress us with constellations and shooting stars. The desert is a place of solitude and a silence so still that you can hear only the sand move and your thoughts swirl. We awoke early to watch the sunrise over the Sahara before packing the Land Rover and preparing for an off-road adventure from Merzouga to Sidi Ali, a journey which would have us trace the Algerian border over rocky mountains, through dry riverbeds, ancient flood plains and fields of bulldust, aka Fesh Fesh.

The trail began with a dusty sand road, rumbled upon by large articulated trucks hauling sand and stone, a sign of progress. Our navigator App showed various tracks, most heading in the same direction and we had to choose which track to follow, some worse than others and many deteriorated while the other tracks seemed in better condition. Criss-crossing the plateau, we arrived at the base of a hill where the road forked. We took a break and enjoyed a lunch of fresh bread, Edam cheese and sweet tomato while planning the route ahead. There were two routes to Sidi Ali - the easier "mountain" route and the river bed route which was suitable for only the most robust 4x4 vehicles. We chose the riverbed route and deflated our tyres again (we had re-inflated after the desert drive) once we descended from the rocky hill pass, the experts will tell you exactly which pressure is best for which road condition, we just play it by eye and performance. The fesh-fesh was deep and thick, I engaged low range second or third gear often and would let the track steer the vehicle, holding the steering wheel lightly and focusing on maintaining momentum. Clouds of white dust billowed from the tyres, covering the vehicle almost completely, seeping into the Land Rover and covering our home with a white layer. Luisa growled. The greatest risk when driving a river bed is the unforeseen flash flood caused by heavy rain upstream, the sky was grey that day, but we had checked the weather forecast before leaving Merzouga - no rain was forecast. We continued along the valley, low mountains to the west, the Algerian border and low mountains to the east. I hear Algeria is magnificent; we shall have to return one day. Emerging from the challenging riverbed the terrain changed to alluvial plain, criss-crossed with trails. Keelan took over the driving, and we were surprised to find auberge's (small hotels) dotted along the trail. The area is a treasure trove of fossils, and the hardy Moroccans understand the value of comfort in the desert. Had we the resources, we would have gladly enjoyed a night in a cold room after a tagine dinner and a relaxed conversation, sprawled on colourful cushions, drinking sweet mint tea. But a life lived on the road requires fiscal discipline and our home on wheels is designed and built to provide our family with the comforts we need.

The valley drew us in and deposited us at the town of Sidi Ali where a weathered, humble and dignified Tuareg man offered a place to park and camp within the perimeter walls of his auberge. A resilient, mountain born river runs through the town, and there is no shortage of firewood, after a refreshing cold shower I made a fire atop a small dune which had been thwarted in its attempt to smother the high, red clay walls. The Tuareg, dressed in blue robes, was attentive but careful to allow us the privacy we sought, he provided freshwater and friendly conversation, a watchful eye - we were in his care.

The night was crisp and invigorating but the morning gusty, the deep blue sky replaced by a fog of fine sand swept up by the wind, which blew from the south and forced a change of plans. Initially, we planned to continue to follow the trail (or piste as it is called in Morocco) from Sidi Ali to Zagora, a diversion which seemed less desirable as the sand storm grew in intensity The decision was made to head west to the incredible Dades Gorge and attempt a piste through the mountains where we were to encounter nomadic families who ran to the trail when they heard the rumble of the Land Rovers engine and offered us fossils and gems, their hands caked with grey dust and their faces streaked in a mountainous terrain without water. The nomads live in tents of black plastic tarp and live on a diet dominated by goat meat and milk; our gifts of fruit were devoured as we struggled to communicate with no common language. A small girl offered a large fossil; we could not accept as we cannot accept gifts, our Land Rover has space only for the practical and useful.

In late 2018, severe storms ravaged the Atlas Mountains delivering feet of snow and devastating flash floods. The trail we had followed up to 2700m disappeared after a series of tight and perilous switchbacks led the path down the mountain and we were forced to drive the Defender in a riverbed twice as wide as it had been before the November storms. With Keelan and Luisa walking the worst sections of the trail and Jessica, fourteen years old, guiding from the passenger seat, the great Land Rover rumbled down, ever down. The pace was painstakingly slow, and the sun soon touched our horizon of mountain peaks and cliffs. And still, we found no track to drive, only occasionally catching glimpses of what remained of a trail recently swept away. Rocking side to side, we continued our downward journey until dark and cold engulfed us until the minutes felt like hours until we grew hungry and fatigued and longing for even the worst road to replace the sea of grey boulders over which we climbed and slipped and pushed and disturbed. If it is our goal to seek, adventure and experience that which very few do, we are certainly successful. Our faith in our own capabilities only grows with each challenge we face and submit ourselves to.

At close to midnight, after almost a full day of tough yet rewarding 4x4 driving, Luisa spotted movement ahead, fuzzy mounds moving slowly and their number growing as we approached. The headlights illuminated a shepherd as we rounded a bend, the mounds his sheep, skittish with the approach of a vehicle, few of which they had ever seen. The shepherd greeted us with a broad grin, and we offered him respectful greetings and the last of our fruit. "How far is the village?". We used hand gestures bemoaning our lack of Arabic. "How far is the road?", there he gestured, pointed to the blackness ahead. We thanked him and continued carefully past his herd and again over the endless grey rock. An hour later a light appeared in the distance, then another and another. A track appeared, and we celebrated. Too soon. The track led only to another tortuous kilometre of rock riverbed but, eventually, we emerged onto a trail which led to a village which led to a camp where a large, friendly man welcomed us with a hot fire and sweet mint tea.

We awoke late the next morning and found ourselves overlooking a field and an ancient village built into the side of a rocky hill. Birds sang, and a crook bubbled beneath us, an old man and his young grandson working together to clear irrigation trenches, a woman preparing her field for spring. The mountains we had scaled behind us, reminding us that we are mere mortals and they are eternal.

From the Atlas mountains, we wound down to the sea and Marrakesh, which we did not tour; instead, we sought out the police head office where we could apply for an extension of our visas. The breakdown in Chefchaouen had eaten most of our three-month allowance, and we only had three weeks left in the country. The police told us that we might not be able to extend the visas as the family was travelling on South African passports and as it was Friday, it would be better if we returned on Monday and applied then.

That night we parked in a large parking area near a mosque and decided that it was time to leave the country, that we should instead get going on the road south than spend too much time and too many resources in a country we had grown to love and which was tempting us to stay.

That morning we awoke to the call to prayer and instead headed southwards along the coast to the sleepy surfing village of Essaouira, where we camped beside a swimming pool, soaking in the last few days of Morocco. Soon we would cross into Western Sahara, and the West African adventure would begin in earnest, best to be rested and ready.

Every so often, we are reminded why we live the lives we do.
The Essaouira campsite is located a short walk to the sea and is popular with German and French motorhomers, many of whom are grumpy, leave me alone types. But there were also families with children who spent days playing in the crystal clear cold swimming pool. Two adorable German children, Luke, the brother six years old and the little sister, Sabine, barely four years old, would play ball games near our camper in the evenings. Keelan and Jessica, who can communicate with any age, joined their game and the children soon befriended the family. Ours is a happy little home, and we are usually laughing and having a good time, the children must have sensed that friendly energy and became attached to us, particularly Sabine, and we would grow very attached to her. In the morning, she would climb into our camper and sit on my bed or cuddle with Luisa. Her mom Sonja, a statuesque voluptuous blonde, eventually realised that if she could not find Sabine, she must be hanging out with us, playing with Jessica's Teddy Bear and Luisa's Monster High dolls. Sabine chatted and coloured in and would happily spend hours with us, a frail angel with wispy blonde hair and the face of a pixie. Luisa and I had spent almost every moment with our children over the last few years, but we still suffered regret, wishing that we had only changed our lifestyles earlier, that we had been more patient, the usual regrets. We had both toyed with the idea of having another child, but Keelan and Jessica vetoed that idea, and all it usually took to convince ourselves *not* to have another child was to take care of a baby - after an hour you want your life back. Little Sabine worked her way into our hearts with little hands and gentle hugs and kindergarten songs.

Two days after we met, Sonja came to the Landy to fetch Sabine for lunch and told us the most heartbreaking story. Sabine was dying. She suffered from severe fits, and every fit made her weaker, reducing her physical and mental capacity, she was not expected to live longer than the age of seven. Sonja, a trained nurse and her husband, a doctor, had made the decision to sell all that they had and to travel and live with their children until Sabine no longer could. At first, because I am cynical and probably because I did not want to accept the truth, I suspected Munchausen by proxy, but we suddenly understood Sabine's lack of strength and Sonja was not interested in our sympathy. We were concerned that Sabine might suffer an episode while with us and that we would not know how to assist her properly, but Sonja assured us that the fits happened rarely and usually late at night. Tell me how is it that devils live to old age, but angels are taken young?

We spent the next few days hanging out with Sabine, showing her on a map all the countries which we have been to and telling her stories, feeding her peanut butter pancakes and playing games, sitting together quietly and swimming in the pool. It was only after we said goodbye and had driven to the next destination that we noticed that Sabine had left her purple beanie on Jessica's teddy bears head. An accidental gift which we will always keep. Be strong little Sabine.

MAURITANIA

Approximately 90% of the country lies within the Sahara and is about six times the size of Florida. The capital, Nouakchott comes from the Arabic Berber, "Place of Winds", you better believe it. It is the eleventh largest sovereign state in Africa. Mauritania is bordered by the Atlantic Ocean, Western Sahara, Algeria, Mali and Senegal to the southwest

1 Ouguiya (MRU) = EU0.24/USD0.27
Ensure that you have EURO's on hand. ATM's are available, but it won't be easy to find an ATM stocked with ample currency

Visas on arrival are generally required for all nationalities. Most European, American, Australian and Canadians pay a fee of EU55 for a 1 to 3-month visa, and African passport holders pay EU40. When applying for the visa at the border, you don't have to use a fixer as it takes the same amount of time and effort. Women are discriminated against and are separated at the border when procuring your visa

Unleaded = EU1/USD1.14 per litre
Diesel = EU0.90/USD1 per litre

Mauritel
Chinguitel

Mauritania is predominantly Muslim with Sunni law.
Atheism, blasphemy and leud acts are punishable by death.
Being overweight is considered beautiful and thin sickly.
Mauritania is notably more expensive than Morocco as most foods and products are imported.
Female genital mutilation, as well as slavery, is still practised

An additional EU10 for the TIP must be paid for at the border, and an additional EU10 at the community/police checkpoint will be requested, argue if you want but after a 4-hour wait, the EU10 seems like small change.
We did not procure insurance, and it was never requested

Police = 117
Ambulance = 101

Valid passport
Vehicle title papers
Fiche - ensure you have several on hand due to the many checkpoints. This fiche will be utilised throughout West Africa

Mauritanians speak Arabic but with a Berber influence

Marhaba - Hello   Ma'assalamah - Goodbye
Shukran - Thanks   Min Fadlik - Please

Simple foods such as pizza, hamburgers, sandwiches, fish and chips are served at several restaurants in Nouakchott or ask your host to cook you a traditional meal of fish and rice
There is not a huge variety in terms of supermarkets. Alcohol is banned but can be purchased at a steep price at a bar or a restaurant in Nouakchott

The Libraries of Chinguetti - UNESCO World Heritage Site
Richat Structure "Eye of Africa"
Port of Nouadhibou, "Backbone of the Sahara", is a 704 km railway line that transports trains of up to 3kms long. Tourists can ride along but keep in mind, the conditions are harsh

Summer - July to October - Low 22C/72F and High of 35C/95F
Winter - Dec to March - Low 15C/59F and High of 27C/81F
Temperatures are extreme in Summer and carry heavy winds, making it unbearable for a tourist

DID YOU KNOW? The official name of the country is the Islamic Republic of Mauritania.
The Richat Structure or 'Eye of Africa' can be seen from space and is 50kms wide.
The Bay of Nouadhibou is home to one of the world's largest ship graveyards with more than 300 ships being dumped once no longer operational.
Mauritania have wild baboons, monkeys, gazelles, hyenas and golden wolves (sometimes confused with jackals)

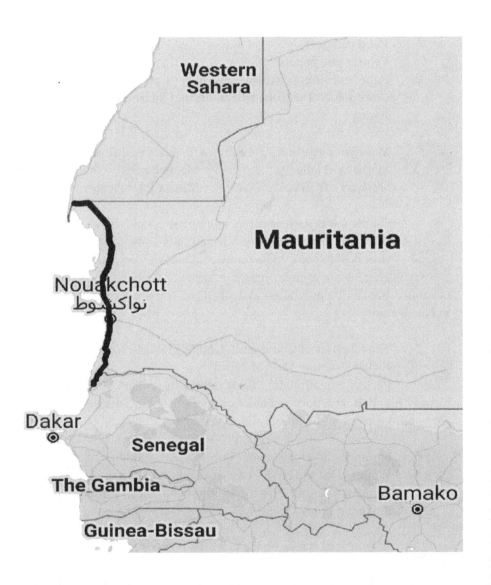

3

Mauritania - A Land of Extremes

One by one, we opened our eyes to a bright, blue sky and a world of silence. Our Land Rover was parked on a sandy cliff behind a knoll which had done its best to shelter us from a powerful wind. To our left lay the endless expanse of the Atlantic Ocean and to our right lay the Sahara. Today was the day that we would leave Morocco and enter Mauritania, today was the day that we would leave the gateway to sublime Europe and enter a world a universe apart. The Moroccans had welcomed us into their world of beauty and contrast, of peace and ancient culture, and they bid us farewell with equal grace and humanity. The kingdom had enchanted us all, and I encourage everyone to invest in a journey to the land, which gives more than it takes.

The Spanish once ruled Western Sahara, and their withdrawal from the region prompted a war between Morocco and The Polisario (a Sahrawi national liberation movement aiming to end Moroccan presence in Western Sahara), a war which was never quite settled, though Morocco did gain control of the endless sands. A wind blew us to the border along an arrow-straight road which terminated at a modern border outpost of large white buildings and dark, wind tormented men. Half an hour later, we drove through a boom, our vehicle scanned and paperwork inspected by a cheerful young man. "Good luck", he said as we drove out of the complex and into another world, another universe. Is it not amazing the difference a line in the sand can make? The border had been mined many years before, and we crossed a real No Mans Land where the unfortunate had driven their vehicles over explosives as they attempted to reach a better life, or return to a loved one, or attempt trade. Some vehicles were merely abandoned and stripped of all value. The wind blew tiny tornadoes between the wreckage as we carefully felt our way along a track which had been dug in the dirt by the brave and desperate. A large truck trundled confidently ahead of us, and we followed his line - there was no real risk of us driving over a land mine unless we left the main track or were incredibly unlucky, the United Nations has a presence at the border, and most mines had, apparently, been cleared. We were not taking any chances.

The gates of Mordor approached. Men in military uniforms and black full-face scarves pointed at a building, "stop there, go there". All we see is a white building, and once we enter, we find a forecourt full of men and a few closed doors, no signs. A metal door opens, a man escapes, other men shout, we are pushed forward, "what's going on?". Behind the metal door is the immigration room where a barefoot man dressed in a thin suit packs Euro notes into drawers overflowing with Euro notes and languidly, eventually issues visas. A small man enters the room often and tells raucous jokes and can't take his eyes off Jessica and Luisa, a fixer tries and fails to push ahead of us in the queue, we are made to stand against a wall and await our turn to be processed, the girls are allowed to go first while Keelan and I wait our turn to be processed. Luisa chats to the shoe-less suit and soon establishes a report. We talk to an elderly, respected man, and the mood of the room changes becomes more civil. The raucous little man returns to the room to throw jokes but is met with less welcome; we cannot be the butt of his jokes if we have earned the respect of the most respected man in the room. The raucous little man engages us directly (in Arabic), but we smile and return to our conversation. Defeated the little devil retreats, we continue our conversations in broken Spanish and English, and we leave the room four hours later with handshakes. We emerge legally into the white sky of Mauritania, a land of great, monotonous beauty.

That first night we camped in a world inspired by Salvadore Dali, where the wind-sculpted rock and the blue sea promised nothing more than a passage to the other universe. Nouadhibou is a small city perched on the tip of a peninsula; the streets are crowded with traders and stores, a sullen people trade goats, live chickens, hot fish and fresh Moroccan produce. The port is notorious as a haven for traffickers who deal in living, breathing human flesh desperate to reach the shores of Spain or Italy. As we drive, we are stopped often by the military and police who demand a "fiche", a document which details our particulars. In order to avoid lengthy delays, we have prepared and printed a stack of fiche; the travelling community had advised us to do so. A weathered policeman asks us for a bottle of water, and we oblige, water is life in a land without water.

The 300-mile drive to the capital Nouakchott is simultaneously excruciating and rewarding, to witness how communities survive in such a barren and hostile land is to be reminded of the strength of the human spirit. The north wind continued to blow us south while extracting all moisture from the air, skin and eyes. We drove through a community of colourful square homes which hugged the road, the lifeline. Mauritanian drivers appear blissfully unaware of the lack of infrastructure which might save their lives when their gambles do not pay off. Overtaking a truck at high speed with traffic approaching is the norm, the approaching drivers are forced to brake hard, even coming to a full stop, to allow yet another battered Toyota Corolla to arrive at his destination a few minutes earlier. We drive carefully and adapt our driving style to ensure our survival. Occasionally we pass a stubborn, beautiful tree, camels, goats, ancient Land Rovers, abandoned trucks and battered villages. Frequently we are stopped by a policeman, some of whom inspect our documents as if they have never before encountered a foreign traveller, but most simply accept our fiche and wave us on through the intense heat. One young policeman asserted his authority by creating an unnecessary roadblock, interrogated drivers, examining licenses and loads before dismissing the driver with an authoritarian wave as he stood battered by wind and sand beside a dilapidated hut. He had irritated his superiors to the point that they assigned him a position in the desert where the hot wind would eventually erode his superiority, and he might return to the town of his family, humbled and obedient. Or he would stand sentry in the desert for eternity.

Nouakchott is an unloved coastal city built to accommodate 15,000 people but home to over a million. We arrive at dusk and, after spending a small fortune on supplies at a "western" supermarket, fight our way through obstinate traffic, on dirt streets between large compounds and cross a littered, derelict piece of land to reach a camp by the ocean where we would sit for two weeks, waiting for the Carnet de Passage which would make our journey simpler as well as Luisa's new passport without which we could not continue past Senegal. The family had all applied for new passports at the South African consulate in Beverly Hills, Los Angeles in 2017. Well, all except Luisa who was adamant that she had enough pages in her passport. Notoriously, South African passports issued to overseas consulates can take six months to a year from the date of application. Put that in perspective. An American or German will have a new passport within a matter of days, but the bureaucratic corruption in South Africa was (and possibly still is) so crippling that every application has to be scrupulously processed. For many years South Africans did not need visas to enter the UK until a scandal broke in the early 2000's - thousands of Indian nationals, living in India, with no connection to South Africa whatsoever, were buying South African passports directly from corrupt officials within the Department of Home Affairs in Pretoria before entering the UK and disappearing into the system. We know of many people who bought South African permanent residence permits under the Nelson Mandela bridge in Johannesburg. In August, Luisa had applied for a new passport at the consulate in Lisbon and in February found herself stuck in Mauritania, unable to proceed until the new passport was issued. We were facing up to three months in the desert, sitting on our hands, eating sand.

Keelan swam most mornings in the sea, bordered and sailed by hand made, colourfully painted wooden fishing boats, the waves large and powerful, the locals in awe of the large young man's ability to survive the waves and currents into which they would not venture. Men gathered on the shore to await a brave and battered water taxi which daily breaks through overhead waves to deliver wet fishermen to their boats. Stray dogs fight for dominance and scraps on the beach, which offers the only glimpse of blue sky in the early mornings or on the distant afternoon horizon. The city is apocalyptic. To get there, one needs to walk down the sandy track, which leads to a paved road. Eventually, a million mile Mercedes taxi will approach and accept you and anyone else they encounter as cargo. Heading south, parallel to the ocean, the taxi passes a million strewn plastic bags and dumped waste, the coast guard guarded by AK47'S, a gas station, the fish market, run-down stores and damaged buildings, stray dogs flattened into the tar and sand perpetually blowing debris across the road. The market is a maze of tin buildings, slaughtered animals blowing in the gale, dark men with dark eyes follow your every move. The only food available is hanging from a hook or waiting in a can; the stores all sell the same products; the colour of your skin determines wealth. We buy eye drops, tinned peaches, sardines, refreshing drinks, bread, a bag of damaged tomatoes, a lift back to the camp which we regarded as shabby but, compared to the city, is, in fact, an oasis. One Wednesday morning we leave the kids in the small, dusty conference room and venture into the city with the Land Rover, heading for the "western" supermarket, at first happy to be out of the camp but instantly wishing that we had not left.

Along our route, we spot a grocer and stop to buy imported fruit and vegetables. An old woman parks her silver Toyota Corolla behind the Landy and catches my eye, for some reason I am immediately suspicious. As I start the Land Rover the old lady starts her Toyota, and as I pull out, the old lady follows suit, but Luisa suddenly remembers that she needs to buy a sim card, I stop and the Toyota stops. I am now watching the silver vehicle closely and have Luisa write down the number plate. Back on the road we know that the Toyota is tailing us, my paranoia has been on form, and there may be a good reason for us to be paranoid, we are in a country with areas off bounds due to Islamic extremism, and my imagination convinces me that an old lady following tourists may arouse less suspicion than a young man doing the same. I can't think of any other reason for her to follow us. To confirm my suspicions, I take an unscheduled turn, the Toyota follows, I speed up, and the Toyota speeds up, I slow down, and the Toyota slows down. After five minutes, we are becoming weary. I pull onto a side road and stop, the Toyota stops next to us and before I say a word Luisa jumps out of the Land Rover and approaches the Toyota aggressively. "Why are you following us?". The old lady smiles and drives forward, Luisa is in Shield Maiden attack mode, "Luisa, get back here, chill out!". We are strangers in a wild city shouting at an old lady; this could end badly for us. Back on the road, the Toyota continues to follow us, and I remember that there is a police Land Cruiser permanently parked outside the bakery opposite the western supermarket, I stop next to them, the Toyota continues 200 meters and pulls into a gas station. While I am explaining to the police that we are being followed, the old lady drives to us and stops to talk to the police, sweetly. They ask questions, and she answers before being told to leave.

Palms up, I look at the policeman and shrug, universal sign language meaning "What does she want?" He responds with a finger rotating at the temple, universal sign language, "She is crazy". The Toyota disappears, and we return to the camp after handing over a fortune for mayonnaise, eggs, tinned food, pasta and tomato paste. Fifteen minutes after returning to the camp we park in our usual spot, reunite with the kids and sit down to make dinner of sand seasoned pasta and dusty salad, Luisa looks out the window. There, parked directly in front of the Landy is the silver Toyota. The restaurant manager arrives at the scene as we jump out of the Landy to confront the woman, but we pause as the manager's hands the woman a large set of keys, the master keys for the camp. The woman smiles at me accusingly, gets in the car and drives away. "Who is that, Omar?" "The bosses mother, she is a little crazy".

We had made friends with the American educated camp owner who wore blue robes over western clothing. I never told the camp owner that his mother had followed us around town, I suspected that he would have been embarrassed.

For two weeks, the wind blew our minds away. A perpetual sandstorm which prevented us from escaping to the interior where we could explore Atar, Chinguetti and the worlds longest iron ore railway from Zouerat to Nouabhidou. Every day was the same - the mornings arrived cool and calm, but by mid-morning, the sky became dusty as the wind, encouraged by the sun, grew in strength. By lunchtime, we could not see further than the end of the nearby restaurant. Flies stirred within the Land Rover; the heat grew stifling, we struggled to breathe and lived for the night, which would bring cool, still air.

We endured the wind, heat, flies and dust until eventually, our documents arrived, by some miracle, and we were free to escape the dire city and drive to the Senegalese border on a road identical to that on which we had travelled to Nouakchott but in worse condition.

Perhaps one day we will return to Mauritania, everything changes, and with a government of and for the people, the country could be transformed. We had befriended the camp staff who had grown to respect us as we respected them. The people of the desert do not freely and automatically respect, while they may be respectful, respect itself must be earned - they inhabit a hard land where resources are few and survival is not guaranteed. We were quiet during prayer, did not expect the unchangeable to be changed and always complimented the cook though her options were few! "You are African too", they told us when we left.

Mauritania is a land of extremes and each day is an adventure of circumstance, and it is the extremity and beauty of the land which deliver a unique experience, the experience which we seek but sometimes leave willingly behind.

SENEGAL

Senegal is the westernmost point of the "Old World/Afro-Eurasia". Dakar, the political capital, is situated at the westernmost point of continental Africa. Senegal is bordered by Mauritania, Mali, Guinea Conakry and Guinea-Bissau. Senegal surrounds The Gambia, a country occupying a narrow strip of land along the banks of the Gambia River, which forms a natural and political barrier between Senegal's southern region of Casamance and the rest of the country. Senegal also shares a maritime border with Cape Verde

 Senegal uses the West African Franc (CFA)
100 CFA = EU0.15 / USD0.17

 All Europeans and most nationalities of the world can enter visa-free for 90 days. For most Southern and East Africans, a visa on arrival can be obtained for one month

 Unleaded = EU1.178/USD1.275 per litre
Diesel = EU0.99/USD1.05 per litre

 Orange
Tigo

 Although Senegal is a secular state, Islam is practised in Senegal and have devout Muslims.
Do not enter mosques or homes with shoes on. Women should try and dress modestly, and homosexuality is illegal in Senegal

 Upon entry at the Diama or Rosso border, you must report to Dakar within five days in order to get your Carnet stamped. The passavant will be issued at the border for an approximate CFA2,500. Carte Brune/CEDEAO Insurance can be obtained at AXA in St. Louis for an approximate EU50 for three months

 Police = 17
Ambulance = 33 889 1515
Tourist Police = (+221) 33 860-3810

Valid passport
Vehicle title papers
Carnet de Passage (highly recommended) or a fee of EU250
payable at the border
Vaccination certificate (advisable)
International Driver's licence

The official language is French

Bonjour! – Hello	Au revoir! – Goodbye
S'il vous plaît – Please	Pardon – Sorry
allez-vous? – How are you?	ça va bien – it's going well

Excusez-moi – Excuse me   Plus lentement – More slowly
Où est…? – Where is…?
Merci beaucoup – Thanks a lot
Je ne comprends pas – I don't understand
C'est combien? – How much is it?

Chebu Jen - fish and rice
Yassa poulet - Onion sauce with chicken
Fattaya - fried dough filled with french fries, sauces, fried egg
Fresh juices made from mango, hibiscus, ginger and bouye (the fruit from the baobab tree) - divine!
French food is standard and available in French-owned supermarkets

Saint-Louis - a bustling port city with tons of French and European influence and culture
Popenguine - a tranquil beach in the Natural Reserve of Popenguine for the bird spotters
Touba - A holy city with an annual pilgrimage, attracting between 1 and 2 million to the Great Mosque with a towering 87metre minaret
Casamance - a beautiful stretch of "coast" along the river that meets the ocean. Dolphins play in the waters and fishing for prawns is a daily treat

Winter - January to May - Low 18C/64F and a High of 25C/77F
Summer - May to Dec - Low 25C/77F and a High of 31C/88F
The rainy season is between July and September

Wresting is a national sport in Senegal and was traditionally an exercise in preparing for war.

It has an island made of millions of mollusc shells.

The Endless Summer (a humorous and exciting surfing documentary) was filmed in Senegal.

Taxi drivers attach a goat's tail at the back of their cab to bring them good luck.

The Paris-Dakar was held from 1979 to 2009 but was moved to South America after the threat of terrorism

4

Senegal. God, Trade and the Harmattan

A lifetime ago, my family and I drove our Land Rover from Peru into Ecuador. The Peruvian coast is an endless sea of sand, dry cities and unloved desert. After dropping down from the heavenly Andes and her endless switchbacks, the straight coastal road is both a relief and a beautiful bore. After days of the khaki desert, you eventually reach the border post and cross into Ecuador to be greeted by green grass, banana plantations, flowers, trees, rivers! We ate bananas, rolled on the grass until we itched, then sat in the shade of a cool tree.

The crossing from Mauritania to Senegal is a similar sensational contrast. But first, you have to negotiate a terrible road to the Dakhla border where the Senegalese welcome you with an elaborate scam - a vehicle travelling without a Carnet de Passage is charged an unofficial fee of $300 US to enter. There exists no legislation to support this claim, but the officials enforce their "law" with a vested interest. We had procured the Carnet from the Automobile Association in South Africa to ensure that we would not fall prey to this and other unofficial costs as we made our way down the west coast of Africa. Luisa has seen us through over a hundred border crossings and knows how to play the game without opening her purse, she laughs and jokes and scowls and protests until the uniform relents and allows us to proceed as we rightly should. We had heard horror stories about travellers being delayed and even thrown in jail overnight, but Luisa negotiated the entire process without paying any special fees. When asked to pay an unlisted fee, she explained that we are Africans too, we should not have to pay European fees, this caught the officials off-guard, and they relented, smiling.

With the sands of the Sahara behind us, we drove into Port Louis as the sunset, amazed by the clean streets, trees, colourful clothing, cheerful smiles, rivers and flowers and grasslands. In the city, over a bridge, we found a neighbourhood populated by blocks of colonial architecture and Frenchmen. A small boutique run by an amicable Frenchman sold us

French cheese, ham, bacon, bread, steak and wine. Our camp for the night lay at the end of a long narrow road bordered by a fish market, fishermen, ice trucks, buses, stalls, goats and the pungent smell of fish not sold. At the camp, a small tent sat in the corner under a tree, occupied but still (the next morning we met the occupant, an amicable and talkative Englishman who had cycled 100,000 miles and was on his way south). Luisa and I enjoyed a legal glass of wine (alcohol is illegal in Mauritania) and the sea breeze while the children relaxed and waited for dinner. That night was to be our first, free of the sandstorms which had assaulted us constantly in Mauritania. But Luisa and I had a rare and unscheduled argument (I can usually anticipate a brewing storm), and we did not resolve the argument before going to bed. Harsh words were said, not by me. We awoke angry and hot, I opened the rear door of the Landy and there, waiting, was the English cyclist.

"Hiya mate, my name is Jason, that is quite a truck you have there mate, I am cycling down to South Africa, yeah a long ways to go, mate, you know. You have kids in there? Ah, mate, they must be having such a great life. Yeah, I have a problem with one of my wheels, but I might be able to get a replacement in Dakar, yeah this one is a different size, and this tyre is expensive but really, really good, so I could use another wheel, but they don't have that tyre here, and I don't want to change the tyre and the wheel coz they use crappy Chinese tyres here, won't last a week without a puncture, you know. Yeah what time is breakfast mate, a bacon sandwich would go down perfect mate, and a cup of tea never killed, haha, just joking mate, you know".

"I just need to go for a leak Jason".

"Yeah, of course, mate, you had a beer or two last night, right? Yeah, I don't drink, but I tell you after Mauritania it must be great to have a cold one. I have a mate, very clever man, works in the film industry, such a clever guy, just makes things happen, you know, we used to have a great time, grew up together...".

We had to leave the camp, once Luisa and I have argued somewhere that place is forever tainted and the best way to get over it is to move on, which might explain why we don't live in a house. I jest, of course.

Unfortunately, the entry to Port Louis was not a sign of the general wealth and beauty of Senegal, but after the poverty and chaos of

Nouakchott, Senegal seemed at least marginally wealthy. But we were back in real Africa! Mauritania is the end of the Maghreb and the regional Arabic influence. The French had left more of a mark on Senegal.

If you have ever walked the streets of southern Europe, you might have met more than a few West African men selling luxury handbags, belts and shoes. The chances are great that the friendly trader in the shadow of Pisa is Senegalese and if he is chances are even better, that he is a Mouride. The Mouride's are more than a tribe; they are a community of traders. The founder Amadou Bamba is said to have stepped off a boat taking him to exile in Ghana. A prayer mat had magically appeared on the water beneath him, and after prayer, he walked on water a hundred miles back to his beloved Senegal. There he began the community on the cornerstones of faith and trust and trade. Not only do the Mourides help their community within Senegal, but they also assist traders to travel abroad where they will practice the principles of their movement and in turn, help other Mourides. Their spiritual home is the city of Touba. We were to encounter the Mourides not only through the traders and signs which alerted us to their presence but also through billboards outside communities where the Mourides had built a clinic, mosque or well.

When I think of Dakar, I have visions of the famous rally - high powered motorcycles and four-wheeled vehicles blasting through the Sahara desert, of helicopter flyovers and spectacular scenery, the well-heeled at play, racing the ultimate off-road machines in the most hostile territory. I envision a sweat-drenched Spaniard, a sponsors cap askew on his head, the torso of his white, red and blue racing suit zipped open as he shakes and aims a large champagne bottle at his teammate and a tiptoeing, laughing but cowering blonde.

The real Dakar is a city on the brink of collapse or meteoric rise. Dakar traffic is terrible, but not nearly as bad as Johannesburg or Lima, or La Paz or Los Angeles. Dakar is a city built by the French and inhabited begrudgingly by the Senegalese. We had come to the city seeking visas for some of the countries which we needed to cross, as we avoided the shorter route through southern Mauritania, Mali and Burkina Faso where Islamic extremists vent their rage (born partially from the failure of ISIS in the Middle East) on foreigners and Christians. We had rushed to the city from the north to be at the DHL office by 5 PM to collect Luisa's new passport and had found a city with suburbs not quite as terrible as we had been told to expect. In fact, if the traffic were not so horrendous, parts of the city would be lovely, liveable even.

After many hours of stop, go, stop, go, we arrived at our camp, Cercle de Voile situated between an industrial area, a motorcycle repair shop and the sea. Beneath palm trees, we watched the world go by as we waited for the visas for which we had travelled across the city by taxi. Mama Nougat cheerfully sold peanut brittle, of which she had eaten too much, her teeth suffering more than her waistline. A thin, elderly man sat all day on the exposed root of a large tree and pondered upon the sea, pop music blaring distorted from his portable speaker, his prized possession. Young men hung out on the beach among boats in dry dock awaiting repair, they played football or danced, flexing and showing off for each other, telling jokes, talking about football and girls. A harassed but smiling French woman prepared pizza and hamburgers, pasta and sandwiches in the large, open restaurant and a dark bar entertained groups of bikers and French ex-pats while accepting only exact change for drinks. The English cyclist, Jason, caught up with us and became part of our family, waiting patiently each morning to be fed our breakfast of small banana and peanut butter pancakes and English tea. Jason left Dakar before we did but cycled more than 100 miles every day, a real feat in the heat and congested or difficult roads we had travelled.

An old man driving a taxi half his age took us into the city where we had the Carnet stamped and then took another taxi to the Ivory Coast Consulate where we failed to apply for a visa. In the heat men worked with sledgehammers demolishing a concrete building, we ate a sandwich and spoke to a Swiss traveller we had first met in Nouakchott and walked faster than the traffic moved. Eventually, we accepted that having any visas issued in Dakar was out of the question as the fees were double the fees charged in neighbouring countries. We waved down a taxi and asked the driver to take us to the Decathlon sporting goods store near the campsite. There were extensive road works taking place, and our taxi driver struggled to find a way around the standstill traffic, we drove for half an hour through side streets, following Luisa's navigation app but found every possible road blocked by the construction of a railway. Eventually, the driver admitted defeat and told us that there was no way across. Then, surprisingly, he refused to accept payment for the lift as he had not been able to deliver us to our destination! This floored us; we were expecting to be charged triple because the ride had taken so long. I insisted on paying, and the driver refused the payment until Luisa took the money out of my hand and handed it to the driver, insisting that he must accept payment. He relented, and we separated as new friends. The walk back to the camp was long and hot; we had to cross the new railway track and then walk beside the dusty road without pavement for three kilometres. We eventually hopped on a bus and hopped off again once we realised that the journey would be quicker on foot. Jessica complained but did not hold us back, once fortified with a cold drink, and we arrived at the Decathlon sporting goods store expecting a wide range but finding only a few bicycles and racks of clothing. While Luisa searched for a new bikini, I watched as the covered parking area filled with men while other men set up a sound system. Eventually, the parking area was full of men standing in rows, this was their Friday mosque, and they prayed together for half an hour. We dared not leave for fear of disturbing their prayer, but there was no ill intent towards us, and we were greeted warmly once prayers were completed. The Senegalese have reason to be proud. When Luisa and I would enter a store at lunchtime, we would invariably find the staff sat together around a large metal bowl eating stew with bread, and we were asked to join the meal, which was delicious with a peanut-based sauce.

We snuck out of Dakar on a Sunday when we rightfully expected traffic to be thin. North Western Senegal is mostly dry grassland, home to many gargantuan baobab trees and villages of brick and mortar where we were either welcomed with waves by all or waves by few, depending on the village. We drove the last freeway we would enjoy for another six months, past the international airport and into a town brimming with suntanned Frenchmen populating large beach houses, coffee shops and bars. At the supermarket, we bought baguette and ice lollies for our children and for the policeman manning the checkpoint we had just crossed and would return to as we searched for a camp for the night.

THE GAMBIA

The Gambia is the smallest country on the continent of Africa and is surrounded by Senegal except for its western coast on the Atlantic Ocean. The highest point in The Gambia is 53m above sea level. The Gambia River (it's namesake) flows through The Gambia. It is said that the range of the British naval guns dictated the width of the country conquered

The Gambia uses their currency, the Dalasi
10 GMD = EU0.18/USD0.20

Most EU nationals can enter visa-free for 90 days. American citizens and all other nationalities can get a visa on arrival. A one month visa is approximately EU59/USD66, and a transit visa for 48 hours is available at the cost of EU9/USD11

Unleaded = EU1.03/USD1.13 per litre
Diesel = EU1.01/USD1.10 per litre

Africell
Gamcel
Qcell

Although a secular country, The Gambia is predominantly Muslim. The Gambia was colonised by Great Britain

Carte Brune/CEDEAO is required for entry of vehicles
A Carnet de Passage is recommended, or you can pay USD10 for the passavant

Police = 17
Ambulance = 16

Valid passport
Vehicle title papers
Vaccination certificate (advisable)
International Driver's licence

English is the official language

Benachin - rice and vegetables
Domoda - stewed meat in groundnut puree with rice
A full selection of British cuisine is available

Gambia River National Park - although expensive you can spot several species of primates
Sanyang Beach - a famous beach for tourists
Bijilo Forest Park - Birdlife, monkeys and fauna galore

Rainy season - June to Nov - Low 19C/33F and High of 33C/91F
Dry season - Nov to May - Low 16C/61F and High of 34C/93F

The official title of the 2nd Gambian President (1996-2017) was His Excellency Sheikh Professor Doctor President Yahya Jammeh.

Up until 2018, Gambians would vote by tossing a marble into a plastic drum for their elected candidate.

Baboon Island in the River Gambia National Park is a rehabilitation centre for chimpanzees. They occupy three of the five islands with over 74 primates.

Crocodile pools are considered sacred in The Gambia due to their powers of fertility.

Some tribes believe the sound of an owl will bring death to their tribe

5

The Gambia and back into Senegal

Protruding into the stomach of Senegal like a long English middle finger is the independent country, The Gambia. It is said that The Gambia is 48 miles wide because the English naval guns had an effective range of 24 miles from the Gambia River. This inconvenient little Colonial hangover lies directly in the traveller's path as they journey across Senegal and the traveller must either pay for a direct 24-hour transit visa or drive around The Gambia at greater expense. Against my better judgement, Luisa suggested that we try and cross the border shortly after nightfall and those of you who are married will know that a suggestion is often not open to compromise, particularly without a convenient alternative. The Senegalese officer barked instructions, "Park here, not there, go there, then go there!". We were learning that we needed to practice humility when dealing with West African uniforms, "Yes, sir", yielded the best results. Stamped out of Senegal, we enter The Gambia in the dark. A voice called out in English, "Park there, not there, go there". In the absence of street lights, we crossed a road and entered an unlit building where we made friends with the head immigration officer (who had never met a South African before) and paid 15,000 CFA/25USD each for the privilege of using Gambian roads. The immigration chief offered us handshakes, his home and office telephone number, email and home address. An hour after arriving at the border we drove into the nearby town, found a hotel where we could park in the parking lot, argued for half an hour over the parking fee (the security guard wanted us to pay the equivalent of a hotel room while the receptionist accepted half that amount) and waited for Jason the cyclist to join us.

A European charity ran a school in town, and Jason joined them for a chat but not a drink as he did not drink, but they certainly did. I said hello to a pink grey-haired man who drained whiskey directly from a large bottle while bosomy dears threw back gin splashed with tonic. Drums beat in the distance and Luisa and I walked through the dark streets to find the drummers who sat three rows deep and pounded a rhythm, while young men danced with great vigour and the scent of marijuana clung sweetly to the air. The absence of women did not escape my attention, and we enjoyed the spectacle from the shadows for half an hour before peeling off and heading back into the darkness and our waiting children. A man grabbed at Luisa's arm, "Gimme a dollar", Luisa did not flinch but regained ownership of her arm. "No, why should I?". The young man smiled. "Where are you from?" "South Africa, Cape Town". "Ah, so you are also African. Welcome to the Gambia".

A new bridge now crosses the river from which the British tormented the French. After a checkpoint we paid the 5,000 CFA fee and drove over while trucks queued for an unnecessary ferry - someone was not going to lose their livelihood without a fight. We drove another 24 miles and 12 checkpoints to arrive at the border where an official demanded another 15,000 CFA each for us to leave the country. "No, that's absurd, we won't pay". After half an hour I decided to play my trump card, "Phone this man, he is the immigration chief at the other border, he will tell you we do not have to pay". The plump female uniform smiled and made the call, the chief answered, "You must pay". Damn, checkmate. With Luisa fuming in the scorching heat, we handed over a pile of cash to the drooling official (it was lunchtime, and we had just paid for a month of lunches) and headed to Casamance, an area of Senegal with a dormant but passionate liberation movement.

Pointe St. Georges is a hidden gem. Accessible only by boat, dirt bike or 4x4, the point is home to a rustic village and a small "backpackers" without electricity or running water. Half of the road to the village is deep beach sand, and our Land Rover worked hard as we chose which line to drive, then committed to getting through the thickest sand to the harder ground where we could make some distance before again hitting the soft stuff which takes control of the steering wheel and shows you who is boss. The deep sand section of road is only 17 kilometres long, but it takes a good hour to eventually emerge near the shore of the lagoon where dolphins play, and the position of the sun dictates the time.

Our room was large, with four beds protected by mosquito nets and a bathroom not yet connected to the municipal water system for the simple reason that such a system did not yet exist. Neither was there electricity. We had come to the point to relax and work, writing and images, and decided that we would simply have to relax and leave sooner than planned. The lagoon lapped quietly at the low walls of the yard where a low table sat surrounded by plastic chairs with shortened legs. Birds flew overhead, the air quiet and relaxed, the laughter of children, a woman singing as she prepared our meal of rice, dorado and prawn, a cold drink in hand (the solar panels near the entranced serviced the fridge and one long-life bulb), we watched the sunset under the dusty sky. Once we had eaten our fill, Keelan began cleaning up and putting leftovers into a Ziploc bag to be snacked on later. Suddenly he asked, "Do you want a bag of cheese?" to no-one in particular. It was completely random and a serious question, he was not joking. We erupted in laughter, and he stood there, red-faced. "What the heck were you thinking about?" He had no answers; he must have been thinking about cheese for some strange reason. "Wanna bag of cheeeeese?" has now become a family saying to be used at strange and inappropriate times. We have other nuggets like "Shu-cho-pie-ho", which means "Shut your pie hole", and "Shooooosh", to be used when interrupting someone's self-defence. "Friend or Foe!" (asked in an upmarket British accent), "Fartmonster 3000" and "the Mother Beast", Luisa's unofficial names. "Jessica stop being sensitive, Keelan stop being annoying" and "is this an imagination conversation? "Slow White", Jessica's nickname. "Dumbass" is still being thrown around in a tribute to Red and Jessica laughs like Kitty from "That Seventies Show" whenever she damn well feels like it.

The Harmattan is a season in West Africa, a time of year when the northerly winds blow Saharan sand and cool air into the Gulf of Guinea. Combined with the numerous cooking fires, the sky wears a haze which obscures the sun and lends trillions of particles off which the sunset can reflect. With a cool breeze blowing away the heat of the day and the beer encouraging relaxed thoughts, we sat and whiled away the time looking at maps, discussing the route ahead. That night we slept soundly, listening to the tide creep and retreat across the sand. I spoke to the owner Louis; I suggested that he should consider digging poles into the beach and installing hammocks, the like of which we had enjoyed in Jericoacoara, Brazil. He listened patiently, and I did not need him to dismiss the idea vocally, I could tell by the look on his face that these were ideas which brought problems of transportation, investment and maintenance. His family owned the point and, with the exception of the small military base, was theirs to sell when the time was right. Soon a French developer would visit and make an offer which could not be refused, then Louis and his family would move elsewhere and live a better life while bulldozers tore down the building they had built and replaced them with large white blocks of Europe, bars, coffee shops, restaurants and supermarkets. It was just a matter of time, and all he needed to do was prosper humbly while he waited.

That morning we took a walk along the beach looking for manatees but found not them but a man in camouflage who informed us that we could not take any photographs beyond a certain point. We swam, climbed an observation tower, chased crabs, watched a woman smoke fish and relaxed in the shade until the afternoon when boats of women arrived to celebrate a wedding. They converged on a large hut at the centre of the village to drink palm wine and dance. We hung out with them for a while, playing with small children who had met few white people and returned to Louis' place for a quiet evening. In a mix of French, Spanish and English, Louis explained to me why the rebellion was important, why Casamance should be free from Senegalese rule. He despised the soldiers who were based in his village for no other reason than to protect access to the lagoon and control the villagers. He despised the soldiers for taking advantage of the village girls and told the story of how one night, many years before, the soldiers had dragged his father from his home and killed him. Louis, a large and powerful man, bristled with anger as he told me the story. He lived in paradise governed by the devil.

With the Harmattan wind at our backs, we drove past signs of Mouride investment and charity en-route to the border with Guinea Bissau. Senegal had welcomed us, and we were sad to leave.

Working on the transfer box, Rif Mountains in Morocco

Graeme taking a walk in Chefchaouen, Morocco

Keelan gathering wood in Chefchaouen, Morocco

Paying tribute to Louisa Vesterager Jespersen and Maren Ueland
in Chefchaouen, Morocco

Being towed from the Rif Mountains, Morocco

Keelan and the punk's puppies in Chefchaouen, Morocco

The Merzouga to Sidi Ali trail, Morocco

Off the beaten track, Morocco

Berber family, Morocco

Berber girl, Morocco

Exploring the Atlas Mountain range, Morocco

Dune camping in Erg Chebbi, Sahara, Morocco

Dune exploring in Erg Chebbi, Morocco

Crossing the Tropic of Cancer, Western Sahara

Port de Peche, Nouakchott in Mauritania

Escaping the sandstorms Nouakchott, Mauritania

Keelan washing up in Dakar, Senegal

A visitor, Senegal

Beach vacation, Pointe-Saint-Georges in Senegal

Drying fish in Pointe-Saint-Georges, Senegal

Cute little Louis in Pointe-Saint-Georges, Senegal

Inquisitive little girl in Senegal

A family portrait, Western Sahara in Morocco

GUINEA-BISSAU

Guinea-Bissau is located in West Africa and covers 36,125 square kilometres, borders Senegal and Guinea Conakry to the south-east.
A country larger in size than Taiwan or Belgium, with its highest point at 300metres

Guinea-Bissau uses the West African Franc
100 CFA = EU0.15/USD0.17

If travelling by road and heading South, apply for your visa in Ziguinchor in Senegal (or at any bordering country). The cost will be an approximate EU30/USD33 otherwise a hefty fee of approximately EU60/USD65 could be charged

Unleaded = EU1/USD1.05 per litre
Diesel = EU0.95/USD1 per litre

MTN
Orange

There is a majority of Christian's, but most claim to still practise indigenous religions. Guinea-Bissau was colonised by the Portuguese

A TIP can be issued therefore a carnet is not necessary, however, please ensure that the TIP is endorsed for the full period that you wish to spend in Guinea-Bissau. Carte Brune is valid in Guinea-Bissau

Police = 112
Ambulance = 119

Passport with visa (if required)
Vehicle title papers
Vaccination certificate

Portuguese is the official language, but Creole is more widely used. French is spoken fluently by most

Good morning - Bom dia (till noon)

Good afternoon - Boa Tarde (till sunset)

Good evening - Boa Noite (after sunset)

How are you? - Como voce esta? — Fine, thank you - Bem, Obrigado   My name is - Meu nome e — Please - Por favor

Thank you - Obrigado — Sorry - Desculpa

Yes - Sim — No - Não

Excuse me - Com licenca — Goodbye - Ciao

Do you speak English - Voce fala Ingles

Most meals consist of fish, rice and palm oil. Tube vegetables such as yams, potatoes and sweet potatoes are farmed for subsistence.

Hardboiled eggs are available at most roadside stalls

The Presidential Palace and the vast amount of islands and pristine archipelago reserve.

Cantanhez Forest National Park - A mosaic of mangroves, savanna and agriculture.

Varela Beach - Exotic beaches along the coastline

Guinea-Bissau has a constant temperature year-round averaging 26C/79F

Locals are called 'Bissau-Guineans' and not Guinea-Bissauans'.

Guinea-Bissau is one of the poorest countries in the world.

There are no power plants in Guinea-Bissau; therefore, most people rely on generators.

Besides subsistence farming, most farmers farm cashew nut's for export

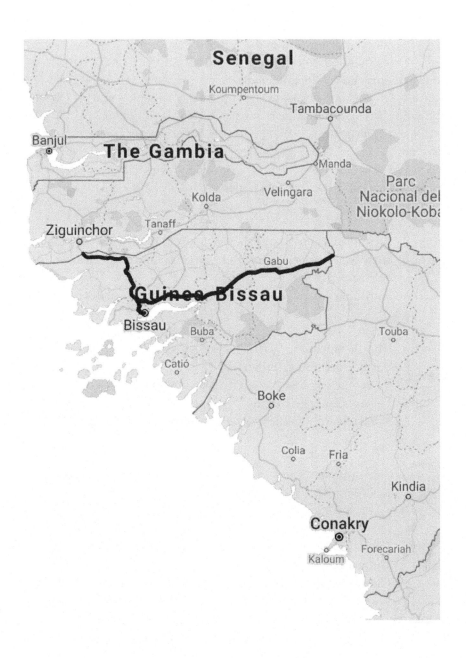

6

The Two Guineas

Guinea Bissau was the only West African territory controlled by the Portuguese. While Angola and Mozambique in the south were larger feather caps for the Iberians, Guinea Bissau was a small foothold into the riches of Western Africa. While England and France (and Spain to a degree) fought over the territory and drained resources through rail, road and port, the Portuguese made do with a small but strategic territory. My family speaks enough Portuguese and Spanish to have a rudimentary conversation in either language, and we were looking forward to meeting people with whom we could have basic but friendly and informative discussions. Guinea Bissau was not what we had hoped to find.

Because of the endless need for expensive visas, we once again found ourselves in a capital city which we would rather avoid. There is no suitable accommodation in the city, and we arrived late in the afternoon to blistering heat, seeking a parking area where we could spend the night before applying for the Ivory Coast and Guinea Conakry visas. After a few hours of searching for the right person, then phoning someone else who sent another person to negotiate with us, a gate was eventually opened, and we were allowed to enter a large concrete parking area where large walls and a building, suffocated any wind which might offer us the slightest relief from the oppressive, stifling heat. For 10,000 CFA, we were given directions to a water tap, the key to a dilapidated bathroom and a security guard who we never saw. It was a long night and an early morning rise to head to the consulates to hand over documents and large piles of cash. As South Africans (with the emphasis on Africans) we were expecting to find that we would need fewer visas than our European brethren and when we did need to apply for visas, we would pay far less. The reality is that we needed more visas than Europeans do in West Africa, and we had to spend as much as they did. Bissau city has very little appeal, unfortunately. Hot and littered and falling apart, the city is small and complicated. Some restaurants and supermarkets close at lunchtime - here is a tip, it might seem obvious, but your bakery might turn a profit if you a serving food when people are hungry and have time to eat. The supermarkets only accept cash for items which are three times the price than in Europe.

After numerous trips to the ATM, we handed over a large pile to a friendly man who said, "Come back in two days but maybe sooner", and an even larger pile to a less friendly man who said, "Come back at 2 pm". At 2 pm we collected the Ivory Coast visas and headed out of the city to a small hotel which offered expensive chalets and, if you asked nicely, might let you camp in your vehicle. We arrived at the auberge to find a short, plump and angry woman who was one moment hostile and dismissive and the next friendly and hospitable. We offered to pay her double the standard rate to park, which brought out her friendly and hospitable alter ego, and after telling us to make ourselves at home, showed us the kitchen and bathroom and swimming pool. We did not care too much about the kitchen and bathroom, but the swimming pool was irresistible. Within minutes we were parked, changed into swimming costumes and lying in the cool water. A German man did his exercises in the pool while we cooled, he glanced at us cooly every so often, then lifted an empty plastic flower pot above his head fifteen times and waddled off to scowl at the short, plump schizophrenic to whom he had pledged eternal love.

We cooked a dinner of prawn and rice, fed the kids and went to bed quietly, stewing in the heat. That morning Short Plump woke us shouting that we only paid 5,000 CFA and were not allowed to plug our small fridge into the wall socket around the corner. "We paid 10,000!". Short Plump went quiet for a moment then stormed off shouting Portuguese words which we understood but did not want to hear. Our problem was that we needed to stay another night if we were to collect the visa for Guinea Conakry the next day and we had no other accommodation than the hot, horrid parking area in the city. Again we were reminded that overland travel in West Africa demands patience and humility. After breakfast, I approached Short Plump and asked her if we could pay double the regular rate to stay another night. She said no, I said thank you and left. While I was swallowing my pride, Luisa had contacted the friendly man who issued the Guinea Conakry visa, and he informed us that we could collect the visa after lunch. Luisa had worked her magic yet again, but I only wish that she had done so before I had treated Short Plump with twice the respect which she deserves. I only hope that my children see humility as a strength, not a weakness. If you are ever in Bissau, please avoid the Restaurant and Residence Almagui.

Back in Bissau, we melted in the heat while waiting for the friendly man to return from a late lunch and finish with our passports. Luisa had struck up a conversation with the man, and I am sure that it was her respect and kindness, which had motivated him to issue our visas a day early. We left Bissau along a horribly scarred and potholed road and endured checkpoint after checkpoint, potholes, terrible drives, speed bumps, speeding overloaded trucks and reckless drivers.

Now, it may seem like I am focusing purely on the negative but the reality is that, aside from a few friendly people, our time in Guinea Bissau was almost entirely unpleasant and even though I desperately seek positives when surrounded by terrible, Guinea Bissau offered bitter few good experiences. Heading to the border was no exception. At one junction, we were stopped at four checkpoints in the space of a mile, each uniform inspecting our documentation as if we had just driven out of the cargo hold of a space ship. A typical checkpoint procedure unfolded thus;

The uniform jumps out of a plastic chair as they see you approach (letting all others pass).

A serious face, a salute.   We greet with smiles and shake hands.

"Documents", the uniform demands.

The uniform then takes half an hour to inspect each passport (often mistakenly reading old visas as if they are the bio page), inspects and studies the vehicle registration, carnet or temporary import document, studies the drivers' license, has a look at each of the occupants and then flirts with 14-year-old Jessica.

When they realise that we will not be handing over any gifts they wave us on.

Do that ten times a day, and the smiles eventually become forced and faded as you wilt in the sun waiting for the charade to play out. After one checkpoint, where the officer read my drivers' license upside down, we stopped at a gas station for some cold drinks. I walked over to stand in the shade near the road to stretch my legs, and two young men stopped walking to say hello with large friendly smiles. I chatted to them until a group of young men strolled over, the "leader" a light-skinned and dangerous-looking young man. I knew something was amiss when the two young men stopped smiling and looked afraid, for lack of a better word. I shook the young man's hand. "Give me money". I patted my pockets, "sorry, I have nothing on me", I said goodbye and walked back to the Land Rover casually. Immediately after leaving the gas station, we reached a checkpoint. A young, tall man walked over and asked for our papers, we smiled, shook his hand and handed over our documents which the young man studied with the intensity of a scientist studying a new bacteria under a microscope. "Your drivers' license is expired, you must pay a fine". Since I have not returned to South Africa since 2012, I have not had the opportunity to renew my license card which expires every five years, but I have a document from the Minister of Transportation confirming that the license is issued without restrictions and is only renewable in terms of South African bureaucracy. What followed was an hour-long argument about whether a mundane requirement of South African bureaucracy is punishable under Guinea Bissau law. It was a shakedown, I knew it, and he knew it, but neither of us would budge until eventually, he relented but then began to ask whether my vehicle had been modified according to regulations and whether I could produce an engineers certificate? He may have been as corrupt as Pol Pot, but he was also very smart. I explained that in terms of South African law vehicles modified to campers with a GVM of 3500kg and under do not require re-registration (which is 100% factual). The song and dance continued, and he kept asking another Short Plump to issue me with a fine. Eventually, I said "Fine, my wife will drive", I handed Luisa the keys and asked if we could leave, Portuguese speaking Pol Pot relented and told us to get lost.

That night we made it to the town of Bafate where we parked in a slim hotel parking area between hedges. The staff were kind and friendly to us, the tonic we needed after a day of hard travel. There are days on the road which are so taxing and difficult that you question why on earth you bother to live this lifestyle, days when you regret the choices you have made and wish that you could just teleport to somewhere, anywhere else. But, all it takes is a smile and a return of kindness and respect for the worst of the day to be forgotten, for faith in humanity to be restored. Those days in Guinea Bissau were challenging, to say the least.

The road to the border was long and unpaved, but the waves and smiles as we passed villages brought a smile back to our lips. At midday, we reached the border and stamped out of a country which most likely is wonderful; perhaps we had been unfortunate to see enough of that and too much of the alternative.

GRAEME BELL

GUINEA-CONAKRY

Guinea-Conakry, formerly known as French Guinea was named after the region of West Africa that lies along the Gulf of Guinea and is roughly the same size as the United Kingdom. Guinea Bissau, Senegal, Mali, The Ivory Coast, Liberia and Sierra Leone border Guinea-Conakry

Guinea Conakry uses their local currency, Guinean Franc
1000 GNF = EU0.096/USD0.10
Ensure that you have EURO's or Dollars on hand, as it's challenging to withdraw local currency at a bank or ATM

Visa's must be applied for before entry whilst in a neighbouring country. The visa costs an approximate EU40 for a one-month visa

Unleaded = EU0.99/USD1.05 per litre
Diesel = EU0.89/USD0.98 per litre

Orange
MTN
Intercel

Guinea is predominantly an Islamic country, with 85% of the population practising Islam. Education is not a priority for most families as women are kept out of school to help with household duties or working the land. A majority of Guinean girls are married off before they turn 18 and some even before reaching 15 years of age and polygamy is the norm within the smaller villages. More than 80% of the female population suffer genital mutilation

ECOWAS Insurance is required

Police = 122
Ambulance = 442020

Valid passport
Vehicle title papers
Carnet de Passage (highly recommended) but a TIP will be issued on arrival
Vaccination certificate for yellow fever
International Driver's licence

The official language is French

Bonjour! – Hello	Au revoir! – Goodbye
S'il vous plaît – Please	Pardon – Sorry
allez-vous? – How are you?	ça va bien – it's going well
Excusez-moi – Excuse me	Plus lentement – More slowly
Où est…? – Where is…?	Merci beaucoup – Thanks

Je ne comprends pas – I don't understand
C'est combien? – How much is it?

Rice and Cassava is the main staple diet and is combined with sauces blended with fish or beef and cooked mango
Pineapples, mangoes, avocados and bananas can be found at any roadside stall
Fried dough balls are served fresh at roadside stalls too

Grand Mosque of Conakry
Iles de Los, an island accessible by boat, perfect for a day excursion
Foutah Djallon highlands has great hiking
Bel Air is a secluded and remote beach to camp for free. It may only be pristine for a while due to a newly established bauxite mine on the same coastline

The climate is tropical and hot all year round
Rainy season - April to November
Dry season - December to March
The average Low is 23C/74F with a High of 29C/84F

Conakry is one of the wettest capitals in the world with 3.7metres of rain in a year.
The Conakry Grand Mosque is the fourth largest mosque in Africa and the largest in Sub-Saharan Africa and can host 25,000 worshippers.

Guinea is also known as Guinea-Conakry to distinguish itself from Guinea-Bissau and Equatorial Guinea.

Although one of the poorest nations in the world, it is the world's second-largest bauxite producing nation

7

Goodbye Guinea Bissau, you will not be missed

Entering Guinea Conakry, which I will from now refer to simply as Guinea, we were greeted with smiles and good humour. The rains had pelted the road to the point that not much road remained, only a weathered and scarred dirt track led from the border to the next town. With the immigration process completed and our carnet stamped we said goodbye and drove into Guinea, first through scrubland and eventually into a landscape of immense granite boulders and flat top mountains, which shadowed gigantic mango and avocado trees. The track was in a terrible condition, and we lumbered forward swaying from side to side, kicking up dust and keeping an eye on the fuel gauge. Children ran to the road to wave as we passed through shady villages, and we stopped to buy mangoes from a group of young women. A young man emerged from a grass walled compound to translate and negotiate, and we were sold a bag full of ripe delicious mangoes for the equivalent of $1.00 US. We actually had to ask the young lady to stop putting mangoes in the bag as she had already given us more than we could eat in two days. The road gradually improved, and with our fuel running low, we entered Koundara, a dry city close to Senegal with wide well-maintained roads and an ATM which refused to do the one thing it should. Guinea uses a different currency to Guinea Bissau, and we were low on fuel, but at least we had mangoes. With a quarter of a tank of fuel, we continued driving towards Labe. The roads were excellent by recent standards, and we found that we could drive at a decent speed, without the fear of hitting potholes or well-hidden speed bumps. We stopped along the road to top up the fuel tank from the jerry cans which we carry on the roof rack for emergencies. Children stopped their game of football to call to us, "Porto, Porto!".

With half a tank of fuel, we set off confidently towards Labe, a couple of hundred kilometres away, if the road remained excellent we would arrive there just after sunset. But the road did not stay excellent, at the foot of a mountain the paved road ended and was replaced by a maintained red dirt road. Luisa, who had been driving since that terrible checkpoint in Guinea Bissau, handed me the keys and I drove up the mountain as the sunset. We climbed up for an hour, surrounded by thick, healthy rainforest and were grateful that it had not rained recently. I was unsure if we were on the correct road and stopped twice to ask truck drivers if we were heading to Labe, they said yes, so we continued. The number one rule of overlanding is "Do not drive at night", but we could not find a secure place to sleep for the night and Luisa refused to sleep in the rainforest, for very good reason. There was very little traffic on the road, so we continued to drive the mountain trail which, I assume, was a beautiful drive in the daylight. The summit rose in the headlights, and we dipped over the crest and wound our way down to a checkpoint where a young man inspected our documents and told us that the rest of the road to Labe was good and we should be there in an hour. By now the fuel light had come on, and we continued on, rolling through towns in the dark to the astonished cries of "Porto, Porto!". At 9 PM we eventually reached Labe, endured a long, officious checkpoint and made our way to the Hotel Tata, a hotel with mixed reviews which offered parking. We arrived tired, sweaty, hungry, relieved and thirsty. The guard greeted us warmly, showed us where the showers and toilets were and handed us a key for each, he then plugged our fridge into the main electrical supply, and we prepared to relax. A group approached us from the restaurant as we were settling in - Americans serving with the Peace Corps. I asked Luisa to get us a cold drink in Afrikaans and one of the Americans, from Philadelphia, asked, "Hey, are you speaking Afrikaans?". He was born in Pretoria but raised in the USA after his family emigrated there. For an hour, we chatted and learned about the Peace Corps, how the volunteers live and work in remote communities and their concern over the effectiveness of their efforts. There were two girls in the group, both slim and pretty and while the brunette spoke with a Washington State accent and displayed her affection for the Philly boy, the blonde spoke with a California surfer drawl, even though she was born and raised in Montana. All three were counting down the days until they could return home, Guinea was much harder work than they had anticipated and they longed for the comforts and normality of home. Despite our exhaustion, we continued to chat to the three until a strange, lanky, dressed for the 70's Norwegian came over to make friends, enthusiastically. He was a musician, and he had stepped out of an Abba concert to learn the flute. "Good for you, man, tell the Americans, we need a shower".

The heat sucks the energy out of a person, the roads and the checkpoints and the simple, pure hard work of getting from A to B drains your energy faster than you can replenish it. The next two days would push us to the edge.

The Hotel Tata has a European touch, and it is always fascinating to arrive somewhere at night and wake up to see the reality of your environment. At night, with simple lighting, the "hotel" seemed well built but run down, and in the glare of daylight under the Harmatten dusty skies, all charm vanished. The security guard was a nice guy and did what he could to make us comfortable, but he did not run the hotel; unfortunately, that job was left to an inebriated dragon. A local woman who had married the Italian who built the hotel, the dragon, sat at a table in the restaurant and drank beer all day while screaming at the staff, breathing fire. At times she would unbutton her blouse to reveal her breasts, and she regarded every one with either unmasked contempt or the fakest of smiles. The dragon was charging us the equivalent of $30 to park in her parking area and use the bathroom. She unplugged our fridge and refused to plug it back in, scowling that electricity was a problem in Guinea, despite having a large bank of solar panels and few clients. Our house battery, the battery which is charged by the solar panel and which is responsible for running our fridge, was severely depleted and in need of replacement. All our food was going to perish, and in the afternoon, when the dragon had left to sleep, I asked the beleaguered young cook if I could have a bottle of ice to cool our fridge.

The next day we packed to leave, paid the dragon and prepared to leave. The dragon was not done with us yet, standing at the back of the Landy, she demanded that we pay for the water. Oh, ok here is 500, the standard rate for a bottle of water. "No, it is 5,000!" she slurred. "You must be mistaken, here, take 1,000, and that's that". Well, it all went to hell from there. She started shouting at us and we, completely out of character, responded aggressively. We gave her back the bottle of water, still partially iced and unopened.

"No, 5,000!". We refused, dragon grabbed our 25m electrical supply cable and ladder and stormed off towards the office, Keelan grabbed the ladder from her. An elderly man who had just delivered bread stood staring in disbelief as the dragon screamed at us and we did not back down. I threatened to call the police, but it was at that moment that I realised that this incident was spiralling out of control and really was not worth 5,000 pathetic francs. I threw the money on the table, retrieved our extension cable and left, furious. In seven years of travelling four continents, we had never been treated with such vile disrespect. But worse still, we had never allowed ourselves to lose our calm and composure, we had responded badly but could not think of another way to react to such blatant aggression. I was infuriated and exasperated, all of the frustration of the last few hard months had come to a head, and I was exhausted mentally, physically and emotionally. As we drove out of the hotel, the delivery man stopped us and apologised, he told us that the dragon was a horrible person, who drank heavily and treated everyone like dirt, her husband had been a very good man, but he could not live with her any longer, and he had left the country. He offered to find us another place to stay and again apologised for her behaviour, "We are not at all like that". We thanked him for his kindness, which had soothed us. We found a gas station and headed off into the country, Luisa driving and all of us in quiet contemplation.

It took most of the day for us to begin to relax again, hardly anyone spoke a word during the drive through beautiful countryside where friendly people waved and called to us, "Porto, Porto!". The American Peace Corp volunteers had explained to us that Porto refers to the Portuguese and had come to mean, white man. We returned happy waves solemnly. We had time to think. Africa is tough, and you have to have your mind in the right place if it is not to get the better of you. The endless checkpoints, bad roads, expense, heat and poverty, had been grinding away at our resolve, energy and patience, and the worst of the journey was yet to come. We needed to get our minds in the right place, we needed to be tough, resourceful, patient and humble, and we needed to be positive and respectful. If not, Africa would chew us up and spit us out; we travelled her on her terms, and nothing would change that reality. As they say in South Africa - Africa is not for sissies.

When we had crossed into Morocco, we had spent the first-night free camping beside the Mediterranean, on a small outcrop overlooking the port of Al Jazeera's. There we had met a Zimbabwean, Dot who was driving West Africa solo in a blue Ford van. She was brave and eccentric, as one needs to be to attempt such a journey, and we were following in her footsteps, driving the same roads as she had. Outside the town of Mamou, Dot had attempted to spend the night camped by a river, but a policeman had told her it was not safe and escorted her to an isolated nightclub where she was given permission to spend the night after buying the policeman dinner. She had loaded the location on the app iOverlander, and we decided to try our luck and ask if we could camp the night after buying a few beers and dinner.

We were greeted by Mohamed, a Sierra Leonean who had escaped the civil war a few hours west. He had come to Guinea with his family and had stayed, building a new life. Mohamed took care of us as if we were royalty, we were not allowed to lift a chair or move a table without being assisted, and he escorted us to the toilet if we needed to go. With loud music pounding, we sat and relaxed with a few large, warm beers and ate a meal of chicken and rice. It had been another tough day, and the beer helped soothe the rough edges. When we asked if we could camp for the night, Mohamed immediately agreed and without our knowledge, sat and guarded us all night once the other patrons had left. A thunderstorm crackled and banged throughout the thankfully chilly night, and we awoke to find Mohamed seated in a plastic chair, waiting for us. We chatted for a while as Luisa packed up and we left, leaving Mohamed with a large tip and a warm handshake. His hospitality and genuine warmth had been exactly what we needed, and we left the restaurant/nightclub with a renewed sense of vigour, an energy which we would need over the next few days.

South of Mamou, the road deteriorated steadily, and we soon found ourselves swerving around, and over gigantic potholes, we passed villagers who waved and children who chased the Land Rover. A young, traditionally dressed young man waved. I returned the wave, and he immediately rotated his hand and flipped the bird. This made me laugh in good-humoured frustration, damn, he got me. That night as we approached Kissidougou, we decided to look for a gas station where we could sleep safely. After a day of hard driving through the rainforest and low mountains and natural palm oil plants, we needed a good nights rest. Southern Guinea seemed wilder but much friendlier than the north-west; there had been many checkpoints, but none too bothersome and the road itself was the most taxing element of the journey. We arrived at a suitable Gas station as the sunset and asked permission to stay the night. The attendant granted permission without hesitation.

The garage forecourt was lit by large spotlights, worthy of a small football stadium. A generator hummed loudly in a far corner, local women filled buckets of water from a hand-turned well, and we camped opposite the well, along a wall and near to the road facing out, in the event that we needed to flee in the night (a precaution which we practice routinely), but we did not feel unsafe. A thick rainforest surrounded us and in the air hung smoke from countless palm oil boilers.

The Story of RayRay

It was mid-April by now and the rainy season was fast approaching. While Luisa prepared a simple dinner, I took photos of the million insects which spun in frenzied hypnosis around the double spotlights two meters from and above the Land Rover. Suddenly the generator died, and instantly the spotlights blackened, the only lights visible were those in our camper where Luisa and the children stood or sat. A scream broke the darkness. It was Luisa. "They are everywhere; they are climbing through the window frames, there are thousands!". The horde of insects had turned their attention to our lights in the dark night and by sheer volume, were able to access a vehicle carefully constructed not to allow insects to enter.

"Turn the lights off!" I shouted.
"I can't; they are everywhere!"
"Turn the lights off!"

Luisa and Keelan swatted and swept and screamed and shouted and swatted and swept and screamed. From my calm vantage, I could clearly see the solution and did not share a fear of being in the dark, surrounded by two million wings and mandibles and thorax.

"Turn off the lights now!"
"That won't help!"
"Do it now!"

Keelan reached over and killed the lights, I opened the rear door and placed a diversion solar light on the bumper of an old Toyota SUV parked behind the Defender.

"Now swat", Luisa and Keelan, and eventually Jessica, swatted and swept and screamed before exiting the vehicle, as did almost every insect.

As we stood in the moonlit dark, waiting for our unwanted occupants to evacuate, a large creature landed on my exposed neck. Quickly and gently with open fingers, I scooped the insect off and flung it aside. It was a beautiful green Praying Mantis, 10 centimetres long. She landed gently on the concrete forecourt and looked around before flying up to land on Keelan's arm. Keelan allowed the creature to clamber over him for a while before placing her on the drop-down sand ladder table suspended on the side of the camper. With the red light of a head torch (insects are not attracted to red light), we finished our evening routine and went to bed, listening to the sounds of the rainforest around us, the occasional insect flitting onto our faces as we fought the heat to sleep.

That morning we found the Praying Mantis clinging to the frame of the drop-down table which we had folded closed before going to bed.

"We should move her Papa", said Jessica.
"No, it's ok; she will leave when she wants to".
After fuelling the Land Rover, we left the garage and drove for eight hours on horrendous roads through sublime landscapes to reach the isolated border with Cote d'Ivoire. It was a gruelling day of mud, potholes and remote wild towns where murals of men wielding machetes standing over the bodies of their enemies decorated the lot opposite the police station and market.

A short distance from the border, we heard a bang, and the Land Rover lost all power to her wheels. My worst fear was that the gearbox had suffered a failure, but after working through the gears, we began to suspect that the fault was elsewhere. Perhaps the rear axle? With diff lock engaged, the vehicle would pull forwards and a horrible grinding sound emitted from the right rear of the axle. We rocked the Landy forwards a few times, and suddenly the grinding stopped completely. I had an idea of what the failure might be and removed the right rear drive member to reveal that it was completely stripped. I used to carry a few spare drive members but, to my horror and disappointment discovered that I had none in my spares box. Luckily we still had access to the internet via our mobile sim, and I sent a message to our friend Rob Keen in Pretoria, he advised that we could drive in two-wheel drive by removing the rear half shaft and engaging diff lock.

We followed his advice and managed to get the vehicle rolling with power to the front two wheels and with the sun setting, reached the border and endured the procedures of importance which a uniform bestows with power. Parallel to the muddy corrugated track which we were forced to drive, a perfect Chinese road waited to be marked with paint and transport resources for the glory of Beijing. After a day of bouncing, shaking, splashing mud and wind, we arrived before midnight at a small hotel in the town of Touba, exhausted but relieved and amazed to find that the Praying Mantis was *still* clinging to the side of the sand ladders.

"Tomorrow, if she is still here we will let her inside the camper".

The next morning she was still with us, perfectly healthy. I reached out my arm and allowed her to climb up onto my shoulder before stepping into the camper with our new family member. She flew from my shoulder and settled on the gas strut which supports the pop-up roof. I never witnessed her fly again.

Praying Mantis are voracious predators with large appetites - they prey on grasshoppers, other insects, small birds and even snakes and to watch them hunt and eat is fascinating. As ambush predators, they blend in with an environment and wait with eternal patience before striking an unsuspecting prey then feeding with glutinous efficiency. But our new "pet" was also incredibly fragile, and we had to be careful not to sit on her or swat her or close the roof on her. While we drove, she sat by the kids, hanging from our Peruvian privacy curtain, or clung to the mattress above the children or clung to the handles suspended from the ceiling. She was not captive, and when camped, we would leave the windows and doors open until the sunset and we had to deploy the mosquito netting. We named her Ray (uncertain of her gender) but then changed her name to RayRay once we realised that she was indeed a she. In Greek mythology, Praying Mantis are revered and believed to guide a lost traveller home, we were not lost, but we were driving back to our birth country, South Africa.

RayRay was the perfect pet - fascinating to observe and self-sufficient, but Luisa was unsure that she was eating enough and in the evenings would have me search wherever we were to find bugs for our friend to eat.

"She is free to leave, when she is hungry, she will hunt".

"Maybe she is afraid to go outside, or maybe she can't hunt, go catch a grasshopper".

And so I found myself scouring trees and buildings and anthills and bushes for bugs. Unlike the rainforests of Guinea, the mountainous grasslands of Cote d'Ivoire support far fewer insects, and I found myself spending hours, Leatherman in hand, hunting. If I was lucky, I would spear a grasshopper, but most often, I would return to the camper empty-handed. What kind of man can't even provide for an insect? We would certainly all perish in the wild.

"She is free to leave; when she is hungry, she will hunt!"
To feed RayRay, I would present her with the bug, held to her with the Leatherman. We discovered that she would not eat dead bugs, and there had to be some kind of movement before she would strike with unnecessary exaggeration and devour her easy meal. Eventually, I found my hunting niche; I would swat a fly softly, then pick it up with the Leatherman and feed her. She was insatiable and could eat twenty flies in a row, devouring the little black snacks entirely.
We had been trained by an insect.

At first, we thought that RayRay would soon grow tired of us and her diet of flies, that one day she would simply fly out of the open window and never return. Camped in a Catholic mission among the hills of a chaotic town called Mann, RayRay would climb out of the camper and explore the surrounding areas, sometimes lying in the shade of the pop-up roof, sometimes taking a walk in the long grass, sometimes hanging out in a pomegranate tree, but always returning to the camper in the evening and sleeping in her chosen nesting spot, above my bed, on the roof handle.

RayRay stayed with us for almost a month, travelling through Cote d'Ivoire, Ghana, Benin and Togo. She became part of the family and seemed to enjoy our company.
But nature has her own way. In Ghana, another Praying Mantis joined us - a large female. Somehow she entered the camper without us noticing and as we slept a territorial ritual took place, Luisa heard fluttering and a commotion in the dark night and we awoke to find RayRay missing a leg. At the Ghana border, we decided to remove the aggressive female from the camper, to protect RayRay. She attacked me as I removed her gently, scurrying up my forearm and biting down into

my skin, a bite which was not very painful at all, but her intention was obvious. She refused to leave and kept returning to the camper until I forced her into a tree and drove off without her. Her name was Jean Pierre, and if you ever drive across the Ghana border into Togo, you might find her in the tree near customs, cursing me.

In Togo, RayRay became weak and would not eat even the juiciest flies or grasshopper, and we awoke one hot morning to find her spinning a cocoon on the roof handle. She had chosen our home to have her babies, and it seems that she had made a conscious decision. We had done our research and knew that once she had laid her eggs, she would die. Weakly she ate her last fat, juicy grasshopper meal and lay down on a paper towel. In the morning, she was lifeless.

RayRays' eggs stayed with us for two weeks until we reached the border with Benin, we had hoped that the 400 babies would hatch and we would be able to keep one of her offspring with us. But a camper is no place for a swarm of Praying Mantis, and we decided to un-stick the cocoon from the roof handle above the kitchen sink and to relocate it to a tree near a swimming pool, in the shade and away from potential predators where they could hatch and nature could take its course.

I never knew that it was possible to love a bug.

COTE D'IVOIRE

Cote d'Ivoire has two capitals, namely Abidjan (economic) and Yamoussoukro (political). Cote d'Ivoire is bordered by Guinea, Liberia, Mali, Burkina Faso, Ghana and the Gulf of Guinea (Atlantic Ocean) to the south

Ivory Coast uses the West African Franc
100 CFA = EU0.15/USD0.17

Most nationalities require a visa to enter. Visa's must be obtained before entry for a fee of approximately EU50. The visa can be applied for online at www.snedai.ci

Unleaded = EU0.90/USD0.98 per litre
Diesel = EU0.89/USD0.98 per litre

Orange
MTN
Moov

Christianity and Islam are the two main religious groups. Cote d'Ivoire was colonised by the French

Carte Brune Insurance is required

Police = 170

Valid passport
Vehicle title papers
Carnet de Passage (highly recommended) but a TIP will be issued on arrival
Vaccination certificate for yellow fever
International Driver's licence

The official language is French

Bonjour! – Hello

S'il vous plaît – Please

allez-vous? – How are you?

Excusez-moi – Excuse me

Où est...? – Where is...?

Je ne comprends pas – I don't understand

C'est combien? – How much is it?

Au revoir! – Goodbye

Pardon – Sorry

ça va bien – it's going well

Plus lentement – More slowly

Merci beaucoup – Thanks a lot

Grilled chicken and fish with fermented cassava

Allocco - fried plantains in palm oil

Seafood is excellent and easily obtained at mos restaurants

There are a large variety of Lebanese restaurants in Abidjan

A vast amount of fresh fruits are available at most roadside stalls

Grand Bassam - The beaches around Abidjan are great to visit but beware of the ocean that can be quite tumultuous.

Abidjan is a fantastic city and one of our favourites throughout West Africa.

Basilica of Our Lady of Peace in Yamoussoukro - largest Basilica in the world.

Tai National Park with an abundant rainforest.

Comoe National Park with wildlife where you can spot monkeys, duikers and perhaps even some lions and leopard.

Mount Nimba Strict Nature Reserve - an excursion made by foot

Cote d'Ivoire has two distinct seasons

November to March - Dry Season- Low of 23C/73F and High of 32C/90F

April to October - Rainy season - Low of 22C/72F and High of 31C/88F

The country was once called the "teeth coast" due to the high trade in ivory.

The Ivory Coast is the world's largest exporter of cocoa.

The Tai National Park is an ancient forest and home to the pygmy hippopotamus.

St. Paul's Cathedral in Abidjan cost USD12 million to build.

Cote d'Ivoire was the second black and non-English speaking country to win an Academy Award for "Black and White in Color" by Jean-Jacques Annaud

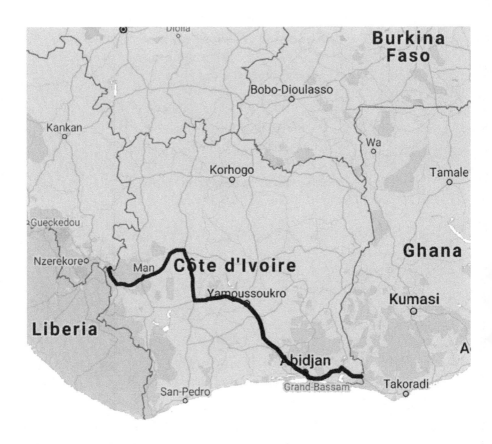

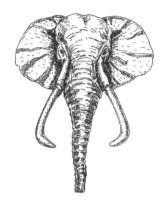

8

Cote d'Ivoire

The city of Man is nestled noisily between massive granite hills and thick green vegetation. After the crossing from Guinea, we were in need of an officious man to stamp our temporary vehicle documentation and a quiet place to rest and prepare for the next leg of the journey. While we waited for the customs man to complete our documentation (and after refusing to pay his $200 unofficial fee), Luisa and I took a long walk to the centre of town where we had heard rumours of an air-conditioned supermarket. We passed a gated and spiked fenced water park where privileged children played under the envious gaze of multitudes of unprivileged children, who spun around to watch us pass. Numerous taxis passed and hooted, but we waved them on, Luisa was having a bad day, and a pleasant walk helps her mood improve. The littered muddy verges of the potholed, uneven paved roads presented us with challenges as we avoided puddles and debris. Eventually, we reached the heart of the bustling town and entered the cool supermarket, the large glass doors held open by a smartly dressed security guard. It was only when the fresh conditioned air chilled our skin that we realised how hot and humid the city was. We were both drenched in sweat while searching fridges for refreshment and fresh dairy products. We returned to the Land Rover, Keelan and Jessica and ate lunch while waiting for the customs official to release us into the country. By late afternoon we were free to leave.

The stark national differences a border represents is perhaps one of the most astounding experiences an international overland traveller can experience. Guinea Conakry was a country rising (from an admittedly low base), but the southern Nzerekore had suffered years of neglect. While the Ivory Coast border post itself had been new and relatively modern, the infrastructure surrounding it was close to non-existent, except for the near-perfect but closed new Chinese road. We did not struggle to communicate in Man though, the people seemed mostly bilingual, to a degree, and a professional young lady escorted us to an air-conditioned wooden building, designed to be erected quickly and bearing the colours of a telecom company, where we purchased airtime and mobile data.

Consulting the iOverlander map Luisa, found a site where we could camp, a Catholic mission built on the side of a hill overlooking the city. We arrived and negotiated a price for a room and free parking for the Land Rover. The room itself was basic, ancient, mouldy and worn down but relatively clean and boasted an old fan and mosquito nets above the beds. There was an outdoor shower where we installed our porta potty as the communal toilets were dirty and popular with the few men who rented the rooms around us. Tall mango trees surrounded the white-walled compound where the grass grew unhindered. Large lizards prowled the trees and buildings seeking prey, and small brown grasshoppers jumped nervously ahead of your feet as you walked. Keelan and Jessica were given the room while Luisa and I enjoyed the space within the camper, an area which is more than adequate for only two occupants but which can be slightly crowded when we are all occupying the same space. At night we sat down to eat a meal of stewed meat, rice and salad, $10 in total and served with fresh bread rolls, more than we could possibly eat.

The staff were friendly and generous, eager to make us feel comfortable. Beside the reception area a large, cool lounge area offered us the opportunity to work on our computers while drinking ice-cold Coca-Cola, I wrote my magazine articles and Luisa worked on the logistics - planning the route, researching visa requirements and communicating with other travellers. The magazine articles represent a large proportion of our income, and I had to be sure to have a couple ready to submit, properly edited, well written and accompanied by images. I was struggling with the images, though. The skies over West Africa are permanently grey, a combination of dust, cooking and clearing fires and the acrid smoke of burned plastic. If you had to ask me what is the scent, West Africa, I would say it is the bitter and disappointing smell of melting plastic. Some genius decided that it would be a great business to produce 500ml packets of water which vendors sell at every opportunity. The water is filtered and usually cold, but the little blue plastic bags are an environmental nightmare, wherever you go, you will see those indestructible blue flowers of "progress" littering roads, fields and walkways and flitting on the breeze, constipating the sewerage systems in towns and cities and floating in greasy black rivers, en-route to the beleaguered ocean. It seems almost all waste is burned in West Africa, there are hardly any municipal waste collection facilities, and you knew that every plastic product you used was destined to be converted into a noxious gas, filling the air of our beautiful blue globe until eventually, one day, the earth will be forced to shake us off for the sake of her own survival. My own selfish problem was that we were struggling to take photographs which did not feature a background of white grey haze. The Catholic mission was a peaceful retreat though, and we were glad to be there while we organised a replacement half shaft to be delivered from Bearmach in Wales to the Johannesburg home of our friend Robert (the Polish South African who had helped us out with the courier in Morocco) who would be flying to Abidjan en-route to Burkina Faso. We had a week to relax and prepare for the road ahead, a week to plan and work and recharge our batteries. Looking back Guinea Conakry and Guinea Bissau was hard work indeed.

We travelled West Africa with an outdated version of the Rough Guides guide, printed in 2008. Due to the civil war in The Ivory Coast, more commonly and officially known as Cote d'Ivoire (or CI to locals and overland travellers), our old guide book did not contain a section on this country. But we did not feel unsafe or threatened at all; in fact, we felt safer in Cote d'Ivoire than we had felt in either of the Guineas. The police and military personnel were professional and courteous when we eventually headed out onto the road to Abidjan; we were waved through every checkpoint with a smile.

Us "Europeans" really did leave behind a political mess in Africa. Didn't we? Our forefathers sailed down the coast to subdue, disenfranchise, exploit and enslave a regional population with a complex ancient social order and squabbled for resources, they built roads and railways from pristine rainforests and new mines and killing fields, and those arteries of commerce led solely from the source to the sea. The slavers recruited one tribe to enslave another, the rubber merchants hacked and burned, the ivory hunters decimated the vast elephant herds and men who had never set foot in Africa divided the continent from boardrooms in Berlin. Arbitrary lines drawn on a map eviscerated ancient tribes and divided the land, nation-states were formed to be governed solely for the profit and pleasure of European masters. After the Second World War, those masters were exhausted financially and had found a limit to their ambition, governing rowdy, vast African states became unprofitable -

democracy and independence were foisted on a people who had only recently discovered that they were Nigerian, or Ghanian, Senegalese or Congolese. The evacuation of the European bureaucracy and ruling classes left behind a vacuum for leadership and tribal dominance which had been kept in check by the colonists. Decades later when Nelson Mandela was released from prison and elected to power in South Africa, he ensured that the white-dominated bureaucracy stayed in place, ensuring that the country would continue to run smoothly until the balanced transition of administrative power could take place. In West Africa, most European bureaucrats either fled or were evicted at independence and these countries were challenged to survive and prosper, while those least qualified for leadership jostled for power. "Big Men" arose from the ashes of post-colonial conflicts and they ruled their countries with impunity, supported begrudgingly but cynically from Europe, often playing both sides of the Cold War and amassing massive personal fortunes while the average African toiled. Had these men invested the profits of vast natural and mineral wealth back into the countries which they controlled, Africa today would likely rival Asia in terms of GDP and industry. In fact, at the time of independence, many Western economists saw the awakening of an African giant but, while Asia re-organised, educated and consolidated resources most African economies slumped into deep, debilitating recession. European industrialists continued their industry of pillage, paying large concessions to the "Big Men", an arrangement which may have suited the Europeans well as they could continue to profit without the hassle of governing these countries or investing in social programs and non-commercially essential infrastructure.

Felix Houphouet-Boigny was the exception to the rule, at least for most of his career. He led The Ivory Coast from independence in 1960 until he died in 1993, a thirty-three year period during which the country enjoyed significant economic growth and enjoyed a peace elusive to their West African neighbours. Houphouet-Boigny believed that financial freedom had to be achieved before political freedom could be realised, and he maintained a very close relationship, particularly with France and with the West in general. And, despite the two civil wars fought in The Ivory Coast after the vacuum of his death, it was evident that Cote d'Ivoire was quite unlike her neighbour, Guinea Conakry.

After three decades in power, Houphouet-Boigny tarnished his reputation forever by building the worlds largest church (according to the Guinness World Records), I assume, in search of salvation. The

Basilica of Our Lady of Peace was built of the finest Italian marble and European craftsmanship in Yamoussoukro (Houphouet-Boigny's birth village) in the late 80's at an expense of between $150,000,000 and $600,000,000. The basilica was built as a gift to the Catholic church, and this offering reminded me of the story of Santiago de Compostela in Galicia, where pilgrims could earn salvation, and the wealthy could purchase salvation. Perhaps Houphouet-Boigny was inspired by the Camino de Santiago, as he hoped that Africa's 75 million Catholics would adopt the basilica as a pilgrimage site. They have not. What is for sure is that Houphouet-Boigny sought to memorialise himself through the construction of the church if you ever visit the "Basilica in the Bush" be sure to look for the stained glass panel depicting the old president ascending to heaven with baby Jesus. Imagine what that money could have done for the people and infrastructure of Cote d'Ivoire? Pope John Paul II showed up (how could he not, there was a villa with a pool built on-site solely to accommodate his Holiness) and consecrated the gift which was built to house 18,000 worshippers and serves only a few hundred every Sunday.

Presidents for life become detached entirely from the reality of their people. Robert Mugabe is an example of an African president who began his career with the greatest intentions and ended that career in shame a few decades later, having pillaged a country which he grew to consider as a personal possession.

Houphouet-Boigny went a step further and established the village of Yamoussoukro as the administrative capital of Cote d'Ivoire. We visited the city with a Spanish family travelling in an old khaki Land Cruiser, we had met them in Man and found ourselves in convoy. John, Nina and their tempestuous daughter, Bianca had already explored much of Europe and Asia in their Land Cruiser, and while Bianca loathed (or pretended to loathe) overland travel, Nina and John were completely as obsessed as we were with a lifestyle which gives more than it takes. We never convoy, never. Perhaps we are too independent, but it seemed like a good idea to convoy in West Africa though The Ivory Coast was peaceful and pleasant. With the slow Land Cruiser trundling along behind the Land Rover, we covered good ground, often stopping to buy supplies, fruit, bread or the occasional ice cream. With the sun setting, I scanned the rainforest verged road for a place to stay for the night. Not far after a small and well-organised town, we spotted a cleared area and what appeared to be a weigh station. We drove in, and John and I asked the staff of the station if we could park our vehicles up in a clearing near the rainforest where two large skips stood waiting to be filled with palm fruit, destined to be boiled to create palm oil. We parked the vehicles beside each other and boiled water for Jon and Nina who had run out of cooking gas, we still had plenty gas, having filled the large 12 kg gas can in Western Sahara. Luisa and I drank a cold beer and chatted, Bianca hid inside the Toyota camper, and Keelan and Jessica retreated to our camper once they realised that Bianca would not be hanging out with them that night. I made an effort to befriend Bianca, I felt that I understood her desire to be back home with her friends and internet and cosy bedroom and school drama, she was twelve years old and had not taken to travel as our kids had. I could make her smile when dark clouds hung over her mood, and I could make her laugh when she really did not want to, but there was only so much that the odd good humour of a stranger can do to alleviate seemingly permanent unhappiness. Jessica was not much older than Bianca, and it was my job to ensure that her mood was even and that her bad days improved.

A man lit a fire outside his home on the verge of the rainforest, we listened to the insects come to life and, not for the first time, I spent a while catching crickets for our pet Praying Mantis to devour. It was a peaceful night, a beautiful night shared with new friends and a discussion of the road south. The roads had been excellent so far, mostly, and we were making good time across a country which we all (almost all) had come to enjoy. Ivory Coast seemed to be in much better condition than that of her neighbours to the north and was a welcome respite from the hard work travel conditions we had come to expect.

We left the camp the next morning in convoy with Jon and Nina and enjoyed a relaxed drive along winding rainforest roads, weaving around and over hills, waving hello to the locals, enjoying snacks of deep-fried bread (we call the snack vetkoek (fat cake) in South Africa) and stopping to buy fresh fruit. The Ivory Coast has the most delicious, peppery bananas and we bought an entire bunch consisting of about twenty hands (one banana is a finger, a grouping of attached fingers is a hand), the bananas were strapped to the roof rack, on top of the small Turkish BBQ and in front of the rolled Moroccan mat, truly international company. The fruit vendors were friendly and cheeky, competing with each other and trying to charge us exorbitant prices, negotiating with them was half the fun, and we soon parted with bags of mango, small green and red peppers, cucumber, tomatoes and pungent red onions. On sale at one stall were massive snails the size of Jon's hand, but neither of us was tempted by the ideas of steak sized escargot. I reminded Jon to drive with his driving lights on; it would be so much easier to spot him as he lagged behind the traffic and on hills but, as always, he forgot to turn them on, his khaki Land Cruiser blending in with the environment in my rearview mirror. They would often stop, and we would often wait. At one checkpoint we were asked for the Ecowas insurance which Luisa produced, but Jon had not purchased, insisting that his European insurance was acceptable. Fortunately (or in my case, unfortunately) Luisa was doing much of the driving as she had a valid drivers license and mine had long since expired, the police studied her license very carefully looking for any discrepancies. After half an hour of to and fro, Jon was permitted to continue with his European insurance, but we had lost a lot of time, the sun was about to set, and there were no signs of a quiet place to camp for the night. We drove through the town of Sahuye and stopped in the yard of a house beside the road, large termite hills towering over our vehicles. I asked the owner of the house if we could camp in his garden and he kindly agreed and offered us water. While Luisa prepared dinner, I searched for insects for RayRay's dinner, I searched the hollow termite mounds, the grass and trees and found only a gecko, a shy cricket and a scorpion. The scorpion was lying in wait next to the ladder at the back of the Landy and soon found himself one with the earth. The cricket was disabled and presented to the fussy praying mantis who swayed on her bright green stilts. She was waiting for movement; her meals had to be alive. The cricket moved it's front legs slightly, and RayRay pounced, within seconds half of the cricket was devoured, and within a minute not even legs remained.

Beside our camp, the sights and sounds of life continued - overloaded cars, trucks and motorcycles continued to blast along, late into the evening. That morning we awoke to find that our host had brought us a small bench and a barrel of rainwater which I filtered with our Lifesaver jerrycan water filter, which was proving to be a literal lifesaver. I wrote an honest review of the Jerrycan which the manufacturers failed to appreciate, though they should have!

"... As a family overlanding the west coast of Africa, we had a few concerns before setting off - primarily safety and health. While violence is an ominous threat, it is malaria and bacteria which have claimed more lives in Africa than any bullets, and it is those two swords of death and disease which we had to deal with daily, particularly in the tropics where there is no shortage of water *itself but of clean, safe drinking water. We knew that we would explore countries of extremes where self-sufficiency is essential and where a simple illness could prove fatal under the worst conditions.*

With this in mind, we built our camper in Florida to tackle the toughest overland routes, and while sophisticated water filtration and purification systems exist, we are analogue in the age of digital - preferring simple manual systems to those which rely on unreliable conveniences such as electricity. While the Land Rover is equipped with water storage tanks, the system is not designed to deliver potable water but rather purely for storage. I had my eye on the Lifesaver Jerry Can for a few years and was delighted to take delivery of the 20 000 UF Jerrycan while in Portugal - this one product would be the source of all our potable water (four gallons a day) as we explored the worlds most demanding transcontinental route. I am not being dramatic when I state that our lives may well depend on this product.

It is worth noting that while we were in Portugal preparing for the trans-Africa journey, our host city was hammered by the worst hurricane in centuries. In the aftermath, we used the Lifesaver jerrycan to filter the municipal water until we were sure that the storm had not compromised the water supply. This water filter is a Preppers dream come true.

According to the Icon Lifesaver website www.iconlifesaver.com the Jerrycan is "a robust and portable water purifier capable of filtering 20,000 litres/5,282 US gallons of clean drinking water, removing viruses, bacteria, cysts and parasites instantly. The LifeSaver Jerrycan holds up to 18.5 litres of water at any one time and is designed to support those with a greater demand for clean water such as group expeditions, adventurers embarking on overland travel, families or those setting themselves up for off-grid living".

To use simply assemble according to the instructions, fill the Jerrycan with the cleanest water you can source (wading a bit deeper into that river to get silt free water will no doubt prolong the life of the filter mechanisms), pressurise the system with 15 depressions of the handheld pump and open the spigot. Drink.

The flow rate is not exactly rapid and while the manufacturers claim a flow rate of a gallon a minute we have found that with daily use for over six months the rate is closer to 3 litres a minute. But, fifteen minutes every morning is sufficient to fill all water bottles with clean, dependable and tasty water.

Based on our six-month daily use of this water purification system, we suggest the following:

- Take the time to read the manual and be sure to assemble the filtration system correctly,

- If using for extended periods in remote places consider carrying a spare spigot assembly, this is the weakest part of the unit and the spout may break if knocked by a huge 19-year-old foot. If the spout does break the shower attachment is unusable. The internal spigot release spring mechanism is also prone to failure but can be repaired in the field.

- The shower attachment is useful not only for showering but also for filling water bottles by hose with the shower rose removed.

- Fill with the cleanest water available and rinse the Jerrycan often,

- Do not allow the Jerrycan to stand dry for long periods once the filtration system is activated in the initial assembly procedure - should the system dehydrate it becomes unreliable.

- Store and carry the can in a cool, shaded place in or on your vehicle as long term UV exposure is detrimental. The jerry can has similar dimensions to a standard metal jerrycan and weighs around 8lb empty.

- Do not over pressurise the system when filtering water and remember that the system works best when the can is full,

- The can is prone to leakage if left pressurised.

If we had to suggest any changes to the design of the Lifesaver Jerrycan we would make only two suggestions - the single central handle should be replaced by the standard three handle jerrycan design which allows for team portage. The spigot assembly should be more robust, preferably an alloy of some sort. This product is approved for military use but needs to be tough enough to be used and abused over long periods by ham-fisted soldiers (and clumsy 19-year-old overlanders, i.e., my son).

Retailing at around $300.00 (depending on accessories purchased) the Lifesaver Jerrycan is an investment well worth every cent. Not only will each litre of clean, filtered water cost less than 0.015c (300 divided by 20 000), but you will also be doing the planet a favour - we noticed immediately how much less single-use plastic bottle waste we were purchasing and discarding when refilling dedicated water bottles from the Lifesaver. We have filled the Jerrycan from wells in Cote d'Ivoire, Ghana and Guinea, from an oasis in the Sahara and have filtered municipal tap water in Dakar, Lagos and Abidjan. The Lifesaver Jerrycan has stored and delivered clean water to our family, and we will, without doubt, continue to utilise this tool as our primary water filtration system for many years to come as a simple filter replacement is all that is needed to ensure another 20 000 litres of piece of mind".

After filling our water bottles with clean, filtered water, we filled Jon and Nina's water bottles, thanked our host and chatted to the policeman who had parked himself at the entrance to the home, perhaps on his own initiative or sent by a superior. We did not feel unsafe at all, and this is a great compliment to the people of The Ivory Coast, a country which had only a few years earlier been plagued by war and associated lawlessness. We were respected and welcomed, protected and accommodated with no ulterior motive. Imagine the most impoverished region in your country, imagine foreigners with expensive overland vehicles and pretty daughters arriving at a strangers home and asking to spend the night. Imagine if they would receive the welcome and respect which we received?

We gathered some cash together and offered it to our host, who initially refused to accept the gift but eventually relented.

The drive to Abidjan was uneventful, the roads in good condition, the police friendly and courteous, the villagers waving and school children chasing the vehicles. I'd imagine that for many West African children living along the main routes, us overlanders are a relatively common sight. There are a few roads leading from north to south, and there are more overlanders now than ever on the west coast of Africa (but, there are many times more overlanders driving the relatively developed and peaceful East African route). We knew of approximately twenty vehicles attempting the passage during our "season", some would start and turn back in Senegal (if coming from the north), or Angola (if coming from the south) as the reality of the West Africa challenge weeded out the less prepared or adventurous. What do those West African children think of us, and what kind of advertisement are we for the developed world? The stadiums and European football matches viewed on communal TV sets were once their primary view into the developed world but now, here are these foreigners in their midst and markets, buying bread, fruit and luxury items, dressed in strange clothing and speaking strange languages. If anything, we encourage interest and perhaps migration as it must be wonderful to be so wealthy that we can afford to travel around the world in vehicles an entire village could not afford. It is a responsibility we bear then to be good ambassadors, to travel with respect and display kindness and humility. Sometimes the attention can be overwhelming when we stopped to buy bread in a village we were often surrounded by children who will clamber over the vehicle if allowed. Our approach when stopping was to be nonchalant, to not engage directly with the children but to stroll towards a stall casually.

The older children would govern the younger children, and the adults would ensure that we were not being harassed. When leaving, we would wave and say our goodbyes and leave a group of smiles waving us back onto the road. The African wave is two-handed, both arms stretched out, a wave which guarantees that you come in peace as you cannot wave with both hands if carrying a weapon. To wave and greet with both hands is a sign of respect and peace, and invariably you will receive in return both a wave and a smile.

Abidjan surpassed our expectations. The city is well maintained and relatively wealthy with tall, modern buildings, well kept public areas and new, wide avenues. In convoy, we searched for accommodation listed on the iOverlander app and found a hotel which offered air-conditioned rooms and a refreshing swimming pool. Luisa and Jon entered the building to negotiate a rate but returned dissatisfied with the price. The security guard suggested that we could park in a neighbouring parking lot where he assured us that we would be safe, but Jon was not happy with the location next to a busy road. We left in the late afternoon heat and drove towards another site listed on the now-ubiquitous app. The second option for accommodation was close to the Ghanian consulate, in a prosperous neighbourhood, but the gate beam of the house was too low for our vehicles to enter. Beautiful women, office workers or residents, walked confidently alone, and a security vehicle patrolled the streets. I made the call that we would spend the night parked beside a tall white wall, opposite a sizeable maroon house. Jon and Nina were not convinced that we were safe, but I confirmed with the security guards that we would be safe, and they assured us that we would not be disturbed. We enjoyed a few cold beers as the sunset, and expensive European sedans found their way home. The night was hot and humid, but we slept well and awoke early to apply for the forward visas, Luisa confiding that she wanted to apply for the visas before Jon had a chance to upset the official, Jon has a very forward manner, and we had noticed that he would often argue with officials, a strategy which was the opposite of our own and which was not always effective.

A blast of cool air greeted us as we entered the Ghanain consulate which was located in a cool leafy suburb which would not be out of place in the wealthy northern suburbs of Johannesburg. Luisa and Jon made a beeline for the counter, while the rest of us made use of the facilities before settling in a conference/waiting room to watch international news on a large screen TV and take advantage of the free WiFi.

A well-dressed family joined us as we watched the news - an Ebola breakout in the Democratic Republic of Congo, a protest against the detention of an opposition leader in Cameroon, a school attacked in Northern Nigeria and the mayor of a small Ghanian city discussing an initiative to educate and empower girls. She, the mayor, stood in the shade of a high school corridor, the walls blue and white, the soil red and splashed against the walls. Palm trees waved in the background, and smiling children hid behind each other giggling when an out of sight authority moved them along. The mayor wore a red and gold high shouldered dress with matching headdress and jewellery, her lips a deep red, her hips and breasts full. She informed the robotic reporter that the greatest tool in the fight against poverty is the empowerment of women, that women must have control of their own minds and bodies, must be able to choose when and how many babies to have and must be educated and empowered to earn and control their own finances. I agree. Woman tend to put the needs of their families before their own, while some men are preoccupied with symbols of status, self-gratification and shiny trinkets. Not all men, of course, there are many who toil every day just to put food on the table but, unfortunately, a modern West African music video or soap opera is an insight into the desperate materialism which plagues the desires of man. American rap and hip-hop culture are partly to blame following an all too tired formula of excess - bling, gold chains, sports cars, loose women, mansions and piles of wasted cash. Footballers and hip-hop stars are role models for millions of young men and the radio and TV stations pander to those desires. West African music used to be renowned internationally, but young musicians are not inspired by Baaba Mal, Fela Kuti or Youssou N'Dor, they are obsessed with fame, wealth and attitude of 50 Cent, Snoop Dogg and Lil Wayne, men who objectify women and live lives so far removed from the West African reality as to be from another planet. And I understand why. For many, there are few opportunities to escape the depressing clutch of poverty, but if you can rap and string a tune together or master a football, you have the opportunity to achieve great wealth.

Our visas were issued within two hours, and together with the Spaniards we drove out of the surprisingly modern city and visited a mall where we ate Burger King hamburgers and bought groceries before heading to the Grand Bassam beach where hundreds of restaurants dot the beach offering palm trees, perhaps a swimming pool and a weekend of noisy relaxation. The Spaniards had found a hotel called La Nouvelle Pailote at Grand Bassam which allowed overlanders to camp in the parking lot if they bought a meal at the restaurant. The hotel was pleasant enough but had few guests aside from a group of short-haired and serious French men who looked out of sorts dressed in shorts and t-shirts as opposed to camouflage and bullets. They were men who made a living seeking a world which we avoided at all costs. We drove back to Abidjan to collect our friend Robert from his hotel near the airport. Robert was flying to Burkina Faso and had offered to transport our new half shaft which we had delivered to his house in Johannesburg. Robert is one of those people who is blessed with intelligence and courage; he works in a country considered hostile and dangerous and is comfortable living a life which would intimidate brave men. He is also a very generous man. In addition to our spare parts, he gifted Luisa a GoPro and Sony Vaio notebook which he no longer used. And he had brought us boerewors from South Africa! That night we made a campfire on the beach, and while Jessica and little Bianca bonded swinging in a hammock, the adults spoke and shared a few cold drinks. The boerewors was grilled and wolfed down while Robert brought us up to speed on the situation in South Africa, we were curious and anxious to see how the country had changed since we had left all those years before. The hammock broke, and the girls tumbled into the sand, the night escaped us, the fire crackled and the sea pounded the shore until Robert realised that it was late and he needed to get a taxi back to his hotel, his flight left early the next morning. Again we were overwhelmed by the generosity of relative strangers, people who we had only ever communicated with online and who became great friends over a fire. Keelan, Luisa and I walked with Robert along a quiet alley and waited beside the clean, wide avenue until an old red taxi arrived and spluttered away with our smiling friend.

The morning arrived sweltering and humid. I quickly installed the new half shaft and had a shower. Bianca, Keelan and Jessica had gone for a quick swim in the large swimming pool the night before, and we were surprised to be presented with a bill for 20,000 CFA; 10,000 CFA, a head for the kids, to have a ten-minute swim, the equivalent of about $38.00 American. We paid, and we left, our penny-pincher egos slightly bruised but, unlike Luisa, I am not going to sweat over ten bucks a head for safe overnight parking. The establishment is a business with bills and staff to pay, freeloading overlanders are not great for business, and we fill the parking lot. We enjoyed a short drive to our next destination, a beachside hotel.

La Bahia Hotel is situated near the end of a muddy track which snakes between hotels along the coast in a town called Assouinde. The hotel has a large parking area, immaculate swimming pool and a beautiful bar with a restaurant. The owner of the hotel blasts about on a new KTM and has a soft spot for overlanders, as he himself has travelled parts of Africa by bike. Again, the unspoken rule applies - eat in the restaurant, and you can overnight for free and use the pool, beach and showers. The Spaniards parked between our vehicle and that of an elderly French couple, we swam in the pool for hours, walked on the beach, enjoyed meals of grilled chicken and chips and relaxed in a haven of tranquillity. But with most establishments we had recently visited, there were challenges of electricity and water, and a friendly young man walked me to a neighbouring, dilapidated old hotel where I was able to fill the jerry can from a water tank. A much less friendly young man stood guard over the electrical connection in the parking area and scowled at me when I asked if we could plug in, understandably there was only so much electricity generated by the solar system.

After two nights, we left the Spaniard and the French couple and drove to the inland border with Ghana, skirting around the Iles Ihotile National Park.

The Ivory Coast really is a special country - safe, beautiful and friendly, with decent infrastructure and well built, relatively modern towns and villages. From border to border, we enjoyed the country and would certainly consider it among the most delightful and rewarding destinations in Africa.

GHANA

Ghana means "Warrior King". Ghana is just a few degrees north of the Equator and is bordered by the Ivory Coast, Burkina Faso, Togo and the Gulf of Guinea and the Atlantic Ocean in the south

Ghana uses the Ghanian Cedi
1 GHS = EU0.15/USD0.17

Most nationalities besides the British and ECOWAS citizens need a visa for Ghana which can be obtained at bordering countries for an approximate cost EU35 or a 24-hour transit visa for an approximate EU10

Unleaded = EU0.85/USD0.93 per litre
Diesel = EU0.83/USD0.90 per litre

MTN
Vodafone
Tigo

Christianity is predominantly practised.
Education is provided for free by the Government's commitment to Free Compulsory Universal Basic Education. Ghana was colonized by Great Britain

Carte Brune Insurance is required

Police = 191
Ambulance = 193

Valid passport
Vehicle title papers
Carnet de Passage (highly recommended) but a TIP will be issued on arrival
International Driver's licence

The official language is English as well as lingua franca

 Soups and stews are popular with ingredients such as fish, chicken and meat with vegetables.
Banku (maize) and tilapia are commonly served in local restaurants.
Fufu, an equal combination of cooked cassava and green plantains, are readily available and sold in bags at roadside stalls

 Kintampo Waterfalls - a hidden waterfall in the forest
Wli Waterfalls - the tallest waterfall in West Africa
Lake Bosumtwi - largest man-made lake in the world by surface area.
Mole National Park - camp on the savannah with lions and elephant
Kakum National Park - Take a canopy walkway tour in the rainforest and see antelopes, monkeys, butterflies and forest elephants.
Explore Kejetia Market, the largest open market in West Africa

 Ghana is tropical with a rainy season in Summer and a dry season in Winter
Rainy - May to September - Low 22C/73F to a High of 31C/88F
Dry - October to April - Low 31C/88F to a High of 33C/91F

 Ghana was initially called "mina" meaning mine by the Portuguese settlers, but when the British took over the region, they called it the Gold Coast.
Lake Volta is the world's largest artificial lake at an approximate 250 miles in length.
Ghana was the first country in sub-Saharan Africa to gain its independence on March 6, 1957.
There are over 650 butterfly species in Ghana's Kakum National Park, which includes the giant swallowtails, which are nearly 20 centimetres wide.
Kofi Annan is one of the most well-known Ghanaians and he served as secretary-general of the United Nations from 1997- 2006

9

Ghana

We stamped out of Cote D'Ivoire and approached the Ghanaian border at Elubo, I parked beside the busy road, and we trudged through the process - report to the Police, then report to Immigration, then report to customs. The border infrastructure was relatively modern and organised, there seemed to be decent leadership and the officials, despite being not particularly friendly, went about their business with quiet efficiency. I suspect that the process would have been a bit more complicated had we not carried a Carnet de Passage and there have been reports from other overlanders of corruption. We had no experience of this as Luisa worked her magic from official to official, breaking down their borders of perception and achieving in one hour what others struggle to negotiate in many.

While Luisa dealt with the customs officials, the kids and I waited by the Land Rover, and I dealt with the aggressive praying mantis which had to be evicted from the Land Rover.

The visa costs were killing our budget, and we had been forced to apply for 48-hour transit visas for Ghana, a pity. The Spaniards had plans to visit the Mole National Park in Ghana, and we were glad to be travelling solo, despite the relative peace of mind which travelling in convoy can afford. There are no straight roads in Ghana, and we meandered from town to town, occasionally stopping at friendly police checkpoints and for roadside snacks of fruit and deep-fried bread dough, known as Bofrot in Ghana. We had no problems filling the fuel tank and found that a quiet gas station was the best place to spend the night under the gaze of the attendants or security guard. We would cook a simple dinner and chat to the locals for a while, check the Land Rover for any mechanical problems, top-up oils and fluids and perhaps enjoy a cold beer or two before bed. Luisa and I would often sit on the Land Rover bonnet and watch the world go by, children playing, moto-taxis zooming, the activity of the day continuing into the night. The smell of dinner cooked floating in the air, the laugh of friends, and the eventual cooling of the air as the sunset. We have been criticised in the past for overnighting at gas stations, but we are quite happy to pass an evening in a safe, free environment, the advantages are that you do not need to spend dusk hours searching for a suitable, affordable place to stay and are close to the road when departing the next morning when in transit we become transitory.

At roughly half the size of Spain and the same size as Cote D'Ivoire, Ghana is a regional powerhouse boasting universal health care, a low mortality rate, declining population and relatively high life expectancy (around 65 years for men).

Ghana is tremendously religious, there seem to be more churches than factories, and there are certainly more churches than gas stations, by double. 71% of the population is Christian, and the country seems a bridgehead, a defence against the spread of Islam. In fact, the largest growing religion is Hinduism. The number of churches is rivalled only by the amount of Evangelist, Pentecostal and Charismatic billboards which litter the roadside, a well-groomed, gaudily dressed man, golden fingers weighing down hands raised in prayer promising salvation. The prophets stop short only of labelling themselves Messiah, though there were a few billboards touting prophets so exceptional, that they might well be a son of God. The churches compete for attention, straddling hills, reaching for the sky, Christianity is a Ghanaian industry unlike any other, and the product they all sell is hope and redemption, miracle cures and personal enrichment. The former president of Ghana (whose name brings to mind either a boxer or jazz musician) Jerry Rawlins believes they are a sad reflection on the state of his country, "If we can behave in such an ignorant manner, should it surprise you that the country is being consumed by so much filth". These tax-exempt churches form a political base, which hopeful politicians must pander to if they hope to win elections. Many churches open their own universities and hospitals, rivalling the state infrastructure.

As we drove towards Accra, the churches increased, and the volume of worship became exigent, particularly at night as worshipers participated in a sonic onslaught. Perhaps God could sleep through that noise, we could not, and we can sleep through almost anything. Businesses bear names such as "God the Almighty Plumbing", and "Psalm 23 Catering". It can all be a bit too much but, while the people seem to be manically religious, they are simultaneously friendly and hospitable. The Accra mall lured us with the promise of Western fast food and South African department stores (Game and Shoprite) where we would find food, snacks and condiments which we had not tasted in over half a decade. The mall itself was modern and noisy, we found a large and well-secured parking space and hunted for wifi before shopping. Imagine our surprise to find a supermarket overflowing with South African products. It was like being back home already, and we wasted no time searching the aisles for our favourite products and found biltong, boerewors, vetkoek, fish paste, Bovril, All Gold tomato sauce, Tex Bars, Mrs Balls Chutney and Simba chips, Appeltizer, Stoney Ginger Beer, Provita and Bacon Kips.

With the clock ticking, we rejoined the N1 highway and made it to the Togolese border as the sun set.

TOGO

Togo is bordered by Ghana, Benin and Burkina Faso. The country extends south to the Gulf of Guinea, where the capital Lomé is located. The 56 km coast of Togo consists of lagoons with sandy beaches. In the north, the land has rolling savanna, and Southern Togo is mostly savanna and woodland plateau to the coastal plain, lagoons and marshes

Togo uses the West African Franc
100 CFA = EU0.15/USD0.17

Most nationalities require visas. You can get a visa on arrival for an approximate EU30. West African passport holders are visa-free

Unleaded = EU0.85/USD0.92 per litre
Diesel = EU0.86/USD0.93 per litre

TogoTel
Moov

Togo's culture is reflected by their many ethnic groups, namely the Ewe, Mina, Tem, Tchamba and Kabre. Togo was colonised by Germany, France and Great Britain

ECOWAS insurance is required

Police = 117
Ambulance = 8200
Valid passport

Valid passport
Carnet de Passage (highly recommended)
Vaccination certificate

The official language is French

Bonjour! – Hello   Au revoir! – Goodbye
S'il vous plaît – Please   Pardon – Sorry
allez-vous? – How are you?   ça va bien – it's going well
Excusez-moi – Excuse me   Plus lentement – More slowly
Où est…? – Where is…?   Merci beaucoup – Thanks a lot
Je ne comprends pas – I don't understand
C'est combien? – How much is it?

Togolese culinary style is a combination of African, French, and German influences. Groundnuts, corn-on-the-cob and cooked prawns can be found at roadside stalls

Kpalime - voodoo town Koutammakou
"Land of Batammariba" - UNESCO site
Fazao Malfakassa National Park - Where duiker, antelopes, bushbuck and crocodiles roam free

Togo has a slight difference between winter and summer
Average daily temperatures range from 25C/77F to 33C/91F
The rainy season is between April to October

Togo means "House of Sea" in the Ewe language.
Worn-out tyres are used to make sandals and toys.
Togo has an extreme undercurrent, and caution should be taken when swimming in the ocean.
Togo's history dates back to only 10 centuries, with very little evidence of ancient civilization.
Togoland was a German Empire Protectorate for 30 years and included Togo and the Volta Region of Ghana

BENIN

Benin is bordered by Togo, Burkina Faso, Nigeria and Niger and is approximately the same size as the state of Pennsylvania

Benin uses the West African Franc
100 CFA = EU0.15/USD0.17

Most nationalities require visas. You can get a two-day visa at the border for an approximate EU15 and can extend it for an additional 30 days for EU20 or apply for an e-visa online. African passport holders are visa-free

Unleaded = EU0.83/USD0.76 per litre
Diesel = EU0.79/USD0.85 per litre

MTN
Moov
Glo

Christianity and Islam are practised, but Vodun (Voodoo) is still recognised as a religion in Benin

ECOWAS insurance is required

Police = 117
Ambulance = 112

Valid passport
Vehicle title papers

The official language is French
Bonjour! – Hello   Au revoir! – Goodbye
S'il vous plaît – Please   Pardon – Sorry
allez-vous? – How are you?   ça va bien – it's going well

Excusez-moi – Excuse me
Plus lentement – More slowly
Où est…? – Where is…?
Merci beaucoup – Thanks a lot
Je ne comprends pas – I don't understand
C'est combien? – How much is it?

Grilled chicken and goat served with beans and rice can be bought at roadside stalls

Pendjari National Park - where 90% of the West African lion population remains.
Grand Popo - a long stretch of beach lined with coconuts
Temple of Pythons, Ouidah - a spiritual temple that houses over 50 pythons.
Ganvie Lake, Cotonou - a village built on stilts

The temperature is constant in Benin with a slight difference between winter and summer
Average daily temperatures range from 24C/75F and 33C/91F
The rainy season is between April to July

Dahomey was renamed the Republic of Benin, a Marxist country in 1975.
Benin is named after the body of water on which it lies - the "Bight of Benin".
Carved wooden masks are what makes Benin famous.
Benin has a high fertility rate of approximately 5 children per woman

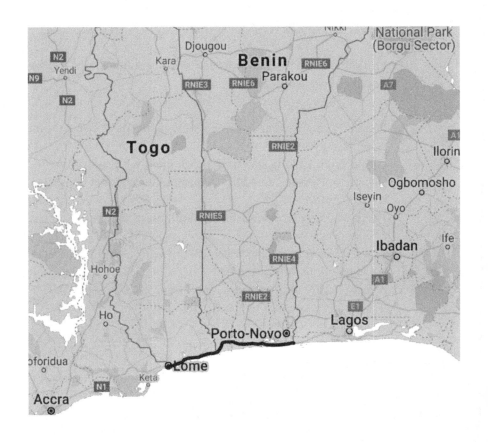

10

Togo and Benin

Our research had determined that we were able to enter Togo by purchasing a visa at the border; however, we were not sure how much we should pay as South Africans. Usually, we would not attempt a border crossing at night (though we had recently crossed into The Gambia after sunset), but Luisa was determined not to spend another night at a gas station, particularly as there was rumoured to be a very nice beach camp near Lome where we could settle in and relax for a few days. I parked beside a large, white building and Luisa headed off with Keelan to negotiate the formalities. It took longer than expected, and we found ourselves being shunted from one office to another until eventually we were all ushered into the office of a large and imposing official who appreciated our humble deference and stamped us out of Ghana with a smile and a handshake - "You are Africans too!".

The Togolese officials were less friendly. Customs procedure was relatively painless, but the negotiation for the visa fee was less than amicable, the official - a short, bald man wearing a stained white shirt and garish faux crocodile skin shoes, refused to budge on his demand that we pay 20,000 CFA per person. Luisa was not amused. A German couple had recently passed through the border, and they insisted that you should pay no more than 10,000 CFA per head. I suspect that not all travellers are truthful in their reports of dealing with corruption, impromptu toll gates and police checkpoints. I believe that it is easier for some to pay up and later report that you fought the good fight and paid nothing. And I was realising that the West African route was home to some interesting characters, you have to be a little bit crazy to drive the West African route, and we had met more than a few overlanders who were plenty crazy, and just plain weird. Luisa took the German overlanders report as fact and refused to pay. The official became hostile, and I realised that we were heading for a stalemate, particularly as the official began questioning our medical inoculation cards and insinuating that the injections were not up to date and there would be fines to pay and that we may not be allowed to enter Togo at all. He was playing the game hard that night. We asked him to show us a price list detailing the visa costs, but that request only annoyed him further. Eventually, after an hour of to and fro, he threw upon a filthy old ledger and pointed at a scribbled figure - 15,000. How could we argue with such an official and definitive document? I had had enough and paid the 60,000 CFA, and half an hour later we left the filthy, un-ventilated white room and drove into Togo.

The city of Lome compensated for the attitude of her corrupt guardian. We drove broad avenues, past colonial hotels and an incredibly and brightly lit port, where gantry cranes heaved endlessly. Eventually, we arrived at Coco Beach and found our way onto the beach where we parked on the thick white sand and ordered a few cold drinks. It had been a long day of driving into and through a capital city and across the bustling border. We needed to relax. While Luisa tidied the Land Rover, I negotiated the camping rate, filtered water and we both eventually relaxed under swaying palm trees after the kids were fed and settled in for the night. This looked to be the kind of camp where we might find ourselves "stuck" for a week, and we were happy to do so.

A day later, I sat beneath a palm frond hut and worked on a few articles which I had penned for The Overland Journal. I felt a light tap on my shoulder and turned to meet a middle-aged British woman who we had known of for years but had never met. She and her husband were driving down to South Africa, and Luisa had been chatting with them online, the idea being that we would convoy through Nigeria together, at least through the most demanding and dangerous parts of the country. Dick and Jane, not their real names, are truly unique, they march to the tune of their own drum, and I soon realised that we would either become the greatest friends or not. With their vehicle camped close to ours, the wifi suddenly vanished, and the sound of the sea was replaced by a voice unwavering in certainty and fact. It takes a special kind of person to travel the world.

I made a small fire one night, and we sat together discussing routes, other overlanders, spare parts, technology and various other topics. A tall, beautiful, surly German girl approached, bordered by two young compatriots. As she moved, her immaculate breasts brushed free and tensely against a boys vest and her little sisters' shorts ended where they might have begun. They had heard that we had a bonfire and looked disdainfully at my small, disappointing campfire. They had heard that we had booze and disapprovingly downed our bottle of Old Brown Sherry, recently and happily acquired at the Shoprite in Ghana. I welcomed them to sit and offered them more food and drink. They had heard that we were South Africans and wanted to know what we thought about the future of Africa. They were disappointed when I suggested that education was the only real cure for Africa's ills. It was soon apparent that they had not come to hear a rational answer. They had come looking for a white South African racist, on who they could unload their anger and perhaps their own guilt for the state of West Africa (Germany had colonised Togo). They were anarcho-communists, and they had come looking for an outlet to their frustration. We did not take the bait, instead offered them an education as people who had been born and raised in Africa. Had they heard of Steve Biko? No? Were they familiar with the Black Consciousness Movement and the idea that Africans must emancipate themselves by rejecting the "white monopoly on truth"? No. With all due respect to my Teutonic friends, I find it a difficult to be taken to task solely based on our race and nationality and the crimes of a system we had no part of, by people whose national past was infinitely more cruel, deadly and destructive than the white South African government ever was. There was never a genocide perpetrated by white people in South Africa through systematic mass industrial murder. The evil Apartheid system was not responsible for the deaths of tens of millions of people. Our historical evil is not equal, Sabine. Sabine, for her part, strung her university friends along with that promise which all vacuous beauties offer, the opportunity for subservience to be rewarded with dull sex. It did not help that our new British overlander friend insisted on regularly proclaiming the fallacy that, "Nelson Mandela was a terrorist"!

After an hour of goading, I eventually lost patience and suggested that Sabine was displaying more leg than intellect which led to a meltdown. Sabine screamed that I was a sexist pig (I was pleased that she did not call me a racist, I had successfully disqualified myself), one of her boyfriends sat on the ground and screamed into his hair and hands with desperate and (hopefully) impressive anger, while the other boy looked at me like I had eaten a cute Togolese child. I stood quietly, smiling like the asshole I can be, offering an opportunity to talk it through, come, let's be civil? Luisa told me to stop being an asshole.

They retreated to their hut to scream at each other in desperation. Later Sabine approached Luisa and offered her lament, did Shieldmaiden Luisa need to be rescued from my misogyny?

The next night the Land Rover caught fire. It was an incredibly humid evening. Jessica and I were sitting in the Land Rover chatting and making dinner while everyone else was sitting near the bar getting to know a German family who had arrived in an old 4x4 truck. A group of Rastafarians were sharing a cottage close to the Land Rover, and despite the humidity, the evening was pleasant. Sabine and her suitors had skulked away earlier that day; their red Land Cruiser pointed towards Ghana, Sabine's one perfect arm hung cooly from the front passenger seat window, nonchalant, attached to a bare shoulder beneath a head swimming in unconnected thought.

I noticed a flash of yellow light and smelled the unmistakable acrid scent of an electric fire. Fire! Our worst nightmare, well one of them anyway. I jumped out of the Land Rover and grabbed the fire extinguisher which is mounted permanently within the rear door. As I rushed around the truck, I looked up to see a Rasta rolling past. "Your truck is on fire, mon". Thanks. Our electrical lead ran from a nearby cottage to the adaptor which lay in the sand beneath the passenger side of the Defender. From the adaptor, another lead led up into the Land Rover. Flames a foot high danced from the adaptor, I gave it a few quick sprays with the fire extinguisher, and the flames blasted out. Had we been sitting in the bar, the result may have been tragic; we might have lost our home!

The consensus was that moisture had formed and dripped down the lead into the adaptor, causing a short. The communists were implicated in a sabotage plot, but that theory was dismissed when we realised that neither of three could have had such a command of chemistry or electricity, let alone both. It was a bizarre accident, the mains did not short circuit, and the adaptors built-in fuse appeared not to have blown.

A week passed. Daily we would walk to the main road to buy fruit, bread and beer from small shops and street vendors. The weekends were as noisy as can be expected. Groups of friends and families came down to the beach and brought with them baskets of food, car batteries and large speakers. Each family had their own music, and we sat unfortunately in the exact spot where four walls of sound met. An Indian family were catered to by a chef who grilled all day, football matches were played, fires burned, jokes told and dances danced. We endured it all until the sun set, we could not complain, this was their beach, and this was how they relaxed. Sunday was noisier than Saturday and Monday dawned hot and quiet. The owner of the bar had kindly taken to refrigerating medium-sized coconuts for me and a swim in the sea each morning would refresh us for the hot, humid day ahead. But, the days had begun melting into each other, and we were itching for the road.

Luisa had spent a fair amount of time with the British couple and the German family, and it was agreed that we would convoy together through Nigeria, a mere 220 kilometres east of Lome.

While a group of French ex-pats joined a group of locals for drumming and yoga on the beach, we packed the Landy and headed to the border with Benin. There is a feeling of nervous relief when leaving a comfortable camp, particularly when you have stayed for more than a few days, and the road ahead is sure to be challenging. At the border when went through the formalities by rote. Luisa worked from counter to counter with her all-important green folder tucked under her arm, and her border attitude switched on. There seem to be a healthy respect for married, middle-aged (between 40 and 60 years old) women in West Africa. Most officials are accustomed to dealing with (foreign) men and are taken aback by a confident, friendly, persistent woman; they react to her well and seem too reverent and embarrassed to be unscrupulous. Her flowing, waist-length red hair and north European features inspire admiration, but Luisa does not suffer fools, they can sense this and are generally well behaved. While Luisa takes care of the customs documentation (either using the Carnet de Passage or a Temporary Import Permit), I will shadow her while Keelan and Jessica will wait with the Landy. We attend immigration offices together. That morning, while Luisa took care of customs, I stood outside the immigration building waiting. I usually do not smoke in the morning, but I decided to kill some time, rolled a cigarette, walked away from the immigration building and smoked, standing on a dirt road twenty metres from the building, next to a car park, of sorts. While I stood there minding my own business, a portly man wearing a blue suit approached with a stern frown creasing his face.

"Smoking is forbidden here!"
"Here?"
"Yes, it is forbidden. You must come to my office, and I will punish you".

I broke the lit tip off of the cigarette and ground it dead with my boot.

"No, you can finish your smoke and then come to the office".

Too late. I followed him back towards the office, and he made a show of pointing at a small, obscured and faded sign high above three uniforms lounging on an old, green patio sofa.

"The sign says no smoking here. I was not smoking here; I was smoking there". I pointed back to the spot where I had stood alone.

"You may not smoke here. Come to my office; I must punish you".

There are days when you have the energy to deal with these charades with humour or obstinance, and then there are days when you are just not in the mood. I was not in the mood, but I managed to fake humble regret.

"I am so sorry sir; I really did not mean to do the wrong thing, I thought that by walking over there I was doing the right thing, I did not realise that a sign here applies to an activity there, I am sorry that you had to interrupt your good work to reprimand me for doing something that I should not have done, I promise that I won't do it again, really, I am really very sorry".

My body language reflected my words - back slightly bent, hands clasped together, oscillating slightly, my head tilted to one side. Unsmiling.

The blue suit studied me for a moment as I looked down at him. Unsmiling.

"You are a humble man. You are forgiven".
"Thank you".

I walked towards the Land Rover, but the blue suit followed me, he now wanted to be my friend. I shook his hand and told him that I needed to leave and turned my attention to a man trying to sell me a sim card, or batteries or a bag of water pulled from a bucket. Luisa returned, and we drove through the police boom and parked beside a tall, white wall and began the process of entering Benin. A smartly dressed official welcomed us dryly to his hut and noted our passport details painstakingly in a large, dog eared journal. The heat baked and we waited patiently before eventually being allowed to leave through an impromptu street market where fruit, deep-fried fish and chicken, clothing and household appliances were sold.

Luisa had spent the last week looking for an apartment or house where we could hole up for a week or two and prepare for the road ahead while getting some work done - the endless obligation of earning and preparation, which ensured that we were able to keep moving. She had found a house, close to the beach which promised all that we needed and we drove along the coastal RNEI1 road looking for the waypoints provided by the owner. Just before the Millenium Popo Beach Hotel, we eventually found the dirt road which led towards the beach and the house, which at first seemed ideal. We were greeted by a slim woman dressed in white, her skin glowing from the effort of preparing the house. The owner lived in France and Maria was waiting to welcome us and answer any questions which we might have. The house was recently built and offered large, airy rooms, a modern kitchen, large garage, flat-screen television and views of the Atlantic and rural surroundings. We unpacked the Land Rover, and I drove with Maria to Grand Popo, the nearest town where we hoped to find a supermarket but found only vegetable stalls and small general stores which stocked the basics. With a basket full of fruit and vegetables, we returned to the house looking forward to a bit of normality, an island of Western comfort. We were soon disappointed. Maria, an educated and graceful woman, introduced us to the caretaker, a wiry, unsmiling man called Fok.

Fok's primary purpose was to maintain the house and grounds and run the generator when the municipal power failed. He lived in a hut in a large clearing between the house and the beach with his wife and four young children. Fok drove a Renault sedan and a motorcycle, he wore new shoes and clothing and was an expert at appearing busy while not doing much at all. Fok's wife and children wore rags and worked the fields surrounding the house, carried water and cooked food, waking before dawn to rake and sweep the path surrounding the house.

On day two, the power went out. It took an hour to get Fok to start the generator, and he demanded money to buy petrol, we had not agreed with the owner to pay for such basics but handed over some cash to Fok, deciding to rather keep the fridge and computers running and deal with the owner later. The house was listed as having high-speed internet, but there was as much wifi as there was power. Fok returned from the gas station eventually with a basket of groceries, half a can of petrol and his ever-present scowl. He spoke no English, we spoke no French, but numbers are a language of their own. Petrol cost $1.00 a litre, we had given him $20.00, and he had returned with 10 litres of fuel but no change. Only a scowl.

The generator sat in a wooden box in the corner of the yard and was controlled externally by a control panel consisting of a large switch, a red "off" light and a green "on" light, mounted to the tall perimeter wall. The generator clattered, banged and hummed loudly, forcing us to close the windows and doors despite the heat. Fok let the generator run for an hour and then switched it off, while we were making dinner and without warning. Fok was going to be a problem. I walked out to speak to him. I had introduced myself and the family when we had arrived. We shook his hand and treated him with respect. Fok did not want us there. He wanted to sleep in the house and use the kitchen and bathrooms and watch the TV and pretend that the house was his own. He wanted to have his friends over for a drink and to park his car in the garage. We were not welcome. I approached Fok as he stood leaning against a tree, I asked him if we could help him with any problem, if he had food or needed anything, I asked him if he could please do his job and make sure that he communicated with us. He stood, arms folded, glaring at me. He controlled the power to the house, and as long as he controlled the power supply, he dictated when we could work, or cook or turn on the lights or enjoy a movie. We needed to remove Fok from the equation as the municipal power was only pulsing to the house for a few hours every day. There was a general election looming and, apparently, the ruling regime was purposefully cutting the power so that the opposition could not effectively campaign or communicate. Emailing the owner of the house yielded no response, so we took matters into our own hands.

The next morning Keelan and I drove to the fuel station and filled a jerry can with petrol. We then returned to the house, spent a few moments studying the generator and control panel, filled up with fuel, checked the oil and pull started the generator. It took a few moments of trial and error to select the switch setting, which delivered electricity to the house and effectively liberated ourselves from the tyranny of Fok. He was not pleased that we had removed his power and skulked about the yard, shooting hateful glares and scheming. The British couple and German family arrived to spend an evening and celebrate Dick's birthday. Fok waited until the fire was going and we were having a good time to interrupt and insist that we had to move our vehicles, the premise being that we blocked the path which only he walked. At night he would skulk outside the house, standing in the shadow of a tree, boiling with rage.

The man must have at some stage been very badly treated, someone took advantage of him or beat him or hurt him deeply, his was an anger learned and which lived so deep within him that there was no opportunity for it to leave. He was, without a doubt, intelligent enough to know what he wanted but not smart or mature enough as to know how to get it. He treated his own family with the same disdain, his wife seemed to bear the brunt of his anger, and she hardly lifted her eyes from the ground. Perhaps Fok is not ideally suited for a career in hospitality.

It was shortly after we arrived in Benin that RayRay died. She had laid an egg pod on the roof handle in the camper just before we left Coco Beach in Togo and we had read that a Praying Mantis will die after laying her eggs. She became lethargic and for days would not eat even the juiciest cricket. One evening I caught her a green locust, and she devoured the poor creature before lying down on a bed of tissue. The next morning she lay still. She had been a good girl and had done the best she could for her babies; nature is wonderful. Now we had a pod of eggs brewing in the Landy, and one day we could expect 400 RayRays to hatch inside the Land Rover. Perhaps not the best idea.

The German family were lovely people. Pia, the mother, is an Argentine-born architect who had lived in Germany for a few years. Petite and open-hearted, Pia loved overland travel and confided that there was little else which she wanted to do with her life. Tim, the father, is a scientist, slim and handsome. The children were two boys named Tiago (13) and Theo (15) and daughter Zoe (10). They drove an ancient Magirus Deutsche 100d11 4x4 truck which we soon nickname, "Das Oliphant". The Elephant. They helped us celebrate Dick's birthday (we bought him a bottle of Vodka from the local market, imported and only twice the price of a six-pack of Coca-Cola), before heading off to Porto Novo, the capital of Benin as they had not applied for the correct visa before entering and their passports had been sent ahead to immigration for processing. Dick and Jane stayed a night longer than planned and then set off to find a nice campsite.

Fok cursed me, and I fell ill, possibly and probably Malaria, but I never felt sick enough to seek out a clinic. I did not trust the Malaria test kits which we carried but vowed to head out to a clinic should I develop a significant fever. Only one of the four beds in the house had a mosquito net, and we slept in the heat, coated in mosquito repellant and our Craghoppers Nosilife clothing, which is embedded with repellant. My energy drained, I had diarrhoea, a fog descended over my mind, and I suffered from flu-like symptoms. Thankfully I was not nearly as ill as I had been in Mozambique, nine years before and I was able to get some work done sitting on the patio of the second level of the house. I had arranged a table and chair facing the ocean and could quietly work on Europe Overland. At face value, the setting was idyllic - the sea pounding 200 meters away, surrounded by rural, coastal Africa, no loud music, few distractions and only the drone of the generator to distract me. But I was distracted by other things. The sky was often grey, and the wind blew endlessly upon the shacks and huts of our neighbours who toiled to grow vegetables in poor, sandy soil. The children worked the land with their parents and often wore no clothing to protect them from the elements. Washed clothing was spread on the earth to dry, the one tree left standing served as a local gathering place for the women who worked the fields, bent double all day long. A cluster of huts near the beach housed a family whose number I never determined and tied to a stake in the ground a large goat waiting for a special occasion. He was a mean old goat. A woman walking past the goat managed to upset him, and he turned suddenly and charged, knocking her off her feet wholly and violently. The woman screamed. A large man emerged from a hut wearing a grey vest and blue shorts, he picked up a plank of wood and beat the goat but left the woman sitting in the dirt, wailing.

The children did not go to school, and there seemed to be at least four children per family, most younger than ten. This was Fok's reality. And look at what European money affords - large, luxurious houses for strangers to live in, strangers who arrive in hugely expensive vehicles and pale skins, speaking foreign languages, eating the best food, drinking liquor and beer, working on expensive computers and staring at smartphones. Strangers who must have more money than a village but they choose not to share their wealth. Fok's anger is the anger of desperation, perhaps. He looks around and sees people living as they have for centuries and people who live as if they are visiting from another planet, a planet of plenty. Perhaps Fok knows a little about colonialism, and maybe he is convinced that the wealth these aliens enjoy today is the wealth which aliens in ships stole from his ancestors while stealing his ancestors themselves. That might explain Fok's rage against us, but not against his own family.

After two weeks we packed the Defender, relieved to be leaving. While Fok was out, we gave the children and his wife tins of food, fruit, vegetables, and clothing before saying goodbye and good luck and rejoining the RNIE1 road east.

The Spaniards Nina, Jon and Bianca had earlier travelled to a northern border to enter Nigeria, and we joined Dick, Jane and the German family at a campsite in Cotonou where we needed to apply for Congo and Democratic Republic of Congo (DRC) visas. The campground was rustic and sandy, a swimming pool full of locals, cooled the kids, as we adults made plans for the road ahead and the Nigeria crossing.

Nigeria has a foreboding reputation - crime, kidnappings, corruption, Islamic extremism, bureaucracy and terrible roads. It had not been possible to apply for Nigerian visas as we travelled south, but there was a convoluted "E-visa", which should allow us all to enter. There were rumours, mostly spread by Dick that the system would change that coming Monday and it was suggested that we should cross on Friday, even though we had no place to stay in Lagos and would have to wait until Monday to apply for the visa for Cameroon. The iOverlander app suggested that there was a construction site in Lagos where we might be able to stay for a night or two, but it had no facilities, and there was no guarantee that we would be able to stay there. Dick was insistent that we leave on Friday, assuring us that he had inside information from a senior Nigerian official that the system would indeed change on Monday.

The Thursday in Cotonou was thus spent driving around the pleasant city applying for visas. The DRC visa was tricky. The rule was, apparently, that you had to apply for a visa in your country of residence but, for some reason, DRC visas were being issued at the Consulate in Benin. The problem was that there had been overlanders who had been granted the DRC visas in Benin only to find that they were not permitted to enter the country from the northern Angolan enclave, Cabinda. They had then been forced to travel east to Brazzaville and pay for a very expensive ferry to Kinshasa before travelling west through the country to enter Angola proper. The other limitation was that you had to provide an exact entry date for the DRC and the visa would not be honoured if you did not arrive on the date. The group decided to adopt Luisa's travel schedule and settled on the 17th of June to enter the DRC. The schedule allowed for enough time to deal with delays or breakdowns or extensive touring, should we find a country irresistible. When we applied for the DRC visas we asked the friendly official if we could expect to have any problems entering the country and he replied, "Of course not. $50 per person please". The Congo visa was equally expensive, but we were issued both visas within a day which meant essentially that we were logistically prepared to enter Nigeria.

While camped, we met a thin, tall Dutchman named Roy, who was riding the entire North to South route on a huge, low bellied Harley Davidson. He had been delayed for a few weeks waiting for a visa and told a story of a man who had attempted to fly across Africa. The man had been stuck in Benin for almost a year as he struggled to gain permission to enter the air space of various countries. Eventually, he had to admit defeat but had another problem; he had to be able to fly his small aircraft all the way to Morocco as he did not have permission to land en-route and had to build additional fuel tanks so that he could fly to Morocco (or was it Algeria). Unfortunately, the weight of the fuel unbalanced the aircraft and the pilot crashed as he landed, destroying the aircraft and his chances of recouping some costs or later attempting the route.

An ancient bridge across yet another river

Another rutted and ruined but exciting road

Perfectly tarred Chinese roads, off bounds

Gorgeous Ray-Ray

Sickly and annoyed malaria ridden Jessica

Yuki hitching a ride

Banana's being ripened

Old Land Rovers and Pinzgauers keep the local economy running

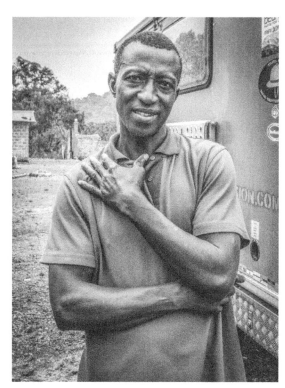

The lovely Mohammed,
a refugee from Sierra Leone

Always smiling

Gorgeous bamboo forest destroyed by Chinese contractors working on the road

Curious kids

Luisa drove more than half of West Africa (the easy parts - G)

"Delicious" snails for sale at a roadside stall

Free camping spot at a weigh station with Jon, Nina and Bianca

The Basilica of Our Lady of Peace of Yamoussoukro in Ivory Coast

Friendly police officer

Brave cyclists touring West Africa

American school bus put to good use

Palm fringed beach in Togo

NIGERIA

Nigeria is Africa's most populous nation as well as the largest producer of oil on the African continent. It is sometimes referred to as the "Giant of Africa", and the tumultuous country is the size of California. Nigeria is located in West Africa, bordered by Niger, Chad, Cameroon and Benin. The southern coast is situated on the Gulf of Guinea in the Atlantic Ocean

Nigerian uses the Nigerian Naira
100 NGN = EU0.24/USD0.26

ECOWAS citizens do not require visas, but all other nationalities need to apply for a visa before entry. There is much dispute, and uncertainty surrounding the procurement of the Nigerian visa and online forums and chat groups should be used to confirm the current situation. Currently, an evisa system is set in place for foreigners entering via land borders. Procure the letter of permission, accompany your escort to the airport and pay for the relevant business visa. If possible, procure the visa before departing from your home country. The visa fees vary between EU80 to EU140 for a one-month visa

Unleaded = EU0.30/USD0.32 per litre
Diesel = EU0.54/USD0.58 per litre

MTN   Airtel
GloMobile   9Mobile

Christianity and Islam are the two main, conflicting religious groups
Homosexuality is illegal in Nigeria

There are many police checkpoints en-route, and probably 90% of them, a bribe of some kind will be requested. Don't give in. We purchased packs of cheap bubble-gum and would give them a few of those, which was usually sufficient

Police = 199
Ambulance = 112

Valid passport
Vehicle title papers
Carnet de Passage (highly recommended) but a TIP will be issued on arrival
Vaccination certificate for yellow fever

The official language is English but with a creole "twang"

Several soups/stews - Afang, Okra, Owo, Pepper, Ground Nut
Plantains are popular and prepared in different ways
There are many Western-style restaurants across Nigeria, especially in Lagos

Yankari National Park - Warm springs
Lekki Conservation Centre - Largest canopy walkway in Africa
Zuma Rock - a beautiful giant monolith
Gashaka Gumti National Park

The weather is comfortable and constant in most areas
August to March - Dry season - Low 22C/72F a High of 30C/86F
April to July - Rainy season - Low 22C/72F a High of 33C/91F

Nigeria is the seventh-most populous country in the world, home to more than 200 million people.
Nollywood is the second largest film producer in the world, after Bollywood of course.
Aliko Dangote is the richest man in Africa and is Nigerian. He has a net worth of USD10 billion.
Five of the richest pastors in the world reside in Nigeria with Bishop David Oyedepo topping the list with a whopping USD150 million net worth.
Evidence of human life in Nigeria date as early as 11,000 BC

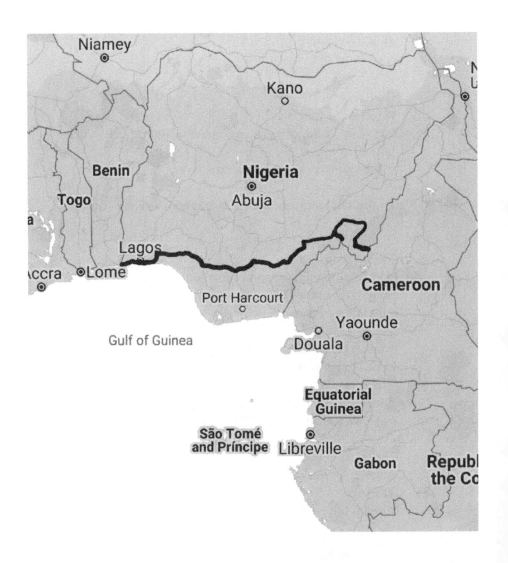

11

Mighty Nigeria

In convoy, we left the campsite in Cotonou and drove the short distance to the Nigerian border. We did not know quite what to expect, and I admit that I was surprised that the Nigerian border facilities were relatively modern and efficient. This was to be close to our 100th border crossing, and it was fascinating to observe how other overlanders dealt with the bureaucracy. Dick faffed endlessly, looking for a short cut, dropping names and buzzing like a fridge. The Germans were happy to follow Dicks lead, and Luisa did what she always does. After waiting in a small office for an hour, an official completed his paperwork and assigned an immigration official to our group. The official would retain our passports, and we would drive in convoy via the Lagos Badagry Express Way to the Murtala Muhammed International Airport in Lagos. The drive was fascinating, as we made our way through organised chaos - every man for himself as Africa's most populous nation fought to get their slice of the limited ground-level resources. Peculiar to the crowded streets of Western Nigeria are Renault, and Peugeot sedans with the rear suspension raised a foot above standard. Fuel is relatively cheap in Nigeria and the black market traders transport barrels of fuel in European family vehicles across the border. The people we passed waved at us and greeted in thick accents. There were 27 police and military checkpoints between the border and the airport but, perhaps, because a uniform accompanied us, we were waved through choked town after choked town. We had left the border at 11 am and drove roughly 75 kilometres to the airport and arrived at 4 pm, a five-hour drive on some of the worst tarmac we had seen yet, with potholes large enough to swallow a Land Rover. We weaved from one side of the road to another, jostling for space with oncoming traffic and at times driving through mud where the road surface disappeared completely.

As we approached Lagos, we drove through neighbourhoods which reminded us of parts of Johannesburg, complete with western fast food outlets, South African clothing and sporting goods retailers, new expensive vehicles and cinemas. There seemed to be two Nigeria's (old and struggling, new and prosperous) competing for real estate. Arriving at the airport, our convoy parked outside a large parking lot and was told by our immigration officer that we could park our vehicles there for the night. The eleven overlanders and our immigration official then marched a long march to the airport, entered and walked through the lobby and up a few flights of stairs to the immigration office where we stood and waited for half an hour before being ushered into the immigration heads office. The boss asked us to sit, and we crowded his small office and large desk. Meticulously the boss studied each passport, asking a few questions and avoiding eye contact. Eventually, he welcomed us to Nigeria and had his lieutenant escort us to the arrivals hall where we sat on white plastic chairs facing a group of men who worked at their own slow pace scanning passports issuing visas and taking payments. A sign above their heads declared that each visa payment would incur an additional $20.00 fee, with no explanation for the surcharge. I was still ill and was struggling to keep my head up as we waited hour after hour to be attended to, and when we finally had our chance at the front, we discovered that Luisa had left the credit card PIN in the Land Rover and had to run off with Keelan to fetch the information hoping that no-one had broken into the vehicle. She returned flustered half an hour later, and we had a bit of a blowout, the entire process was exasperating. The immigration officer then quietly told Luisa that he could not issue our visas because we needed an invitation letter which his friend could supply, at a cost. Luisa refused as the invitation letter was not on the list of documents required and insisted that she would have to speak to the supervisor or go up to see the boss. Eventually, the official relented and issued the visas, which we had to pay for individually via the credit card. We waited for the German family and the Brits to finalise their visa process and eventually returned to the car park at midnight to negotiate a fair fee for parking overnight. It had been a very long and stressful day; we were all exhausted and grumpy, sweaty and hungry. After a quick snack, we went to bed and did our best to forget the day, while relieved that we had been issued the visas and were finally able to focus our attention and conversation on other matters.

That morning, we set off to drive into Lagos and, being a Saturday, the traffic was relatively light as we drove across the Eko Bridge from where we witnessed skyscrapers fringed by a shanty town extending from terrafirma to shacks on stilts above the oily black water, full of floating plastic. From Lagos Island, we passed the Lagos Yacht Club and crossed the Ahmadu Bello Way Bridge onto Victoria Island. The iOverlander app indicated that there was a building site on Ozumba Mbadiwe Avenue where the security guard apparently would let us camp behind high walls for 5000 Naira a day, about $14 per vehicle). The Germans truck almost didn't make it under an overpass, and Dick drove past the "camp" site, but eventually, we established where we could camp with the help of a Lebanese building site supervisor, who was perplexed as to why we would be looking for a place to camp a stone's throw from the Radisson Blu Hotel, in the middle of Lagos. Relieved to have found a place to stay, we squeezed the overland vehicles into the compact parking area and settled in for a few days. Dick, Jane, our kids and a few of the German family took a taxi to the Palms Shopping Centre to watch the new Avengers movie which Dick was over the moon excited to see and had not stopped talking about since Benin! Luisa and I visited the South African Shoprite Supermarket at the Centre and stocked up with our favourite food. We had thought that we would have to wait until we reached Namibia to get our hands on Ghost Pops and Pecks Anchovette, Bovril, Marmite, Mrs Ball's Chutney, All Gold tomato sauce (ketchup) Tex Bars, boerewors, vetkoek (deep-fried dough), Appeltizer, Crunchie and Beacon chocolate. We were amazed to find the Shoprite had almost exclusively South African products at fair prices (as it turns out, cheaper than in South Africa, go figure. Which reminded us of buying British products from a Tesco in Hungary at half the cost in Britain). While we were browsing and drooling in the confectionery aisle, we heard a commotion. A young man had brought his girlfriend to the upmarket supermarket, dropped to one knee and proposed to her! She accepted, and the gathered crowd cheered. The message was clear; this is the life I am going to give you, this is where we will buy our groceries, we will hit the big time. Or maybe they had met there, and I am over reading the situation. You just never know, and the truth is often stranger than fiction.

We were having a financial problem - our American bank cards were refusing to trust Nigerian banks and were not issuing cash at the ATM, which dispense a maximum of 20,000 Naira ($55.00) per transaction! We had the Cameroon visas to pay for and surprise, surprise they were not cheap. Dick and Jane, who had no problem drawing money and paid no bank charges, offered to lend us the cash we needed to pay for the visas after we spent two days searching for a solution. This was very kind of them, and we paid back every cent a week later via Paypal. So far the convoy had been getting along fine. I was sick and quiet, Tim was aloof, and there was never a dull moment with Dick around. Pia, Luisa and Jane got along well, and there was a growing camaraderie between us all. There were four children and Keelan, who kept each other occupied and endured the hottest parts of the day attacking each other with water pistols and water balloons. Saturday night we had a bit of a party and Dick and Jane, who both seemed rather homely, revealed a secret. They were Ravers. Yes, they pumped out dance music we had never heard before and told stories of going to a hundred festivals and Jane, and I even danced a bit, potent Nigerian flu medicine chasing the ill away. Then, Luisa, Pia and Jane danced for the next couple of hours while we sat in a circle, in a construction site parking lot, with the hum of generators and dim of traffic and bright lights blasting away the dark. Sunday was spent tidying up the vehicles, doing repairs, washing ourselves with a bucket beside Dick's Land Rover, chatting about the road ahead. The German family announced that they were going to explore the waterways and shantytowns beside the lagoon. We told them that it was probably a bad idea and wished them good luck. They returned exhausted and irritated - they had been conned by a water taxi who quoted a fee and then demanded triple that fee when they were in the middle of the black, oily lagoon. He took them to a church which demanded a donation and then a preacher demanded a personal donation. On the return, the water taxi driver again stopped the boat in the middle of the lagoon and demanded more money. They were followed by groups of teens through the shantytown and returned exhausted, tired and dehydrated.

Monday morning we awoke to blaring horns and endless traffic, the air choked with exhaust fumes and noise pollution echoing off the high buildings which surrounded us.

Luisa called an Uber to collect us from the construction site, and we drove the few blocks to the Cameroonian Consulate where we waited to be attended to and then spent most of the morning walking from ATM to ATM trying to find a bank which would pay out a Moneygram transfer which Luisa had initiated in an attempt to procure cash without relying on ATM's. Unfortunately, Moneygram does not officially honour transactions in Nigeria. The ATM would only issue $55.00 per transaction (when indeed we found an ATM which would dispense cash), and there was a fee of $15.00 per transaction. Most of the morning was spent walking around Victoria Island in the sweltering heat until eventually, we were able to return to the Cameroonian Consulate with almost enough cash to pay for the visas (Dick helped us to pay in the difference, and we repaid him the total amount via Paypal). There were two possible direct routes from Nigeria to Cameroon - through the Nigerian highlands or via the Ekok border which was rumoured to be closed due to the civil war in Cameroon. We asked the consular staff whether it was possible to enter Cameroon via the Ekok border, but they insisted that that crossing was impossible as the government was not in control of the area. This was not great news as we would have to travel to the Niger Delta and north to the highlands through areas infamous for lawlessness and kidnapping.

So far, our Nigerian experience had been varied. The bureaucracy and road to Lagos had been exhausting, and we still had a lot of ground to cover before we crossed into Cameroon. Nigeria is a country of extremes and has an ominous reputation. In South Africa, Nigerians are feared. There is an inner-city suburb of Johannesburg called Hillbrow, which in the '70s and '80s was considered one of the trendiest suburb in South Africa. At night the many nightclubs and cafes hummed with young urbanites - students, artists, musicians and revellers, who travelled to the city from the surrounding suburbs to experience city life and mingle with open-minded people. The suburb became one of the first racially mixed areas, a hotbed of anti-Apartheid activity and was considered a safe haven for homosexuals escaping the confines of conservative urban and rural South Africa. With the demise of Apartheid, South African borders were opened to all and in the late 90's many Africans, including Nigerians, made a beeline for Johannesburg, the wealthiest city on the continent. Most Nigerians were economic migrants but within the Trojan Horse of legal immigration and legitimate enterprise, hid a criminal element, the Nigerian "mafia". The decline of Hillbrow, in general, coincided with the arrival of migrants from many nations and soon horror stories emerged from the city. Entire apartment buildings were "hijacked" and the residents held hostage, murder, rape and assault spiralled out of control and drug use and dealing reached epidemic proportions, Hillbrow became a no-go zone. In public perception, the Nigerians were central to the horror story of Hillbrow, deserved or not, and most South Africans grew to consider Nigerians synonymous with criminality. The gangsters living among the "Fokken

Prawns" in the movie District 9 (filmed in Johannesburg by South African director Neill Blomkamp) are Nigerian, and they sell cat food to the aliens (some aliens are cat food addicts) and run a prostitution ring supplying human woman to the aliens for sex. The leader of the gang is nicknamed Obasanjo (the naming of the gang leader is particularly offensive to Nigerians as Olusegun Obasanjo is a former Nigerian president) who harvests body parts from the aliens to be used for witchcraft. It can, of course, be argued that the film is in many ways satirical with elements of allegory, offering commentary about the treatment of strangers among us, but that message might escape many South Africans, of all races, who paint all Nigerians with the same brush. We took to asking our Lagos Uber drivers what they thought of South Africa, and the consensus was that South Africa is a very dangerous country, much worse than Nigeria. A few of the drivers had lived and worked in Johannesburg and assured us that they had no intention to return to our home country, they would instead try and build a life for themselves in Lagos or Abuja than risk living down south where xenophobic attacks are the new norm. The South African police chief, Beki Cele, insists that the attacks on foreigners are not xenophobic; they are the criminal in intent and motivation. Another new norm in South Africa are riots (labelled "social delivery protests"), poverty-stricken South Africans take to the streets, burn schools, loot businesses and block highways with burning tyres (all while the treasury reports that the African National Congress ruling party cannot account for 800 billion Rand (approx 56 billion dollars) and all government departments are bankrupt). The elite loots the treasury while the poor loot the streets, there are many victims, but African immigrants are specifically targeted.

Internationally Nigerians are infamous for the 419 email scams and the Nigerian mafia in Italy as well as the violent militant group Boko Haram.

When our South African friends and family heard that we would be driving across Nigeria, we were told that we were being reckless, that we were bad parents and that we were making a deadly mistake. Now, we have been accused of these things before travelling across dangerous countries, but the message was crystal clear - be very, very careful. We had been escorted to Lagos by a uniform, but now we would be venturing into the country un-escorted, and we were all apprehensive.

By the time we returned from the Cameroon Consulate to our construction site camp, it was too late to consider leaving Lagos, and it was decided that we should leave in the morning and head towards Benin City, along the coastal route and against the morning traffic. The road was in very good condition, and we trundled along, past apartment blocks, office buildings, a circus, a stadium, supermarkets, a golf course, signs of development. We pulled into a gas station and were greeted with a phrase which we were to hear often over the next week, "Yor welkom", you are welcome. A few locals stopped to chat with us and take photos of the three rigs, lined up for diesel at $0.60 per litre. With full tanks, we headed back onto the expressway and continued until we left Lagos state and entered Ogun state where the roads deteriorated significantly. We encountered a few police checkpoints but were waved through without delay. At the junction of the Epe Ljebu Ode Road and the West-East A121 Highway, we encountered road works, a bridge was being rebuilt, and there was a narrow detour to the right of the road which led through a residential area. There were no barriers restricting access to the bridge, but as we sat pondering which route to take, a large tanker truck drove through the thick uniform cantaloupe coloured soil-cement covering the bridge surface. The mud was obviously an aggregate of some sort and was at least two feet deep. The tanker emerged from the mud and without a word (we had two-way radios for communication) Tim gunned his old truck and attacked the mud at speed; ploughing across the bridge, spraying the muddy soil cement in waves. Dick and I chose to rather take the detour and met up with Tim and his muddy, now orange truck on the A121. Tim liked driving fast, as did Dick. As the road deteriorated to a muddy obstacle course of deep holes, we noticed that the camper box at the rear of Tim and Pia's truck swayed violently as he drove rapidly through the largest road craters when the road eventually evened out, and we triumphantly selected fifth gear, Tim's truck struggled to keep up with the lighter Land Rovers and the old trucks cooling system battled to cope with the hard-driving, long hills and steaming heat.

It was getting late in the afternoon, and we were driving through a hilly, forested area separated from the other vehicles in the convoy by locals. Luisa was driving, we turned a corner, and both spotted something irregular lying next to the road. The traffic was heavy on the tight single carriageway, and tall trees threw shade onto the road. There was no mistaking the shape lying next to the road; it was a body! Luisa braked slightly, and we both shuddered as we realised that man was long dead, his blue clothing faded, the smell of death wafting through the window. We have seen more than a few disturbing things as we travelled, including corpses but what shocked us most was that it was evident that the body had been there a while. A kilometre later, the single carriageway became a dual carriageway, and we noticed two policemen sitting beside the road. We stopped beside them. A thin, dark officer with sallow skin and yellow eyes approached the Land Rover.

"What you brought for us today?"

"Nothing my friend. Listen, there is a dead body lying next to the road about a kilometre back. Can you go have a look?"

"That no problem. What you brought for us?"

The officer leaned in and eyed a packet of strawberry biscuits between the front seats.

"You brought us dem biskits?"

We handed the officer the biscuits and drove away. If we had not been concerned about Nigeria before, we were certainly worried now. The most dangerous countries in the world are those where life is cheap.

It took almost six hours in total to drive the 207 kilometres from Lagos to the small city of Ore, where we had agreed to spend the night. Turning off the A121, we drove into a bustling market street (the most populous nation in Africa is always bustling, there are over 200 million Nigerians, and 80 million are under the age of 18).and stopped to stock up on bread, cold drinks and some vegetables for dinner, we then proceeded to follow our navigation app in the wrong direction and found ourselves attempting a u-turn in a narrow alley choked with traffic, locals laughing and guiding us as we Austin Power'-ed the long Land Rover out of the alley and back to the main road to rejoin the convoy which had thankfully not followed us. I had still not recovered from my illness, but, thanks to the potent Nigerian flu medicine, I was able to get through the day. Jessica seemed to be falling ill, and we were eager to get her into a cool hotel room where she could relax, and we could assess her situation. We arrived at the De Choice Hotel and negotiated with the owner. Well, Dick negotiated with the owner, the idea being that we would rent a room and share the bathroom, Jessica and Luisa would stay in the room, and we would all pay extra to park and sleep in the parking area. The hotel manager emerged from the bar and Dick, and he spoke for a while. The owner suggested that we should pay double what we knew we should pay, 10,000 Naira as opposed to 5,000 Naira as listed on iOverlander. Dick flipped out. He refused to be ripped off and climbed back in his Land Rover insisting that we should all leave but, with an ill child, we were not interested in driving around town for a few hours to save a few dollars. Luisa and I spoke to the manager, and he agreed to rent us a room for 8,000 Naira, and we could pay 7,000 per vehicle as we had many occupants - eleven people in three vehicles. Dick still refused to accept the negotiated amount *on principle* until Tim and I offered to pay the difference for him and Jane.

With that matter settled, we made ourselves comfortable, buying cold Gulder, Star and Hero beer from the bar. Jessica had a fever and low energy and, after we had all washed, Luisa helped her shower and then put her in the bed to rest. The room was relatively clean, had deep red walls, a double bed and a fan. The toilet had no seat, which is common in West Africa, and the "shower" consisted of a large barrel full of water and a small bucket with which you scoop the water and pour it over your head. The hotel compound consisted of a large cream coloured double story building flanked by the bar and a water tower. Water was pumped to two large tanks from where water was gravity fed to the hotel. We parked behind large walls adorned with rolls of razor wire, and two large gates were swung closed after dark. We all kept ourselves busy as the sunset - applied reflective stickers to the Landy, hoping not to fall foul of traffic laws, thereby inviting opportunities for extortion. Tim busied himself repairing his truck camper body which had suffered damage from the violent swaying and worked to unclog the radiator and low hanging air intake which had been caked in the orange soil-cement from his earlier bridge crossing adventure. Dick kept himself busy planning the route ahead. Our next scheduled stop was the city of Onitsha 222 kilometres east of Ore. It was the 14th of May 2019, and it was difficult to conceive that we had been in Spain a full seven months earlier.

The next day was as sweltering as the day before and all the days before it, and we set off relatively early after settling the bill and filling up with fuel. Jessica had not improved overnight, and we stopped at a pharmacy to purchase new Malaria test kits, Coartem (the cheap and effective Malaria treatment), flu medicine and some immune booster. The drive to Onitsha was relatively uneventful. It rained at midday as we drove through Benin City and we stopped to fill the tanks with fuel and give Tim an opportunity to have the truck chassis and engine power washed. The orange mud was still restricting the old truck's radiator, and the engine was not cooling sufficiently. While we waited for Tim, Luisa and I worked on the Land Rovers electrical system - the glow plug light flickered, constantly and we could not figure out where the fault was. Unsuccessful, we killed time chatting to Jane before buying six litres of 5w30 engine oil from the Total garage. The oil bottles each had a scratch strip which concealed a verification number; you sent a text to the number provided and in return received a text confirming that the oil was a legitimate, genuine Total product. Good old Nigeria. We had heard rumours of fake engine oil (and branded beer) and were hoping that we were not being scammed, particularly as we were purchasing the oil directly from a Total garage.

With Tim's truck cleaned, we eventually rejoined the road to Onitsha and arrived at the commercial hub on the eastern bank of the Niger river that evening to find a hotel. The sky was grey as we pulled into the Cyson Hotel, Luisa was ill, Jessica was ill, we were all tired, and there was not much conversation before bed. Keelan and I wanted to go for a walk, but the hotel security guard stopped us and told us, "This is Africa, not Europe, It is not safe". Without a burning desire to explore the dusty, busy city, we took his advice and returned to the vehicles for a quick dinner. Luisa was struggling with the flu now; she was losing both her voice and her patience. The next morning Tim, Pia, Luisa and I stood discussing the route. The Cameroonian professor I had met in Dakar had suggested that the Ekok border would not be a problem as long as we paid the rebels bribes and, looking at a map, it was tempting to at least try to cross into Cameroon at Ekok. Dick walked over and became very agitated when he heard that we were discussing the Ekok route. He refused even to consider the route and, loudly, informed us that he had inside information and that it was ludicrous even to discuss the border as an option. His agitation became anger, and he railed at us as if we were inexperienced and unintelligent. It was at that moment that the cracks deepened and the convoy began to fall apart. We argued that we were simply discussing the option, that we could get better information closer to the border and that I had spoken to a few locals who had said that the Ekok border crossing was open and possible (a Polish couple crossed at the Ekok border just over a month later, although they did encounter a lot of armed separatists and strongly advised against crossing at Ekok). Dick vetoed the conversation completely, which no-one gave him the authority to do. This is why we do not travel in convoy.

We drove to the Onitsha mall and found a Shoprite supermarket and stocked up on supplies, visited the pharmacy for medicine and then searched for a printing company. I had been sharing the driving with

Luisa (who drove at least 50% of the sealed roads on our West African route) for the simple reason that my driver's license had expired in 2016! I had not been back to South Africa since 2012, and there was no way to renew the license without applying in person. We did have a letter from the South African authorities that the license was valid and without limitations, but that was just an excuse for some roadside cowboy to issue us with a fine and delay us further. Besides, I was sick, and Luisa is a very good driver, there is no good reason why she should not drive. We were amazed to hear that Jane did not drive at all and that Dick drove even when he was extremely ill. Pia drove the truck often and was, in our opinion, a better driver than Tim. We were delayed for an hour while Luisa attempted to print and laminate a fake drivers license for me to show the police but unfortunately, the little print shop, the tenth which we had visited in the last month, was no better than any of the other little roadside print shops and Luisa was able to produce only a sorry-looking little document. We would take our chances with my expired passport then, at least Nigerian Police could read and speak English, and we could argue our way out of any fines. We passed a burning truck as we drove out of town and found ourselves ahead of the convoy, which had left us at the mall and had taken another route. We parked beside the road after driving through a pleasant neighbourhood of large, colonial-style houses and ate fried chicken while waiting, a group of men and women chatting happily nearby as they waited for a bus. I discarded chicken bones out of the camper window and worried about the days ahead. The police and military checkpoints had increased substantially, and while most let us pass without problems, there are always a few rotten apples which we sweetened with gifts of bubblegum.

The A232 road to Enugu was in a poor state in places, there were many checkpoints, and an article of camouflage clothing was enough to grant someone authority. We were stopped at one makeshift checkpoint, a tree branch across the road attached to a slumped man by a rope. The "policeman" wore camouflage shorts, a white vest and flip flops. He demanded our passports and, with a smile, I asked him if he was a policeman, he said yes! I asked where was his uniform. He pointed at his shorts. Look, camouflage! We smiled and handed him a pack of gum before confidently selecting first gear and moving forward. He let us pass with a mischievous smile. Five friendly checkpoints later we were stopped by a soldier standing in mud with a perfect uniform and shiny boots. He stuck his head in the Land Rover and asked for my driver's license. As he studied the license, I distracted him by asking questions about the road ahead, is it safe, how far is Enugu? He spotted Jessica, and a smile spread across his face.

"Is this your daughter?"
"Yes, how much further to Enugu?"
"She is very beautiful. Does she want to marry me?"
"She is 14".
"No problem'.
"It is illegal".

Jessica had to endure these propositions daily, but usually only from men in uniforms or young men surrounded by friends in a market. And nothing made us angrier. Pia told us one night that Zoe, at ten years old, suffered identical harassment at checkpoints and border crossings even though the adult men *knew* that she was only ten years old.

By the time we checked into the Toplog Hotel in Enugu, we were convinced that Jessica was suffering from Malaria. Luisa tested her twice, while I changed the Defenders engine oil, and both test kits confirmed that she indeed had Malaria and we informed our convoy partners as we sat outside the little pub on yellow plastic chairs, our vehicles parked behind a wall fifteen feet high and Jessica resting on our sheets in an air-conditioned room with a lumpy pounded mattress. Dick told us that we were wrong, that the tests were wrong, that because Jessica had taken flu medicine, the results of the tests were wrong. He insisted that there was nothing wrong with her except the flu and that she would be fine. "No, Dick. She has Malaria. We are going to take her to the clinic tomorrow". Dick scowled, if we took her to the clinic they would obviously say that she has Malaria so that they can put her in hospital and then they will keep her there for a week. Dick was concerned that his schedule would be interrupted. I was concerned that we were heading into one of the most dangerous parts of Nigeria, and my fourteen-year-old daughter had a potentially fatal disease. Understanding that we would hold up the convoy, I clearly told Tim and Dick that they did not have to wait for us the next day. I awoke at 8 am, checked on Jessica who had shivered throughout the night, had a shower and walked back outside to the Land Rover. Our convoy mates were gone without a goodbye to myself or the children.

I had the tall, slim and pleasant receptionist call a taxi while the short, fat and unpleasant receptionist lay on a couch watching a soap opera. The taxi arrived and took us up onto a wide avenue bordered by large trees and grand estates. At the Enugu Teaching Hospital, we were guided to the Paediatric ward where we were greeted warmly, filled in forms and waited for a doctor to attend to Jess who was almost too weak to walk but was well hydrated. The doctor called us into his basic but equipped office and tested Jessica for Malaria using exactly the same test kits as we used, telling us that these were the gold standard for Malaria kits in Nigeria. He took blood and urine samples to be positive and evaluated the results an hour later, confirming again that Malaria was indeed at fault. We were prescribed an immune booster, a course of anti-biotics and Coartem and we returned to what the South Americans would call a "love motel", beside the full volume, Lord's Chosen Charismatic Revival Church. The consultation and treatment had cost less than $10.00, and we put Jessica into bed after giving her her medicine. Throughout the entire ordeal, she did not cry, she did not complain, and she apologised for causing a delay. She is the kindest, warmest, most wonderful girl I know, and it breaks our hearts to see her ill. We monitored her that entire day and night, and by morning the fever had broken, and her appetite and sense of humour returned.

Dick sent Luisa a message saying that they and the Germans were waiting for us in a hotel parking lot in a town called Katsina-Ala. We were surprised that they had decided to wait, as we had accepted that we would have to complete the Nigerian stretch of the journey alone, a situation which was in some ways preferable to travelling in convoy. We really do not enjoy travelling in convoy for a few reasons and the experience of the last few weeks had served only to confirm our bias. I had posted on social media that the convoy had moved on and Dick was not pleased that we had eluded that they had "abandoned" us. Unfortunately, the most dangerous stretch of the journey lay ahead of us - from Enugu to the highlands where we would then have to follow an off-road trail through the Gashaka - Gumti National Park to reach Cameroon while avoiding the civil war there. We would have preferred to continue travelling without the convoy, but safety comes first, and there is safety in numbers, apparently. We would have also preferred to allow Jessica a few days in the Enugu Hotel to recover, but we had to catch up with the convoy and Jessica assured us that she felt fine and we accepted that we would have to make her as comfortable as possible and monitor her condition constantly. Our frustration was palpable.

Fortunately, we had built the Land Rover for precisely these kind of situations, Jessica was able to lie comfortably as we drove, had we still had the rooftop tent and double cab layout there would be no way that we could continue.

We packed the Land Rover and left Enugu reluctantly. The road condition en-route to Ogoja was at times good and then absolutely terrible and then not too bad, then quite good, then shocking. There were numerous roadblocks where we were usually welcomed.

"Welkom to Nigeria!"
"Thank you"
"Where are you going? Cameroon. OK. What did you bring for us?"

We would hand the policeman a pack of gum, and usually, that would be enough to satisfy them. The Germans strategy was to hand out packets of cigarettes, but we hardly ever saw West Africans smoking and Nigerians were no exception, tobacco held no true currency.

At Ogoja, we were stopped by a policeman who asked where our front number plate was. We told him that it was displayed on the front of the roof rack and he spent ten minutes staring at the number plate before returning to ask for my driver's license which he contemplated for another ten minutes. Eventually, a colleague approached and said,
"Don't be offended; we are the Nigerian anti-kidnapping unit".

The presence of an anti-kidnapping unit did not make us feel safer, quite the opposite. Our spirits were relatively high despite the roads, heat, Malaria and constant roadblocks and we arrived in Katsina-Ala late in the afternoon, located the Smile View Hotel and drove into the secure compound where the British and German trucks stood waiting for us. Luisa booked a room for Jessica and Keelan and put Jessica to bed immediately. It was amazing how quickly Jessica's health had improved, Coartem is a fantastic drug and renders Malaria impotent effectively (if only there was an equivalent pharmaceutical for the flu-like symptoms which continued to plague Luisa and me). That there are still a million malaria deaths each and every year in Africa is a shocking statistic, despite the best efforts of NGO's and aid organisations distributing nets and treatment. We are fortunate that a handful of dollars to treat such a dangerous disease is easily spent and not soon missed; the majority of Sub Saharan Africans do not enjoy the same luxury.

With Jessica safely in bed watching a movie on her tablet and the Land Rover prepared for a night parked between high concrete walls and a tall, green steel gate, I sat with the hotel staff and watched Tim work on his truck, again. Tim spent most of the evenings working on the truck, repairing the camper panels, preventing leaks and maintaining the vehicle. This evening he was attempting to fabricate a raised air intake. The hotel staff and their friends were friendly and relaxed, helping Tim, telling jokes and chatting to me about South Africa and Europe and the USA. We had a pleasant "camp" arranged between the three vehicles, all facing the main, single-storey building shaped like an L, with the main building of rooms and reception and a wing which extended to the left of our parking lot camp. The sun had just begun to set and a cold beer at the end of another steaming day relaxed us all. Pia fed her children dinner, Tim tinkered, Luisa tidied the Landy while Dick and Jane, Dicked and Janed. The laughter of our conversation filled the air.

A shot rang out! A scream. Loud and very close, too close. Our new Nigerian friends scattered as one and without hesitation, running and cowering as if expecting a hail of bullets, they ran into the hotel and disappeared, leaving us bewildered, on our feet, alarmed. We kicked into action, quickly and quietly locked the children in the room and had Pia hide her children in the truck while we packed away our tables and chairs, bottles and plates, removing the evidence of our relaxed late afternoon. Sporadically locals ran onto the property through the large green gate (which was eventually slammed shut and locked) and another smaller gate at the end of the left wing, they too rang cowering, shoulders slumped, heads protected from feared bullets. The sun vanished, and night arrived suddenly dark and ominously quiet. The entire town became absolutely silent, as all her residents hid from the dark men who terrorise. Time stood still. A large, powerfully built man dressed in fatigues rushed into the courtyard, a Kalashnikov assault rifle in both hands, ready. He ran into the hotel shouting and emerged with two tall, thin, young staff members who he ordered to lay on the ground. As I stood with Luisa in front of the Land Rover, two metres away, far from the comfort of the shadows, the soldier picked up a long metal pole and began beating the men, shouting.

"Where is the gun! Where is the gun!" (He might have been shouting "Where is the girl").

The prostate men shouted that they did not know; their hands held open before them, protesting and protecting.

The aggressor looked us over and then left, taking a few men with him, and absolute quiet returned.

Soon Dick started chatting to Tim excitedly, while Tim noisily mounted his bicycle on the back of his truck, their loud, conspicuously European voices breaking the silence, I asked them to be quiet and to remain hidden, explaining that when the locals return to normal, only then can we relax. Tim, Dick and Jane then left the parking area and entered the hotel, I stood in the shadows, ready to act, not being a hero or a fool but prepared to intervene to protect my family and friends, ready to diffuse a situation, hoping to ensure that we could all stay safe and unmolested in this, the infamous Nigerian kidnapping zone. I was determined not to allow our worst fears to come to reality and felt strangely calm. The militant returned, his attention now turned to our vehicles. I stepped out of the shadows and offered my hand.

"My name is Rob, what is your name?"
"My name is Commando; I am Nigerian special forces. Where is your security detail?", he barked.
"They are coming now, five minutes", I lied.
"Where are you from?"
"I am South African; we are heading to Cameroon", I responded.
"A woman was murdered now, outside the gates. Are there men here with guns?"
"No, sir, I only saw the staff".
"Stay inside. You are safe".

With that, he left, and we waited, unsure what would happen next. Pia emerged from her truck. We spoke for a short while, but she was very concerned about Tim, he had not told her where he was going, and together with Luisa, who emerged from the locked bedroom, they went looking for Tim who was enjoying a chat and an air-conditioned room with Dick and Jane. Pia was not happy that Tim had not stayed with the family, and after a short, terse conversation, Tim collected his towel and toiletries from the truck and headed back to the hotel room. As he approached the entrance, two young men emerged from the hotel and greeted Tim with huge smiles of relief, clapped their hands and declared, "You are free! You are free!".

Tim ignored the men and brushed past them. I approached the one man and asked,
"Why are you surprised that he is free?"
The young man's smile faded, "No, everything is OK, I am just happy to see him".

I continued to question the one man, but, he refused to confirm what I already knew. The conversation spooked me; eleven "European" travellers must have presented a very tempting target for any professional kidnapper gang. It was going to be a long night.

The town came back to life, radios played, vehicles drove, people chatted, and an air of calm returned to Katsina-Ala. I was surprised that Dick and Tim had been so nonchalant about the entire episode, these were not military men with years of experience and hardened hearts. They had been born and raised in safe and secure countries, where the prospect of sudden and discriminate violence was as foreign to them as the country they now found themselves crossing. Growing up in South Africa, I had experienced another world - late-night assault rifle fire very close to my boarding school (at the edge of the Munzieville township (after a visit by the firebrand Winnie Mandela), our hostel master patrolling the corridors with a pistol), bomb drills, witnessed unrest and a few guns being shoved in my face over the years. I could only assume that they could not fathom the true danger of the situation we were faced with that night.

Luisa and the kids locked themselves in the room, and I sat in the Land Rover for two hours watching and waiting. Eventually, at midnight I slipped out of the Land Rover and locked up, before joining my family in the room and pushing a large armchair against the door. There I sat all night, trying to stay awake, listening to every sound, armed with hidden tear gas and a hunting knife. It was a very long night indeed, and when a large storm broke, I permitted myself to sleep for an hour or two before we prepared to leave. Dick and Tim slept well; it seemed. At 8 am precisely, they drove out of the compound, ignoring our request to wait a few more minutes to prepare. Luisa had not slept either, and Jessica still had Malaria. Ten minutes later, we received a message stating that they were waiting for us at a gas station. We packed up and drove out onto the road and took a wrong turn and found ourselves at a military checkpoint which, luckily, was not too interested in us. Eventually, we found the correct gas station - old, ramshackle and surrounded by long grass. We topped up with fuel, fuming with anger, our patience wearing very thin. Dick took the lead and drove off quickly as soon as Tim had finished filling the trucks large tank.

The road to Takum was in a poor state of repair with very little traffic. We spent most of the morning dodging potholes and stopping at police checkpoints, the more remote the checkpoint, the more inebriated the policeman seemed. The countryside had changed - green rolling hills of wet grass bordered by ancient trees, the sky grey with clouds, not smoke and villages few and far between. There were two route options for us, the track via Bali and the national park or, a much shorter but much tougher route via Gembu and a forging of a river. Dick had expressed no interest in driving the tougher, shorter route even though a lone German had driven that route a week before. Imagine our surprise when Dick then lead us down the Gembu road, despite our protestations that he was, in fact, taking the Gembu road, he refused to stop driving until we reached a police checkpoint an hour and a half later down a winding, muddy yet dusty red dirt road. At the checkpoint, we were told by the large friendly policeman, that the road to Gembu was terrible, but a truck driver told us that the road was OK. Dick was still struggling to admit that he had led us down the wrong road, going so far as to tell me, "You would know where you are if you had a map". It is true; navigation is not my strength or duty, Luisa takes care of the navigation with help from Keelan, I go where they tell me to.

Travelling with Dick would have been funny had it not been so inconvenient. Dick is the kind of man who is not made for this world. He is intelligent, but it is his intelligence which makes him socially awkward if not impossible. I imagine that he was bullied severely at school, his friends were his comics, books, toys and computer. He lives in a world where he is king, and he is always right, to admit being wrong would be to compromise his foundation. He told me that he could have millions of followers on social media, but chooses not to, that he could make videos with a million views on YouTube, but he chooses not to. At first, I had felt an affinity for the man, I know what it is like to be an outsider, and we could have been good friends, under normal circumstances. But, I soon began to realise that, that which does not please or suit him does not have the right to exist or is, in fact, just plain stupid, particularly when a situation is beyond him. I have taught myself great patience and humility, but, my friend Dick had spent the last week pushing all the wrong buttons.

Tim and I had a chat and thought, since Dick had already led us so far down this road, we might as well continue. We walked up to Dick's Land Rover and proposed the idea. Dick started shouting, as he had when we had brought up the idea of the Ekok crossing. He refused even to consider the idea and insisted that the German who had done the Gembu road before us was a raving lunatic and we were mad even to consider taking that route.

At this point, I am starting to ask myself why I was putting up with this constant insanity? The answer is simple; I needed to convoy to ensure the safety of my family, at least through this most dangerous part of Nigeria. I needed to bite my tongue and count to ten and remember that soon we could separate and we would never have to see Dick again. Tim, being relatively inexperienced, was relying on Dick to do all of the thinking for him and Dick had convinced him that he was a big deal in the overland world. We were very found of Pia and her kids and Jane, and being in convoy with us was evidently better and safer for them if the events of the previous evening proved nothing else. So I had a responsibility to my family and Pia and her children, and I would have to endure the enormous egos until I could at least bear responsibility for my family and my family alone.

Reluctantly we turned the convoy around and drove the hour and a half back to the road to Bali, where the route across the highlands would begin. We stopped for fuel, Dick led us down another wrong turn (admittedly Nigeria can be challenging to navigate) but eventually we joined the correct road and tried to make up for the three lost, precious hours. Our destination was the town of Bali (Beli on some maps) where we exited the dangerous zone and would begin the climb up to the national park. We endured police checkpoints on average roads but could not make up for the lost time, and the sun began to set as we approached a small village 100kms from Beli. Unfortunately, Dick was still leading the convoy and I trailed him with Tim at the rear. As we entered the town, we approached a police checkpoint, tired and anxious to find a safe place to spend the night.

A tall, wiry policeman stepped into the road and brought our unhappy convoy to a halt. Watching from a few meters behind, we witnessed the policeman approach Dick and, after a few words, instruct Dick to open the back of his vehicle. Dick was agitated and began arguing with the policeman. He reluctantly opened the back of the vehicle and stepped inside with the official, refusing to open certain drawers, being as uncooperative as possible, all the while berating the officer, asking him how he would feel if Dick came to his house and started going through his possessions? Luisa and I looked at each other; this was not going to end well, we had been through enough checkpoints and borders to know that a bad attitude leads to bad situations. While the officer continued to search, Dick nudged him out of the vehicle and locked the doors, aggravating the policeman. Dick then refused to cooperate any further, climbed in the vehicle and started to drive away. We and our children (and the German family in their vehicle) watched incredulously as the officer grabbed an assault rifle, ran to the front of Dick's Land Rover, cocked the gun and, with a finger on the trigger, aimed the rifle at Dick aggressively and shouted at him to stop and get out of the vehicle. We watched nervously, hoping that Dick would regain his composure and do what he was asked. The officer searched Dick's vehicle and eventually approached us, assault rifle in hand, locked and loaded with the safety off. We now had the pleasure of dealing with a very angry and agitated policeman. Thanks, Dick.

I opened the back of the Land Rover, introduced him to my family, welcomed him inside, offered him a cold drink and a pack of bubble gum,

"How are you today sir, Nigeria is very beautiful, we are from South Africa, here are our passports, yes, we are African too, is there a nice hotel in town, would you like some chocolate, here is my driver's licence, do you want the papers for the vehicle, in here we have food, look. And in here we have clothing and some books, under Jessica's seat is a water tank, under Keelan's seat is another water tank. Jessica has Malaria. Here is a gas tank and there are our shoes and this is a toilet. Yes, that man is crazy. I am sorry, sir".

The officer poked around for a while in the vehicle; he explained to me that there are a lot of kidnappings in this region and it is very dangerous, that he has a very dangerous job and his duty is to protect us, but we have to do what we are told. I agreed with him and thanked him for his patience. By the time he had moved on to the German truck, he was calm and spent less than ten minutes searching their vehicle.

An hour had passed since we had stopped at the checkpoint and the sun lay low on the horizon when, a short drive further into town we stopped at another checkpoint, I had taken the lead and spoke to a large woman dressed in white who began to issue me with instructions. I asked the lady who she was, and she apologetically produced a police identification card. The town was not safe, and we were to follow one of her officers to the police station where we would spend the night under their guard, and the next day a police convoy would escort us to the national park. We thanked her, relieved that we would not have to search for a hotel and that we could sleep safely, hopefully. We followed the policeman and entered a compound beside the main road, where we were directed to park on a large overgrown lawn. There was a barrel of water beside the building which we could use and a toilet at the back of the building. A few of the higher ranking policeman approached, and we had a conversation about Nigeria, they warned us that it was incredibly dangerous and they said that we were welcome and we were safe. With the pleasantries and introductions over with, we all set up some chairs and prepared food.

A low wall and a road separated us from a noisy market, where we were able to buy some supplies under the watchful eye of a police officer. The sunset, the eleven of us sat in a circle; we tried to relax, we tried to avoid speaking to Dick, but we were all incredibly agitated. Keelan decided to talk to Dick about the checkpoint, asking him if he knew that he had provoked the officer. Dicks response was that Keelan did not know what he was talking about, this young man who had grown up travelling the world! I bit my tongue. Pia suggested that there may have been a better way to handle the situation, Tim agreed that it was a scary moment. Dick responded,

"You can all go fuck yourselves".

It was all that I could do to stay seated; nobody speaks to my family that way. I let Dick know how we felt and put him in his place firmly and with no doubts, that there would be repercussions if he did not zip his lip and behave himself. I had eventually reached the end of my rope, as had Luisa. I was raised to be a gentleman, I always try to be, and after a few minutes of calming silence, I offered Dick the opportunity to be a man and move on from this. He refused, "I won't sit here being bullied, this convoy is over". Thank all the Gods!

The next morning we packed up, Dick and Jane sat sulking in their vehicle. Tim seemed unready to leave, and I asked him what he was waiting for, he said he was waiting for Dick to speak to the police about the escort. Keelan and I walked over to a group of policeman chatting under a tree, introduced ourselves, told them that we are also African and that we love Nigeria. We asked to speak to the chief and explained to him that we were absolutely fine that we did not need a convoy and that we were confident that we would be safe. The chief seemed satisfied in the security and innocence which a fresh morning brings. We walked back to our fractured convoy and told Tim that the police agreed to let us continue without an escort, upon hearing this, Dick kicked his vehicle in gear and sped out of the compound leaving us all relieved and smiling broadly. We worried only for Jane.

I soon realised that though Dick may have physically left the convoy, he had not left at all. There was only the one route over to Cameroon, and he knew that if experienced any problems along the way, we would only be a few hours behind.

Without the volatile Englishman, we left the compound and travelled at a sedate pace, stopping at leisure to buy fruit and bread and then to eat a sandwich beside the road at the foot of the mountains. From Bali, everything changed; the people seemed calm and friendly, healthy and helpful. The land itself opened up and embraced us under immense blue skies. A huge weight had been lifted from our shoulders, and we travelled peacefully to the mountains along the Mambila Plateau Road.

There were two particularly interesting roadblocks that morning. At first, we sat talking to a young officer for a few minutes, a field to our right, a rocky cliff to our left. A voice called out from the cliff, "Where are you from?". We looked across at the rock face and could not see the source of the voice, until the soldier moved, so effective was his camouflage uniform. We have a pet rubber snake which sleeps on the dashboard and does a very good job of keeping strange limbs from entering the Land Rover. It was a source of constant amusement to see a rough and ready, "seen it all" policeman jump back in fear and surprise when spotting the still, yellow, black snake. Some would not approach the Defender again and immediately told us to leave, and no-one ever touched the snake. At the second roadblock that wonderful, liberated morning a very large and heavily armed policeman approached the waiting Land Rover. In the distance, rolling green hills beckoned, and beside the road, a square building and a group of policemen sat in the shadow of a large, majestic tree. The policeman approached the Land Rover, started to talk and then stopped as his eyes landed on the snake.

"Is it real?"
"No, sir".

He reached in and touched the snake, withdrew his hand cautiously, looked at Keelan and said, "Watch this". He picked up the snake, hid it behind his back and walked casually towards the group of men laughing beneath the tree. He threw the snake onto two young, muscular officers sitting on a low wall. The group scattered, screaming and one of the two young officers did not stop running until he was at least 50m's away, our new friend laughing so hard that he had to rest his hands on his knees.

The closer we got to the national park, the more peaceful the area became and we had one last significant checkpoint beside a large and beautifully located military base, where a serious and professional soldier checked through our documentation. We passed friendly people selling fresh fruit and vegetables transported by ancient Pinzgauer 6x6 vehicles and Land Rovers, a clear sign that we were headed for some epic roads. After climbing a mountain pass, we stopped one last time to look back on volatile Nigeria, a country which had been at times wonderful and incredibly challenging. A group of children ran out to greet us as we took photos of the plateau which we were leaving behind, along with the kidnappers, cops, great roads, horrible roads, wonderful people, terrible few and endless surprises. The clouds grew thicker as we continued along up into the mountains; the people changed but remained friendly. We suddenly found ourselves back in the rolling green beauty of the Colombian coffee region. Here and there we spotted a large farmhouse or homes built of stone. At a traders market, where men in robes covered the hills with herded cattle, the navigator had us turn left, from the good paved road, through a crowded, narrow market where Tim had to drive carefully to squeeze the big old truck past the many colourful stalls. We emerged onto a muddy track, and as if on cue, the heavens opened.

We were now on the infamous highlands trail to Cameroon, and we were nervous for what lay ahead. First, let me paint a picture for you. By now we were accustomed to the typical images and perception of West Africa - the crumbling, busting villages, the hustle of everyday life, great poverty endured daily and occasional opulence enjoyed by few, dusty streets, and a natural world sapped of every available resource. The highlands are unique to Nigeria as if another country on another continent. Here, fields of rich green grass and rolling hills are bordered by ancient forests under a misty sky (a typical montane ecosystem) where livestock grow large and slow and calm, cash crops grow full and sweet, and the Fulani people live with a degree of serenity unknown to their compatriots. The Fulani have permission to graze their livestock on the fertile grass of the southern reaches of the park, but there has been conflict in the past, and tribesmen recently murdered a park ranger. The Gashaka - Gumti National Park was created by joining two game reserves is 1991 and is Nigeria's largest and most diverse national park. Deep within the park are herds of elephant, troops of chimpanzee, buffalo, wild dogs, crocodiles, hippos, antelope and 500 species of birds. It is hoped that lions will eventually return to the park. The southern sector, which we had recently entered, has a rugged, mountainous terrain of steep cliffs, valleys and gorges, waterfalls and raging rivers while the northern half of the park is grassy savanna. There are rumoured to be a thousand kilometres of muddy 4x4 tracks crossing the large park. It is also rumoured that criminal gangs and Boko Haram take advantage of the seclusion of the park, to conduct their nefarious business and take advantage of the porous border with Cameroon. We hoped to avoid both.

Our first obstacle, aside from the mud, was a bridge made of planks of wood over a log frame. Our Defender is not as heavy as she may appear and certainly a lot lighter than the old German truck. Keelan, Luisa, Tim and I inspected the bridge and decided that we would layer planks to reinforce the track and that the Land Rover would cross first if the bridge showed signs of weakness we could then further reinforce it for the heavy truck. With the rain falling heavy and steady, we drove over the bridge and up the track until we found a level area to stop. With Keelan and Tim guiding, Pia drove the truck over without any problems despite a few creaking and bending planks. Pia had taken over the driving for the 120 km off-road trail, and she was proving to be a mature and competent driver, which was a good thing indeed. For a few hours, we drove in the rain, climbing steep hills and dropping down into valleys as rainwater filled large potholes and ran beside the trail, collecting in streams at the base of each valley. Fortunately, most of the trail had a substrate of rock which allowed for plenty of grip, but there were large muddy sections which required more attention. Overall we were gaining altitude (the highest point in Nigeria would be near the Cameroon border, Chappal Waddi at 2419m), the further we drove, the more beautiful the highlands became, we found ourselves often stopping to marvel at the natural splendour of hills, cliffs, forests and dramatic skies and enjoying the fresh, cool air. This was the first time in months that we were not coated in sweat. If Nigeria were not so tumultuous, this would be the perfect location for five-star boutique lodges where nature lovers could hike, raft, explore, game view (in the more secluded areas of the park) and enjoy a unique environment, climate and experience. Without a doubt, this was one of the most beautiful places we had ever set a boot.

We found ourselves driving in low range often, not because the trail was so demanding but rather because there were hardly any sections of the trail where we could drive faster than 20 kph. It was simpler to rumble along at low revs, climbing and descending, than it was to try and keep the turbo spinning and running through the gears. The German truck was slow, and we had no intention of rushing them, we had already established that pushing the truck hard was not a great idea. With the sun dropping towards the horizon, we began looking for a good place to park up for the night. We had seen very few people, except for farmers travelling on motorbikes and the occasional old Land Rover loaded with bananas. The track continued to impress, and it was soon apparent that there was a love for the land - many fields were fringed with tall, evenly spaced old trees which served to establish borders and as natural fences. It was on a plateau, next to a long row of tall pines that we decided to stop for the night. I spotted a shepherd tending his flock; he was seated on large granite boulders which framed an exceptional view of a forested valley and rolling, rocky hills to the horizon. The rain had stopped, and we walked over to the shepherd and asked permission to camp on the road, which was wide and almost level. The shepherd greeted us with a warm smile and told us that we would be very safe and were welcome to stop there for the night. Pia parked her truck in front of the Land Rover, and Tim busied himself stretching a tarp between the cabin and the camper box of the truck where rain often found it's way between the concertina walkway walls. We ate bananas and mango and enjoyed a pasta meal while watching the sunset and

Tim fly his drone. That cold night, a storm raged and soaked the road, lightning and thunder electrifying the air. We welcomed the crisp air and were pleasantly surprised that there were no mosquitoes to plague us with buzzing, bites and Malaria. We slept better than we have for a very long time.

The morning arrived fresh and wet. A few motorbikes passed us, and we were surprised to witness a large, red articulated truck ploughing along the red, muddy road. It is mind-boggling what people are able to achieve when they simply have to. We were reminded of the muddy trail through the upper Amazon from Linden to Lethem, where large trucks defied the elements for the sake of commerce but often fell victim to the elements, either becoming hopelessly bogged or flipping onto their sides. We took the presence of the large truck as a good sign for the road ahead, particularly for Pia and her truck. A Muslim family approached from the left of the field before us, as goats ate the banana and mango peels which we had thrown into the field. The mother and her daughter remained a short distance away, while her sons came closer to say hello. A man arrived on a motorbike to ask us where we were from and where we were going before leaving and returning with a man in a white and gold tunic riding pillion. His name was Ibrahim, and he was the chief of the nearby village, Dungwa Bongo. Ibrahim exuded the authority of a respected man, and he welcomed us to Nigeria. Surrounding him respectfully, were six of his thirteen children, and he was proud that he had only one daughter in his personal army. The sons were dressed in old and weathered clothing, but their smiles were rich and friendly. We chatted for a while about Nigeria, South Africa and Europe, and he reassured us that we were welcome and safe. After chatting for a while about the road condition ahead, we said thank you and goodbye and left as the rain began to fall. The village of Dungwa Bongo was built of cement and brick and evidently suffered a lot of rain, the walls stained with splashed red mud. There were no signs of a general store, but we had enough fruit to keep us all going for a while, in fact, there were few signs of life aside from the smoke of cooking fires rising out of almost every home. Once through the village, we climbed a long, wet hill and emerged into a thick mist which obscured the green world around us.

It was to be a long day of driving but one of the best days we have ever had in Africa. There were no checkpoints or roadblocks, no flies or pollution or maddening traffic and the cool air was comfortable. This was an adventure! The Land Rover was working hard, and we realised that we had a few issues to deal with - the glow plug light continued to flash, the reverse gear was jamming, and I was struggling to change from first into second gear, the brakes needed to be bled and we were still suffering from the fuel leak caused by the reckless mechanics in Turkey. Despite all these issues, the Landy soldiered on, never missing a beat and making light work of even the muddiest, gouged incline. In low range second gear, she would climb like a mountain goat, and there seemed nothing she could not conquer in first gear, low range, diff lock. Our friend Billy had helped us to get a set of General Tyre X3 mud terrains in Portugal, and these tyres were proving to be indestructible and gripped like an octopus on a dive mask. People often ask us why we use a mud-terrain tyre, and the reality is that you don't *need* a mud-terrain tyre until you really NEED a mud terrain tyre. I suspect that the reason we have hardly ever needed to use our winch for self-recovery (we have rescued many others) is that we have had the grip we needed when others did not. Before we crossed the Amazon, we invested in 33 inch MT's and that investment paid off as we ploughed through feet of thick mud around other stricken vehicles and we were relieved to be running a tyre capable of dealing with the thick, red clay mud which we were driving now in the Nigerian highlands. The mud itself was like a greasy clay, coating the rocks and lubricating the steep hills, adding significant weight to the Landy as it clung to the chassis, inches deep. This was the mud of legends.

Now, to be fair, you do not need mud-terrain tyres or even 4x4 to drive this route - in the dry season. A sixty-year-old woman named Dot Bekker, had a month before, driven this route in a 2x4 Ford van and she had been able to make it through to Cameroon because she drove in convoy with an American driving a massive 4x4 beast. When her blue Ford could not make it up a hill or through a mud patch, Bruce (the American) would do what he had to to get the Ford moving. Sometimes they had locals help to push, and sometimes the Ford needed a pull. When people ask me whether a 4x4 is essential for travelling around the world, my answer is, "Well, it depends". The vast majority of roads you will encounter around the world do not require a 4x4 with mud terrain tyres, the Amazon route which we drove solo in 2014 had just been completed by an Argentine couple in a little Renault delivery van with horrible ground clearance. 4x4 comes into its own when you are a solo, independent traveller who likes to go to places many do not visit, and you like the idea of not having to wait for someone to tow you out or over what a 2x4 (or 1x4) vehicle cannot pull itself over or through. The Argentine couple knew that the Amazon road had traffic and knew that someone would pull them out of the mud as they blocked the road. Dot had wisely arranged to drive the highlands trail in convoy with Bruce, who apparently is the kind of man who does not hesitate to help another, even when he has his own plate full. The take away is that you can travel the world in just about any vehicle, but you may have to ask for help when the going gets rough.

The highland route is not possible in a 2x4 in the wet season. Well, it may be but you will certainly need a lot of help along the way and may find yourself sliding towards a cliff or into a river. Occasionally, we would pass a small village or a farmer on a 125cc Chinese motorbike, or an old Land Rover loaded to the sky with thick, green bananas. We were always greeted warmly and made a concerted effort not to churn up more mud than we had to and to make way for locals using the road - they were working, our goal was secondary to theirs. The scenery became more spectacular the; further, we travelled, and often we found ourselves parked on the side of a road just soaking in the beauty of green paradise, the Garden of Eden. Often we had to stop for a while to wait for the German truck to catch up or to guide them through some of the worst sections. I had given Pia some advice - as slow as possible, as fast as necessary - and it was soon evident that she was a courageous and excellent driver. The massive truck with its enormous tyres had no problems with the mud or the middle hump, but it was in heavy articulation that the vehicle struggled the most, particularly with body sway. At times the trail became narrow, the road formed by nature, heavy rains eroding the hills and decades of road maintenance digging the trail two, three or four meters below the level of the earth surrounding us. The recent and continuous rainfall had washed away rocks thrown into holes by local road users, and occasionally we would stop to fill the holes and repair the road. The wide truck at times brushed the muddy, stony banks and Pia had to drive at a snail's pace to prevent the body from swaying into the banks. We were learning as much as Pia was, it seems. Our impression had always been that the large trucks were not nearly as capable as a compact 4x4 like a Defender or Land Cruiser, and I am sure there are terrains where the trucks suffer particularly (soft sand, pebble beaches) due to their weight and a constant battle with gravity. On this road, the truck was more than capable as was her driver. Little Pia stood just over five feet and weighed as much as one of my legs, but she has the heart of a lion and the mind of a scientist.

At midday, we dropped into a village, muddy but cheerful. When I say dropped, I mean precisely that. The road down was winding, steep and churned by the wheels of vehicles heading up. And at the other end of the village, another track fought back up the side of an incredibly steep hill. In low range second gear, we idled up, up, up and grinding over a lip where the hill met a plateau. There was an "escape route" gouged into the hill beside the trail which Pia wisely branched onto. We were now deep into the Bamenda - Adamawa - Mandara mountain chain which borders Nigeria and Cameroon and we were loving every second of the journey now that we could travel at a good, gentle pace - enjoying the beauty, sights and sounds, not rushing at Dick's pace. We saw no evidence of Dick except for tyre tracks. We could see where they had stopped, which line they had taken over the worst of the obstacles and where they avoided puddles, which they did religiously. The depth of the tracks and sharpness of their edges suggested that they were only a few hours ahead of us and that it had not rained since they had passed there and that there had been little traffic. I couldn't track a fat rabbit through a snowy field, but I know how to find a heavy Land Rover.

At lunchtime, we entered Mayo Ndaga, a town which has two gas stations but only the one had diesel, which we did not need but we topped up regardless, it is always a good idea to have a full tank of fuel when crossing remote areas, you just never know what might be ahead, and we have suffered before with the assumption that fuel will be available in the next country. Besides, Nigerian diesel, while not of very high quality, was cheap and we love cheap fuel. The village was built of brick and mortar at the top of a hill, surrounded by rivers and the road that ran between tall buildings, the road so narrow and slippery that we worried for Pia and the truck. The slick red cobblestones led us to the Centre of the village, and we had to turn right, in a small square and descend a steep and glutinous hill which terminated at a dark river carrying fertile run off to the lands below. We had bought fresh bread, and after churning slowly down to the river, we reversed the vehicles against a bank and had our lunch of peanut butter smeared thickly onto chunks of bread. We then shared a melon with the German family.

Theo, Tiago and Zoe were well-loved and well-behaved children. Zoe would occasionally perform like a child much younger, but we are all forgiven strange behaviour under trying circumstances. Tiago and Theo, handsome and soft-spoken, seemed well at ease while travelling - they helped their parents often, and each had to take turns making meals for the family. Their speciality was spaghetti made twenty different ways, served with water and fruit. I would chat to the boys often, more often than I would chat to their father Tim, who seemed to be having a German language only issue with Pia, who was having a Spanish language only issue with Tim. It was none of our business and is none of yours, but we have learned through many years of experience, that an international overland journey is a great test, if not the greatest test for marriage. As this was the families first serious overland journey, it was to be expected that the issues which could be ignored at home would mushroom into an existential crisis which would have to be confronted and a compromise found, or not, in which case the marriage would most likely not succeed (the good news is that at the time of writing they are together). Theo, Tiago and Zoe missed their friends and their school and their sports. They missed their house and their bedrooms and the luxuries of a normal life. But, for the most part, they had adapted to life on the road, smiled often, hardly fought and were a great testament to their parents. We understood that unhappy children would quickly ruin a journey and we made an effort to interact with the kids and keep them smiling, which is only a natural extension of the daily efforts of keeping our children happy and motivated, no matter how despondent and fed up we may be. We chose this life for them; we must ensure that it is a satisfying and rewarding life for them.

After lunch and a short exploration of the river banks, we drove across the metal bridge and up a long, wet hill, churned by the wheels of the now ubiquitous 6x6 Pinzgauer and Series Land Rovers (we had only once passed an old Hilux, but it was beaten and broken beyond repair). If you search this highlands route on Google Maps or similar, you will notice that there is no official road and that may be a good thing as only those who live there and intrepid travellers have the privilege of enjoying what must be one of the greatest "trails" in Africa. We were having an excellent adventure! Jessica had by now fully recovered from Malaria, and we were all in high spirits. The fact that we were having such a good time, despite the sometimes treacherous roads, is attributable to a few obvious factors - we were cool and comfortable, there were almost no checkpoints or corrupt officials, the scenery was superb, our company enjoyable and the trail challenging. I imagine that in the mid 20th century, the West African route was incredibly tough on man and machine, but I also imagine that there were very few police and military checkpoints. And it is those checkpoints and dealing with corrupt or officious officials, which take more energy and patience than even the worst road. Being stopped up to twenty times a day, having to play the same game, being genuinely friendly and patient and respectful, having the vehicle searched by men who flirt shamelessly with your teenage daughter, that drains the joy out of your soul, pours vinegar on the day and adds hours to your travel time. Granted, not all countries are equally corrupt or paranoid, and the truth really is that bad roads lead to good people. Unpaved roads may have an official at either end but are generally peaceful; paved roads are heavily policed.

The highland road had been challenging bliss, a slice of deep rural Colombia, but all good things end, and we found ourselves rolling into a small village surrounded by perfect fields and huge, old oak trees.

We debated staying in Nigeria one last night, but the consensus was that we should continue to Cameroon. Together the nine of us sat in the immigration hut, the immigration officer enjoying our company and painstakingly listing the details of each passport in a large ledger. Our two families sat across from each other, on wooden benches, separated by a mud floor. The hut was cool and cosy, a small window framed a perfect green hill in the distance but could not brighten the dark room. The immigration officer sat at his old desk, a desk lamp throwing yellow light across the old ledger and the pile of passports, and called out our names as he worked through the pile.

"Loosa?" Luisa
"Greemie?" Graeme
"Killer" Keelan
"Jessica?"

He then turned his attention to the German family.

"Teem?" Tim
"Pia?"
"Theo?"
"Zoo?" Zoe
"Tiger?"

Tiger? Tiago, who looks like a young James Dean, arched his back and clawed at the air with his right hand. "Raawwr". Jessica drew a deep breath and laughed nervously, Dios Mio. The room erupted in laughter,

Jessica blushed, and Tiger blushed, a beautiful moment in that happy little hut.

Before leaving the hut, we asked to check the immigration ledger; we needed to be sure that Dick and Jane had survived the highland trail, if they had not crossed, we would have to either wait for them or go back to find them if they did not show up within 24 hours. They had crossed that earlier that day. From immigration we walked to the customs official who quickly stamped our carnets, a boom was lifted, we were free to leave Nigeria. We left with mixed feelings. Nigeria had been both wonderful and terrible, we had never felt as unsafe, and we have hardly ever met such friendly people. We were almost always welcomed with the phrase, "You are Welcome", and were usually treated with kindness and respect. That might have all been quite different if we were in Nigeria a few months later. South Africa is a country which has been teetering on the edge of chaos for many years now. Immigration is a hot topic, and there have been numerous xenophobic attacks over the years. South Africans accuse foreigners of stealing their jobs and Nigerians are perceived as drug dealers. In late 2019, xenophobic attacks exploded across the country - Nigerian, Zimbabwean, Malawian and Somalian migrants were beaten, their homes damaged and businesses looted, 12 people were killed. In Nigeria, the public in major centres responded by attacking South African owned stores. MTN outlets (a cellular network company), Shoprite supermarkets and Game stores and South African nationals had to be protected by private and governmental security agencies. We have a friend, an air hostess who is based in Lagos, who could not leave her home or go to work for fear of reprisals. We sought out Shoprite stores as often as possible, we travel on South African passports and a South African flag on our Land Rover, and if we had been in Nigeria at the time of the reprisals, well, it is difficult to know what could have happened given the volatility of that country. We might have been just fine, or we might have suffered greatly, Nigeria is not shy of violence.

CAMEROON

Cameroon is known as miniature Africa and is slightly larger than California or Sweden. The country is located in Central Africa, bordered by Nigeria, Chad, Central African Republic, Equatorial Guinea, Gabon and the Republic of the Congo. Cameroon is not an ECOWAS member state but is considered geographically and historically West African. The country exhibits all major climates and vegetation of the African continent, including the coast, mountains, desert, rainforest, and savannah

Cameroon uses the Central African Franc
100 CFA = EU0.15/USD0.17

ECOWAS citizens do not require visas, but all other nationalities need to apply for a visa before entry. The visa for Cameroon can range from EU50 to EU100 dependant on the country of issue, the duration and your nationality

Unleaded = EU0.95/USD1.07 per litre
Diesel = EU0.87/USD.84 per litre

MTN
Orange

Christianity and Islam are the main two religious groups
Homosexuality is illegal in Cameroon
Do not shake hands with your left hand
Cameroon was colonised by Germany. France and Great Britain

No specific insurance was requested. We endeavoured to purchase insurance in Yaounde but could not find any insurer to assist

Police = 117
Ambulance = 112

Valid passport
Vehicle title papers
TIP will be issued on arrival
Vaccination certificate for yellow fever

The official language is French

Bonjour! – Hello	Au revoir! – Goodbye
S'il vous plaît – Please	Pardon – Sorry

allez-vous? – How are you?   ça va bien – it's going well
Excusez-moi – Excuse me   Plus lentement – More slowly
Où est…? – Where is…?   Merci beaucoup – Thanks a lot
Je ne comprends pas –   I don't understand
C'est combien? – How much is it?

Available meats are added to cassava, maise, potatoes or fufu
Hot spice is preferred with meals
Doughnuts are available at most roadside stalls along with a large variety of fruit

Mount Cameroon in Limbe - an active volcano that you can explore
Waza National Park - Great place to view wildlife such as elephants, giraffes and hyenas
Kribi - great beaches to camp on with local seafood cuisine
Mefou National Park - a primate conservation camp
Lake Nyos, The Bad Lake

The temperature does not differ much during seasons but will be cooler in the highlands
December to February - Dry season
March to November - Rainy season
A regular low of 20C/68F and a high of 31C/88F

DID YOU KNOW? Cameroon is named after a crustacean, "Camarões" in Portuguese or in English, "shrimp or prawn".
50% of the population in Cameroon earns less than USD2 per day with an average monthly salary of USD35.
The forest in Korup National Park is reputedly Africa's oldest remaining forest.

Over 2,173 species of butterfly are from Cameroon; the highest number in Africa.

The goliath frog is found only in Cameroon and Equatorial Guinea. It is the largest frog in the world, can weigh up to 3.25 kilograms and can grow up to 32cms in length.

.CM is one of the world's riskiest domain, with about 35% of the Cameroon websites posing a security risk.

Mount Cameroon is the highest mountain in West Africa and is an active volcano

12

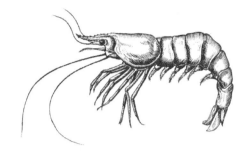

Cameroon

To reach the Cameroonian immigration office, we first had to descend from the highlands. The road twisted down, and as it did, we emerged from the clouds, the deep red soil gave way to clay, and the rolling green fields became scrubby rocky bush. The heat returned with the sun, and we were soon sweating and sweltering and longing for the highlands. With the German truck behind us, we eased off the mountain range in low range, happy to be descending, the trail deteriorating as the effect of flowing water magnified. There was a river crossing just before the first Cameroonian village which Luisa had been worrying about since the beginning of the trail. If the water level was too high, we might be forced to camp a while and wait for the water level to drop. Our Spanish friends had taken a video of their crossing a few weeks earlier, and their Land Cruiser had to work hard to climb the muddy exit bank. We arrived at the river after the long winding descent, both vehicles caked in mud. Luisa and Keelan took their shoes off and walked through the river; it was less than knee-deep but flowing strongly. No problem, we had driven through much deeper water before. The exit bank was as muddy as it had been in Nina's video but presented no problem to the Landy with her large mud-terrain tires, but the bank was heavily eroded and rutted and demanded a low range second gear approach. With groups of locals standing beside the road cheering us on, we climbed up and drove away up the trail to wait for Pia to drive her truck up the bank, which she did without too much drama.

The muddy village invited us, and while a group of children helped me to pump water from the well, Luisa, Pia, Tim and Keelan visited the local stores and bought fresh bread and fruit, cold drinks and canned food. The immigration building resembled an old schoolhouse, a Cameroonian flag waving atop a tall flag post in the yard where unloved but loving dogs greeted us. At the top of the entrance stairs, we were greeted by the young immigration officer and asked to remove our muddy shoes before entering the office and sitting before a wooden table on old chairs. The young official studiously wrote down our passport details in his own large, ancient ledger and we chatted as he worked. He was from Yaounde and had been sent to this post recently. He was from a good family and well educated and missed the city. With nine passports to process, it was a while before we were able to get back on the road. iOverlander suggested that there was a place to camp beside the river a few hundred meters from the immigration office, but we found only an exposed, muddy area.

The road itself was a mud pit, and I made the mistake of letting Tim drive ahead of me. The truck's huge tyres gouged deep ruts into the mud as the truck struggled to gain traction, wheels spinning and the vehicle sliding sideways towards a muddy knoll. We followed the truck but soon realised that we had no control of the steering, the mud so thick, slick and glutinous that the Landy slid sideways towards the truck. I rocked the steering slowly and accelerated gently, hoping that the mud-terrain tyres would find something solid to grip. The strategy worked, and I found that I was able to control the slide to a degree and avoided contact with the Oliphant. The bridge over the river was cast concrete with walls roughly twenty centimetres high on either side of the bridge itself. The large triangles of cement leading to the bridge had no walls, allowing the rain and mud to escape down the steep bank into the river below. Ahead of us, after the bridge, waiting for a steep climb up the side of a muddy hill. We walked over to inspect the road and found that it was simply a trail of mud defying gravity. I suggested to Tim that the Land Rover should go first and, looking back at the massive ruts torn by the truck, we agreed.

Luisa, despite being incredibly well-travelled, brave and hardy, has one character flaw - she panics. She screams, she tries to prevent calamity with sheer volume and a wall of unbridled fear. This sucks, especially when I am trying to drive a difficult off-road route, and she is freaking out, distracting me and making the situation ten hundred thousand times worse. Poor Keelan is his mother's child, and while Jessica and I laugh, they scream. A great example of this was that nightmare ride atop the tow truck in Morocco - Luisa screaming, shaking and panicking while Jessica giggles and I film the excitement and Keelan's wide eyes watched us sway from the relative safety of the truck cab. To be fair, that was one of the most stressful days of my short life, but, at least, I did not panic.

With Jessica resting in the back of the Land Rover (all signs of Malaria now passed) I aimed the Land Rover at the bridge and pulled off in low range third gear, centre diff locked. The Defender pulled off straight but soon began to slide uncontrollably towards the sheer riverbank, I geared down to second gear and repeated my strategy of accelerating gently. Five metres from the bank, I still had no control, and Luisa started screaming, naturally assuming I had absolutely no idea that I was sliding towards a watery death. The more the Land Rover slid, the louder she shouted and Keelan, set off by his temporarily deranged mother, started shouting instructions.

"Jesus. Shut up!"

Their cacophony distracted me to the point of severe irritation. Did they not believe in me? Had I not driven them safely hundreds of thousands of kilometres? Was I ordinarily incompetent? My pride hurt that they were not cool while I was under fire. Unfortunately, they could not hear me over their own wailing, and when I eventually regained control of the Land Rover, a meter from the drop-off, I stopped the vehicle and shouted at them they were not to shout at me, that when I am driving in dangerous conditions, I am fully aware of what is going on and DO NOT need to be screamed at. They screamed back.

"You almost went over the edge!"

No shit Sherlock. I call them the panic mechanics. With that drama behind us, I drove onto the bridge and prepared for the mud climb. "Are you ready, Jess"? Jessica, as cool as a cucumber, sat beside me. She was ready. We pulled forward steadily in second gear, low range, diff locked, exited the short bridge and began the climb, invisible deep ruts dictating the direction forward. I held the steering lightly and let the ruts guide us as I controlled our acceleration, the rear of the camper shunting from side to side as the ruts meandered, a loud clunk from the suspension as the wheels fell into deep holes.
The Defender kept moving steadily, mud flying in all directions, up we ploughed. We heard the loud bang! of a rear coil spring trying to dislocate as we bounced through a very deep rut, close to the top of the hill. It had taken a while to climb to the top curve in the road, but the Land Rover did not miss a beat despite her recent electrical maladies and badly behaved gearbox. I drove down the road to a level area and parked, startled as we stopped by small children emerging from the

dense rainforest in the glare of my headlights, with buckets of water on their heads. I left the Land Rover and returned on foot to watch Tim tackle the hill, the trucks tall tyres digging deep and leaving behind wide tracks to be filled slowly by oozing mud. He parked the truck at the summit and together we watched a red pick up attempt the hill, the driver gunning the engine mercilessly, plumes of black smoke belching from the exhaust. The pick-up ground to a halt mere meters of the bridge, and we realised that we would have to help. Tim and I prepared recovery ropes in the hope that the pick up would make it far enough up the hill for us to be of assistance. Keelan stepped up to the back of the pick-up and gave it a huge push, the driver gunned the engine and gained enough traction to get going. Five men appeared and proceeded to push the pick-up up the hill, perhaps inspired by a foreigners willing to help. Tim packed away the recovery ropes and drove the truck off the track, so that the steaming, exhaust red pick-up could pass and continue his journey to wherever his home might be. Luisa, Keelan and Pia climbed up the muddy hill and joined us in the everlasting semi-light of dusk. Our goal now was to find a place to park up for the night, and we drove slowly searching the darkness for a clearing until we spotted a suitable area, grassy, level and large enough for two or three vehicles. A fantastic find.

We set up camp, and while the Germans prepared a pasta dinner, I made a fire and arranged a couple of jerry cans for Luisa and me to sit on. The night was peaceful and dark, with the galaxies glittering above us. Twice a couple of men rode past us on a small motorbike, and we determined that we were parked on a trail which led back down to the river. With a cold beer in hand, we relaxed, feeling the jubilation, confidence and relief of a completing a day of adventure. At the end of a tough day on the road, I experience a feeling of great strength; I feel like I can take on anything, with no doubts in my mind. Until the morning. Then the doubts return, and the tightness in the chest reappears only to fade after an hour back on the road, once the sky has not fallen on our heads. I ask myself, what is there to fear? We can handle almost any mechanical failure and do what we can to avoid finding ourselves in that situation, but it is the dread of the unknown which plagues me. I feel that same anxiety at each and every border crossing, not as anxious as I once was but a border represents a choke point where bad things can happen for whatever reason. We have done well over 150 border crossings in our time, but I remain anxious when approaching that boom. It is the fear of the unknown, and we all have to learn to deal with that at some time in our lives.

Luisa and I sat peaceful and grilled peri-peri chicken for the family and enjoyed another cold drink. This woman has been by my side through the thickest and the thinnest, and here she sat with me, enjoying my company and I enjoying hers. I "fling snot" at her occasionally but never let that confuse how I feel for her, and how she feels for me. Twenty years and lifetimes lived together side by side almost 24 hours a day for the last 12 years; you really get to know someone when days are long, challenging and uncomfortable. We are not perfect people, we have our flaws, but we believe in ourselves, and we have each other. Keelan and Jessica are incredible young adults who have been to hell and back with us, and they love us as much as we love them. They know that we will always do what is best for them and we give them all that we can to make sure that they are happy and comfortable, especially when times get tough. But, they hardly complain, they soldier through it with us, knowing that with the rough comes the smooth and that they are living extraordinary lives.

With a hot meal in our bellies, we washed up as best we could before climbing into bed, the family happy, each in their own space ready to dream. While we slept, a storm broke, and we awoke to a fresh, green world, the Nigerian mountains in the background, birds playing in the sky. This was not the battered landscape we had grown accustomed to over the months in West Africa, this was a landscape of exceptional beauty, similar to the highlands in topography but instead of green fields, we found forests so varied as to be called a rainforest. After a cup of Pia's excellent coffee, we set off to explore Cameroon.

With the sun shining warm, we drove down the muddy trail towards a town called Banyo, where we would finally be able to stock up on supplies. The drive was beautiful and rugged, the trail winding through rainforest and streams. We communicated with the Germans as we drove using their small walkie talkies, "The road here is quite bad, there is a river crossing coming up, after the river there is a steep hill, stick to the left, we just saw some monkeys". We would often stop to wait for the truck to catch up with us, the road was too wet to be dusty, and we enjoyed every moment, occasionally passing a farmstead or locals working their fertile fields. Slowly the land became more populated, and people would wave as we passed, little children running after the

Land Rover laughing, their mothers working the fields, their fathers tending livestock or selling produce. This corner of Cameroon seems a rural nirvana; there is no hunger, plenty of land to work and a lot of fresh water. We drove through a field of perfect plenty; a beautiful young woman stopped her work to stand and smile and wave as we drove towards a river crossing with steep banks. With the German truck behind us, I drove into the river and stalled the Defender in the surprisingly deep and thick river sand. It is not a good idea to start a vehicle in water, especially if the exhaust pipe in underwater as there is a danger of water being sucked through the exhaust into the engine. Luckily we were not deep enough for that to happen, I started the Landy and reversed out of the river, engaged low range third gear diff lock and attempted the river crossing again, Luisa warning Pia of the deep sand. The Defender ploughed through the river and climbed the steep bank without any further fuss, and we continued towards Banyo eventually tiring of the dirt roads and looking forward to the silky-smooth speed of a paved road. The day wore on, and eventually, we spotted what seemed to be a paved road surface. After days on end of off-road driving, we were all relieved to finally drive on a flat, smooth surface, floating on air, no squeaking, creaking, swaying or bouncing. And even fourth gear cruising. The paved road had been built on the side of a steep hill, and we soon found that the paving was temporary. Only the worst sections of the road had been paved, through villages and on hills, a compromise.

We drove down a paved hill and crossed a small river and found a grassy area beside the river where we decided to call it a day. It was an early stop, but we all agreed that driving around Banjo looking for a place to stay was not high on our list of priorities and it would be nice to enjoy a quiet afternoon before entering populated areas. Tim and I kept busy working on our vehicles. Tim borrowed my grease gun after I learned that Dick had refused to lend Tim his grease gun as he was afraid of "contamination" and I topped up the transfer box oil. The transfer box had been leaking since we entered the USA four years before and I had not been able to fix the leak. It was also a good opportunity to lubricate the prop shafts and check the engine lubricants and fluid levels. I was not happy with the viscosity of the oil purchased in Nigeria, and the engine had become louder and smoked more than usual. We would have to replace the oil as soon as possible, and hopefully, no serious damage had been done to the engine. When parking the Land Rover, the reverse gear seemed stuck as if the handbrake was fully engaged and we had to reverse in low range. Our list of problems had grown, the electrics were acting up, fuses were blowing, the glow plug light flickered constantly, the headlights and indicators worked intermittently and the second and fourth gear continued to be problematic. The last thing we needed now was a breakdown but try as we may, we could not solve the problems we had. After working on the vehicles, we washed up and relaxed by the river, swimming and exploring. A group of women came to the river to wash, a herdsman brought his cows to drink, and a public works vehicle pulled up to wash tools and faces. We had camped in the middle of a community resource but were greeted only with smiles. Later that afternoon, when the locals had all left, a young man approached on a motorcycle. He parked beside the road and walked towards me, and we greeted each other. The young man, dressed in a white shirt and blue jeans, a backpack on his back, politely demanded to see the vehicle registration papers and our passports.

"I am sorry, are you a policeman?"

"No sir, I am a customs agent"

"Well, I will be happy to show you our documentation, but first you need to show me identification proving that you are a customs official".

The young man took the backpack from his back, zipped it open, reached inside and produced a blank customs form.

"That does not prove that you are customs", I said smiling.

He reached into the bag again and withdrew a large and battered 9mm handgun. He did not do so with menace, but my smile faded. He returned the gun to the bag, and we stood looking at each other for a few moments. I said nothing, and he realised that I now felt threatened. We did not speak again until he zipped the backpack and returned it to his shoulders. I invited him to approach the Land Rover and fished out the passports and vehicle registration, all the while keeping an eye on our new friend or foe. With the bag, and the gun within, out of reach on his back, I felt more secure, but there would be no more friendly banter. A line had been crossed, and he knew it. Luisa cleaned the Landy, while Jessica slept and Keelan relaxed by the river. After inspecting the documents, he handed them back to me, and I stashed them in the Land Rover before walking him over to the truck at his request. Tim and his sons had not yet returned from exploring the river, Pia and Zoe sat inside the truck.

"Pia, this gentleman says he from customs, he would like to see your documentation".

Pia, ever friendly, popped her head out of the truck, said hello and please wait a moment and a moment later emerged from the truck with her documents. The young man inspected the documents and informed us that we must report to the customs building in Banyo before continuing further into Cameroon. We agreed, said thank you, and I escorted the man back to his motorcycle, watched him leave and listened until I could no longer hear the whine of his motorcycle.

Cameroon is a nation at war with itself. First the Portuguese (who named the country Rio dos Camaroes, River of Shrimp, which became Cameroon in English) explored the region in the 15th century. Fulani soldiers then established the Adawama Emirate which established powerful chiefdoms. Germany colonised the country in 1884, and after World War 1 the country was split between France and the United Kingdom. The contemporary conflict in Cameroon is known as the Anglophone Crisis and has killed more than 3,000 people and displaced half a million. The power struggle is rooted in the divisions created by the colonial past, and the conflict escalated through 2019 and into 2020. We were less than 40 kilometres from rebel-held territory, camped beside that idyllic river.

That night a storm raged again, as it seemed to every night and the river swelled. The morning was clean and fresh as we made our way to Banyo along muddy trails and short sections of paved perfection, eventually entering the town at the end of a hot morning. Luisa, Tim and Pia attended to the customs procedure, the young armed man nowhere to be seen. An hour later, we sat parked in the middle of the town, bewildered by all the activity after almost a week of peace and quiet. Luisa, Pia and Tim searched for a bureau to exchange dollars while a small man dressed in clean Western clothes stood beside the Land Rover and argued with anyone who would engage with him. He was young and full of rage, mocked by the other young men who towered over him. Perhaps he could not find a woman; perhaps he had a drinking problem, perhaps he was disrespected due to his diminutive stature. He was wound tight as wire; arms held taut to fists, legs wooden, eyes glazed. He presented no danger to us and did not engage with us but performed beside us. Young men would walk past and slap him on the back of the head and howl with laughter as he feign lunged at them. Their mocking fed his rage, and he barked louder, the louder he became, the more he was mocked. A group of people stood nearby, buying mobile data from a kiosk. Some ignored the man, some watched him with disinterest, and a few encouraged him to calm down. The small man shouted at a group of young men passing, they laughed and grabbed him, holding him by the arms and neck, joking. A woman shouted and emerged from a house behind the kiosk, the young men pushed the angry little man towards her, and she marched him down an alley to return to the room where he would fume and rage for eternity.

Despite the commotion, the town was pleasant, clean and tidy with colourful stores and well-built buildings. Luisa returned with a pile of cash, and we stopped at a bakery to buy fresh bread and a general store for eggs, mayonnaise, sardines, cold drinks, vegetables and fruit. Tim disappeared for a while; he was forever searching for pipes or ropes or connections, screws, nuts and bolts with which he could repair leaks, ruptures or breaks. It was nice to be back in the real world, but we yearned for the highlands.

There were two roads to the capital Yaounde. We could take either the shorter N6, N15, N1 Tibati - Yoko - Yaounde route or the longer N6, N4, N1 route via Bafoussam but Luisa had chatted to a man we had met at the border who informed her that the shorter route was in a terrible condition. We took his advice and headed out of town towards Bafoussam. At first, the road was excellent, paved and winding up, out of the town. We passed peaceful homes and smiling, friendly people and enjoyed the great road which descended from a mountain past into a valley bordered by mountains, a veritable Jurassic Park, thick green rainforest and deep blue skies. Descending slowly from the mountain, the road remained paved, but we could see a long, arrow-straight road in the valley floor below. The paved road ended, and we were once again travelling a muddy trail. Occasionally a truck or taxi packed well beyond the legal limit, would approach or pass us, the occupants crammed like sardines in the sweltering heat and oppressive humidity. The vehicles had long since abandoned the idea of comfortable suspension, and we could hear metal meet metal as the taxis, usually, Citroen or Peugeot family vehicles, banged past us. We could not imagine what it must be like to drive those roads every day, hell for the drivers and worse for the passengers. Occasionally we would drive through villages - Nyamboya, Kimi, Magba, Manki - where people rested under large avocado and mango trees and watched the world go by. Schoolchildren waved or chased the vehicles, and we wondered how long it would be before progress arrived with good roads, well-stocked schools and clinics, service stations, ATM's, grocery stores and public areas. It might take decades, or it might take only a few years, it all depends on the road and the willingness to build them. The track was wider through the villages, which it seemed had been built in anticipation of new infrastructure and the journey became monotonous - trees, blue sky, mud red road, a village, a truck, a taxi, second gear, third gear, second gear, third gear, all day long. Approaching the town of Foumbam, we were halted by a boom across the road. A female soldier lazed in a yellow, white plastic chair, and an older male policeman ordered us to stop. We were hoping to be waved through, but the arrival of two overland vehicles heralded the highlight of the policeman's day, and he approached the driver's window with a broad smile. He proceeded to check our papers, inspect the vehicle and search through our belongings. He flirted with Jessica and tried to charm us with his wonderful English and well-used jokes. He searched under every seat and in every cupboard and asked endless questions; he was no ordinary policeman, he also carried with him the powers of a customs officer. After half-an-hour of banter and searching, he finally left us and played through his routine again with the German family, taking his time. To kill time, I chatted to the female officer in her perfect uniform and shiny boots, I asked if I could take a photograph of her and she stood at attention, a PM MD. 63 Romanian AK47 variant slung across her chest, a red beret with large gold insignia adorning her head, lips pouting. Luisa made lunch, our now staple baguette with sardines and mayonnaise and we ate slowly, waiting to be released. Eventually, the policeman grew bored and allowed us to continue up into the town along muddy, winding roads. A terrible road is less bearable when you are not expecting it; I had been under the impression that it was all paved, smooth sailing once we reached Banyo, other travellers focus so much attention on the highland road that they forget to mention the 150 km of muddy track which stands between Banyo and Yaounde, a road which is harder work than the cool Highlands trail. It seemed to go on forever, and it was with great relief that we rounded a corner and were met by perfect tar before the town Foumban. With the new road came a new world of lovely houses, irrigation ditches and traffic lights, general stores and street lights, cement pavement walkways, social areas, football fields, retaining walls protecting the road as it wound between hills, a military base, a bakery, modernity. What an absolute pleasure and a wonderful surprise. We made good time, enjoying the speed the new road afforded. "Fourth gear. Fifth gear!" We had not used the fifth gear in so long and driving along at 100 kph felt like flying, Luisa asking me to slow down, thinking that we were driving much faster.

Unfortunately, Das Oliphant could not keep up with our pace, and we had to stop often to wait for them to catch up. As we approached Foumban, the sun began to set. Jessica and I waited while Luisa, Keelan, Tim and Pia searched for an ATM and supplies and it was dark before we pulled into a gas station and filled up with fuel for the first time since Nigeria, the night before the fallout with Dick. We were running low on fuel and had only one full jerrycan and a quarter of a tank left, and while we waited for Tim to fill his tank I bought eight litres of engine oil, Luisa bought cold beer and drinks for the kids, and we soaked up the air conditioning. The attendants at this service station must believe that overlanders are horrible, dirty people as none of us had had a proper shower in almost a week. We could not smell each other, but I am sure that others could, unfortunately.

With spirits raised, we drove on in the dark, Das Oliphant behind us until we reached the turnoff to a monastery, turning in the black of the night without functional indicators. Pia followed us as we drove the long dirt road bordered by palm trees and came to a tall red brick wall. We followed the wall for a while and turned into a property and parked in front of a tall gate beside long grass. A watchman came over to talk to us, I feared that we were in the wrong place, but Tim spoke to the man in French and confirmed that we were at the monastery, but we needed to wait for the monks to complete their prayers before we could ask permission to stay for the night (and pay a small fee of CFA 3000 per person). After an hour of waiting, the watchman opened the gates and allowed us to enter, instructing us to park beside a long white building. Before us, a domed cathedral channelled worship for an hour before a reed-thin and friendly monk approached us. We were welcome to stay the night and were instructed to drive to the main building where we would be given keys to a bathroom. Hallelujah! We took turns showering, parked beside the large and well built white building. The shower washed away a week of dust and mud, as each person returned from the shower we were amazed how powerful the smell of soap is and realised how badly we must smell. The shower washed away the bad memories and left us with mostly good memories; we felt new, revitalised, fresh and comfortable. Sitting in the drizzle beside the Land Rover, completely unfazed by the precipitation, we drank our cold beers and chatted about the days behind and the weeks ahead. Pia and Tim would leave us here and drive at their own pace; we had spent enough time together and had seen each other through some very challenging days. We were happy to be on our own, travelling in a convoy is something that we do only if we have to and we looked forward to travelling at our own pace, stopping when we needed to, diverting at will and not having to worry about two vehicles.

The morning wet and fresh. Arriving at night at a destination comes with the promise of an interesting morning as the sun reveals all that was hidden by darkness. The monastery accommodation was solid but simple, the rooms basic and devoid of any decoration other than crucifixes, the building built to be sturdy, practical and solemn. The poverty of the living areas was juxtaposed by a garden so lush and vibrant as to compete with any botanical garden. An elderly gardener worked quietly trimming hedges and pulling weeds under a magnificent, ancient tree where birds sang and played. I complimented her work, and she smiled glumly and continued to toil. We showered again, paid the monk and said goodbye to him and our convoy friends. We did not know when again, we would see them.

The road to Yaounde was in very good condition, and we made good time. The checkpoints were few and far between, and we arrived in Yaounde in time for the afternoon rush hour. iOverlander suggested that there was an orphanage on the outskirts of the city where we could park for a few days. The city was relatively clean and pleasant, and we made a few wrong turns before eventually arriving at a Carrefour supermarket where Luisa insisted we stop and stock up on supplies. It was the first vaguely Western supermarket we had seen in a while, and we left with bags full of goodies. Driving to the orphanage, we thought that we must be heading in the wrong direction, but at the end of a muddy little road we came across a large wall with green gates, we knocked, and a tall young man opened the pedestrian gate and welcomed us. The gates swung open and we drove in to find a green lawn, a beautiful modern white house, throngs of smiling orphans and Dick and Jane. We parked in a small "alley" beside the house and set up camp. I walked over to greet Dick and Jane.

"Hello, so you made it"
"Yes"
"Any problems?"
"No"

That was the last time we spoke. The next morning they packed and left without a word, avoiding eye contact. With them gone, we were left with a French couple who we had last seen in Togo, but who spoke little English. The Polish priest spoke only Polish and French and could not communicate with us and thus gave us a large berth. The kids were curious but not intrusive, and we settled into this little island of calm. Overlanders came and left over the next few days. Roy, the tall slim Dutchman travelling on the massive old Harley Davidson, joined us and we celebrated his birthday with cold beers and fillet steak from the local Dov Supermarket. Pia and Tim arrived two days after we did and stayed for four days before leaving. The French couple left, and for a few days, we were alone at the orphanage. We were working on the Land Rover and had to have some spare parts brought in from Bearmach namely a heavy-duty rear half-shaft, service kits and a wheel bearing kit. They sent the parts, they arrived two days later, and we then endured almost a week of fighting with the customs office to have the goods released. When we attended the customs office in town, we were asked to pay an import fee of $200, and we refused. We returned twice more to the customs office before they eventually released the parts after we had a long and interesting meeting with the head of customs who fished for a baksheesh but gave in when it was clear that we would not be handing over any cash.

Our days at the orphanage were busy and productive. I fixed as many of the issues as I could on the Land Rover and finally replaced the horrible Nigerian oil with good, thick oil. We played with the orphans, teaching them how to ride bikes and kicking a ball, teaching them words in English and trying to be good friends to the little people who had lost so much before life had even started. We felt powerless to help them, and it was heartbreaking to realise that the solution to their problems did not lie with us but with their own people, that we could do what we could for these poor little people but the long term the solution for them lay in the betterment of their country, in the development of infrastructure and education and health care, in the resolution of old conflicts and the respect for human rights. Yes, those are lofty ideals, but that is the reality, I believe. Pia thought that I was being heartless when I explained this to her, but I had grown up in Africa and like to think that I have a deeply considered understanding of Africa and her challenges. I may be wrong. It would not be the first time.

We became temporary residents of Yaounde - we knew where to get the best food, spare parts, soft-serve ice-cream, pizza and vegetables. Almost daily, we walked the two kilometres to the Dov, and the locals began to recognise us as we trudged along the muddy streets. At first, they would call to us from the safety of the stalls - Kss Kss, or making a kissing sound, which is enough to drive us crazy. It is not considered rude to make these sounds in West Africa, where the sharpness of the Kss or the kiss sound cuts through the constant chatter and noise. Eventually, they left us alone and accepted that we would only buy our fruit and vegetables from certain stalls and that we would return eventually from the Dov with heavy bags. We had discovered that the Dov butchery sold large sausages and beef fillet at decent prices and perfect for the occasional braai.

A young Polish priest appeared at the orphanage one morning in a white Land Cruiser. Gregarious and relieved to have a conversation, he told us of his assignment near the border with the Central African Republic where a civil war has raged for decades. He laughed as he spoke, telling us of the atrocities he had witnessed and the terrible conditions under which people struggled to survive. His laughter was not mean; it was reluctant as if every act of barbarity surprised him. The priest was also, and possibly, more importantly, a medical doctor. The work which he did was incredibly important to the community which he served, and he served them with the bare minimum of resources. It was obvious that he was crucial to the community and equally important to the rebels who occupied that area. We asked whether he felt threatened by the rebels and he responded that while he knew his situation was precarious and he was only allowed to operate (literally) with the blessing of the rebels, he was valuable to them as the rebels demanded priority medical treatment, he worked for both the Catholic church and the rebels, essentially. When we had first entered the orphanage, we had parked between the resident priests' impressive house and a large collection of medical equipment covered with a tarp. Soon after the young priest's arrival, a truck arrived and loaded all of the medical equipment (operating tables, wheelchairs, beds, cabinets) and returned with the brave, dedicated priest to Central African Republic (CAR).

When I was a young fool working in Israel, I had met another slightly less foolish young man, his name was Hippo, and he was from the CAR. Hippo worked hard and saved all of his money, spending each extra cent on clothing, he had a weakness for Levi clothing, and after a few months, he had a great wardrobe. We spent a lot of time together, working in a small factory making tortillas beside a hot oven and spending the evenings and weekends together either at the beach or hanging out at the hostel talking to girls. Hippo's travel mate Kareem and I never saw eye to eye but Hippo and I clicked, and it was only after I left to stay in another part of the city that we lost contact. One day, months later I returned to the Dizzengorf area in Tel Aviv and was stood on a corner waiting for a light to change when I saw Hippo sitting comfortably in the back of a sedan, his arm around a pretty Israeli girl. He asked the driver, the girl's father, to stop and we had a quick reunion. He told me that he might have to soon return to the CAR, the police had caught him working without a work permit (almost all young travellers working in Israel did so without a work permit). He was worried, he had grown to like living in Israel, and there was not much waiting for him back home. I often wonder about Hippo, he was a good man, and I hope that he found the future he dreamed of.

A tall young man named Papa was our host at the orphanage - he organised everything needed by guests and took care of the children with quiet patience. One warm Friday morning Papa called a taxi for us, and with the blue skies of a fresh morning, we were whizzed towards the centre of Yaounde where we needed to visit the customs office to collect a parcel from our parts supplier. Yaounde is built in the hills, and that always makes for an interesting city, San Francisco has so much more character than Pheonix, and Cape Town is a million times more livable than Johannesburg. The Yaounde city centre is relatively clean and organised, more like Abidjan than chaotic Lagos or Dakar, and we soon found ourselves standing outside the customs office which is located between a DHL and a restaurant, prepared for a fight. We had received a phone call from the customs office, informing us that we needed to pay $120 for our shipment to be released. That was not going to happen. We entered and were shown to a white waiting room where some people stood and waited, some sat in plastic chairs and waited and some buzzed from office to office. We were eventually shown to a small office where a group of customs workers sat chatting happily. We presented our waybill and asked for our package but were handed a piece of paper with an amount written on it. $115. We argued that the shipper was responsible for all costs and were told that we needed to have the shipper complete a declaration form. It took a few hours for a customs agent to present the form and by the then it was too late for the shipper to complete the form as their accounts department alone had the authority to complete the form and it was ten minutes before hometime, and they closed earlier on a Friday. Our contact Danielle made a nuisance of herself with her accounts people and was able to have the scanned form completed and returned to us just in time for the customs officer to announce that there were other forms which needed to be completed and the declaration had to be approved by the office manager, and the sky was not quite blue anymore, and we would definitely receive the package at an uncertain time in the future, they were closed on Saturday and Monday we would have to return. Or we could pay the fee and move on. Well, we don't roll that way. West Africa had already proven to be incredibly expensive, and we were not in any great rush; besides, there is a principle at play - if we do not fight corruption, then we are part of the corruption, and we have always refused to grease palms, palms which would only demand more from those who follow. I was tempted to pay though, but Luisa can be as stubborn as any customs agent with a lifestyle above his income, we would return on Monday with all the paperwork required and fresh determination. Monday was spent waiting at the office, being friendly and patient, asking to speak to the office manager, pestering the customs agent every time he dared show his face. We spoke to the other victims waiting for parcels, most were office workers running errands, some were NGO's and aid workers, and we soon had a murmur spreading discord. Many Africans have resigned themselves to the corruption they face every day, it is part of their lives, but they despise when foreigners, particularly tourists, are subjected to graft.

Almost everyone you will meet on the road is proud of their country and want you to leave with the best impression; it embarrasses them that you might be treated unfairly. A few of our fellow inmates began to implore the customs officer to help us and, perhaps sensing a larger problem on the horizon, we were eventually called to the office managers office. A slick young man sat very well dressed behind a large desk empty except for our customs clearance papers. He welcomed us with a smile and shook our hands. We chatted for a while about South Africa, and he exclaimed, "You are Africans too!" Yes, we are. He indicated that we would need to pay a discounted $93 and we replied that we were prepared to pay $10 and handed him the shippers declaration assuming all costs. He smiled and looked over to the customs agent perched on the corner of another desk. "OK, because you are Africans too, I will waive the cost". Thank you, shake hands, leave. Half an hour later, our package was handed to us, we phoned our taxi driver and returned through the Monday afternoon bustle of a capital city to our orphanage home on the outskirts of the city.

While I installed the new heavy-duty half shafts, Luisa made dinner (choripan - large sausages served in a baguette with a spicy salsa of tomato, onion and peppers) and Keelan informed her that he was not feeling well. He had "crashed" during the day and was lightheaded with a fever. After devouring paracetamol and a huge choripan, he allowed himself to endure the malaria test, insisting that he felt much better. Luisa is mildly hemophobic, and the idea of making her infuriating, precious son bleed breaks her heart. For the test to be effective, a large drop of blood must be extracted from a finger using a sharp needle provided with the RDT (Rapid Diagnostic Test) kit. The blood will then be squeezed into a well and mixed with a flushing agent, and after a few moments, the results will appear negative or positive and for which type of Malaria. Simple.

Well, not if Luisa is doing the test. First, she has to pluck up the courage to poke the finger, and she has to do it hard enough to actually draw blood. She squeals and pricks the finger and squeezes until the tip of the finger turns purple - no blood. Squeals again and pricks again with the same result. It is a death by a thousand cuts, and she refuses help. Watching her try and test herself is both worrying and sadly funny, as her instinct to protect herself overrides all logic, fight and flight are equally strong with poor Luisa. After watching her struggle with herself and Keelan's tortured finger for ten minutes, I washed my hands and took the needle from Luisa and jabbed. Blood. "You are a cruel bastard". Right. Unfortunately, the pain did not end there for poor Keelan because fight or flight then took a back seat to a mothers paranoia, what if the test is incorrect? Well, we will have to do another test, and another and another and if eventually, all the tests come to the same conclusion then we medicate.

Unfortunately, all the tests were positive for cerebral Malaria, and we began a course of Coartem and immune boosters and organised a room for him so that he could rest and recover, but he did not want to be alone. Luisa joined him with a laptop and a hard drive full of movies. Keelan was not worried about having Malaria; he had seen Jessica deal with it, and if anything, he was pleased that he would have a few days off from all chores and responsibilities. But then the Malaria hit him and walloped him, his fever peaked, and he was freezing cold in the scorching heat, he felt dizzy and tired and terrible. We had planned to leave the orphanage on Tuesday, but it was agreed that we would wait until he had a chance to recover fully, close to medical assistance and pharmacies. For two days his body fought the Malaria, and we cared for him attentively, Luisa hardly ever leaving his side feeding him soup and checking his temperature regularly. When Luisa did leave Keelan to sleep, he would wake and stumble over to the Land Rover to be with us, and we would take him back to his bed and stay with him. The love this family shares is immense, and it reminded us of the plight of the orphans who surrounded us. Their parents had themselves been killed by Malaria or war, or extreme poverty and they really had only each other when Malaria struck or loneliness or despair. These children did not have a mother or a father to fret over their precious fingers or give them soup and cold towels; they had an uncertain future waiting for them in a land where family ties are paramount, and they were beginning their lives without the love, care and support that so many of us take for granted. But, the children of the orphanage were the lucky ones. Yes, they live in a barracks while the priest lives alone in a grand, double story house and yes, we had seen some of the older children and "carers" be selfish and uncaring, but they were not being exploited, they went to school, they had medical treatment when they needed it. And they had Papa. Papa impressed me always with his kindness and hard work. At the age of 21, he was already a father to twenty children, and he took care of them diligently, quietly, compassionately. We never saw Papa lose patience or reprimand the children; he did not need to - they respected and loved Papa, and when we were eventually ready to leave I realised that I would miss all the children and I would miss my friend Papa.

With Keelan testing clear for Malaria, we packed the Land Rover and headed out of Cameroon towards the Gabon border, saying goodbye to all our new friends and leaving behind gifts of clothing, toys and food.

The road to the border was in good condition, and we made good time along good, paved roads. There were a few checkpoints, but we were allowed to proceed without problems and arrived at the border shortly before sunset, crossed a boom police checkpoint at a town called Abang-Minko and proceeded to the border, stopping at a checkpoint where lazy uniforms sat, watched and waited for one uniform to stand up, check our documents and search the vehicle. We then snaked down the winding road surrounded by rainforest and tall green grass until we reach another checkpoint. As it grew dark, we were permitted to enter a large, paved area the size of a football field but home to only a small booth and a shack built beside the paved area. At the booth, we were told that we had not done our customs-exit paperwork and that we would have to return to the town. I was annoyed with Luisa (her job is logistics and research would have clearly indicated that the customs office was in the town 6km before the border). She was annoyed with me because I am not allowed to be annoyed with her. We returned to the first boom and were allowed through and then were stopped again at the lazy central boom and allowed through and made it to the town before dark. Luckily the customs official was still at work, and he slowly processed our papers and phoned the uncertain customs officials at the border and informed them that our paperwork was in order. We rushed back to the border, waiting for the lazy boom to magically open and arrived at the border boom as the sunset, only to be told that the border was now closed and no, we could not camp beside the boom.

With that, we returned to the lazy boom to incredulous stares and laughs and returned past flaming green grass to the muddy town where we found a muddy little hotel where we could park beside a wet white building and use a bathroom and throw buckets of cold standing water over our hot bodies. It was challenging to find the little hotel hid behind market stalls, but we had had the assistance of a friendly policeman who also told us that the area was safe and we could buy cold drinks from the corner shop. While Luisa and Keelan headed off to do some shopping, Jessica and I set up the Land Rover and made a simple noodle dinner. It is worth noting that Jessica is able to remember precisely which meals were eaten where she does not remember where we slept or the hundreds of checkpoints or the villages and towns we pass, but she remembers that the night Keelan fell ill he ate a huge and entire choripan and the night we were at the Cameroon/Gabon border we ate noodles. The mosquitoes plagued us, and the walls of the hotel compound blocked any breeze which may attempt to refresh us. Many nights I spent lying with the woven Portuguese fan in hand cooling the family equally before falling asleep for a while until the heat woke me and I fanned the family again. The only respite being the two hours of cool which descended every morning before sunrise.

That morning we awoke and took turns washing again with the bucket shower and taking the time to chat with the family who ran the empty hotel and lived in a small abode beside the parking area. With the heat descending again upon us, we drove back through the checkpoints and were finally allowed to proceed to the small shack which served as the immigration office. Two elderly officials, a man and a woman, processed our passports, writing the details in the now ubiquitous large ancient ledgers. We told them that we thought Cameroon to be a beautiful country with a great future and they agreed, adding that the war must end and the country must be allowed to progress. I would like to be the president of Cameroon. We would live by example in a simple home surrounded by bodyguards (the initial changes will not be popular with the ruling elite) as we appointed the best and brightest to positions they earned and deserved while stamping out corruption and engaging international companies and corporations to sustainably invest in the country and improve the infrastructure of road, port, rail and communications while establishing plants to process raw materials into exportable products using Cameroonian labour. We would recruit successful farmers to work the fertile land and teach the people how to farm collectively and negotiate wholesale trade. We would invest in health care and education and hire consultants from Scandinavia to establish systems of trade and government which would benefit all and protect the natural resources, establishing vast reserves where local communities could benefit directly from tourist and wildlife populations could flourish. Jobs would be created through communal improvements and communities which progress most would be rewarded while being held as an example for all. Presidential terms will be limited to two terms of three years, and politicians would be paid a healthy but reasonable salary which could only increase in line with the improvement of the economy and capped eventually. Diversity would be celebrated, free-market principles encouraged, education prioritised, and corruption punished intelligently. Cameroon would be a secular, democratic state with checks and balances, an effective judiciary, micro and macro lending and intelligent social security infrastructure. When people are educated and have opportunities, they are productive, and productivity creates markets, which creates consumers. Essentially we would take the best from every country and adopt those principles with a Cameroonian context.

But what do I know? I am just a traveller.

GABON

Gabon means "cloak" in Portuguese, which is almost the same shape of the Komo River. Gabon is located on the west coast of Central Africa, on the equator and bordered by Equatorial Guinea, Cameroon, the Republic of the Congo and the Gulf of Guinea. It has an area of approximately 270,000 square kilometres

 Gabon uses the Central African Franc
100 CFA = EU0.15/USD0.17

 Most nationalities must apply for a visa before entering via the evisa portal at https://www.dgdi.ga/e-visa/ and the approximate cost will be EU75 dependant on your nationality

 Unleaded = EU0.92/USD0.99 per litre
Diesel = EU0.89/USD0.96 per litre

 Airtel
Gabon Telecom

 Christianity and Islam are the two main religious groups. Gabon was colonised by France

 No specific insurance was requested

 Police = 177
Ambulance = 1300

 Valid passport
Vehicle title papers
Hotel reservation
Carnet de Passage (highly recommended) but a TIP will be issued on arrival
Vaccination certificate for yellow fever
International Driver's licence (required)

The official language is French
Bonjour! – Hello   Au revoir! – Goodbye
S'il vous plaît – Please   Pardon – Sorry
allez-vous? – How are you?   ça va bien – it's going well
Excusez-moi – Excuse me
Plus lentement – More slowly
Où est...? – Where is...?
Merci beaucoup – Thanks a lot
Je ne comprends pas – I don't understand
C'est combien? – How much is it?

The French have influenced the food in Gabon, but staple foods such as rice, chicken and cassava or potatoes are consumed daily with hot spicy flavours. Bushmeat such as monkeys and antelope are widely consumed and sold along the roadside

Loango - a fantastic amount of wildlife that roams free from gorillas, to wild elephants to dolphins in the ocean.
Pongara Point - turtle conservation
Fernan Vaz Lagoon - Gorilla conservation
Ivindo National Park for organised tours
Reserve de la Lopé - a fantastic sanctuary and camp

May to September - Dry season
October to April - Rainy season
With a year round average low of 23C/73F and a High of 31C/88F

Gabon has a fair amount of gorillas; however, illegal hunting is putting them at risk to become critically endangered.
"Survivor" Season 17, took place in Gabon in 2008.
Gabon is one of the few places on Earth where tropical rainforest extends all the way to the beach, with 80% of Gabon being covered by rainforest.

13

Oh Beautiful Gabon

Entering Gabon, we drove a short while until we encountered a bridge and a boom. A small brick and mortar pegoda, where four uniforms representing different branches of government waited for us. Travelling with South African passports, we were visa-free to enter Gabon, but there was a quirk of an entrance which held fast - we needed to provide a hotel booking, and if the booking was not confirmed we could not enter the country. Luisa might not have known where the customs office was in southern Cameroon, but she knew that this was a requirement to enter Gabon. She had made the booking and had the proof, and we sat chatting to the officials while they went through the rigorous procedure of confirming our details and phoning ahead to confirm our hotel booking. The hotel receptionist was unable to confirm the booking immediately, and it took a few calls before the uniform was informed that we did indeed have a booking, his crisp white shirt disappointed that it had been robbed of the opportunity to exercise a display of authority. While we were waiting, an overloaded red sedan approached and disgorged of occupants - a few rotund men and a sharp looking old lady. The vehicle was searched, their passports stamped, and they were free to leave in ten minutes, while we sat and waited into our second hour, an old AK47 propped up in the corner behind me. I grabbed the AK47 and sprayed the uniforms with lead screaming, "Set us free!" Blood sprayed across the old white walls, Luisa grabbed another AK, and together we crossed the hillside road and hunted the off-duty cop in his white vest and green underpants running away from the blue sedan he was washing with adoration. Tatatata tatata. Hahaha! "We are free!".

My mind had begun to wander. Back in the real world, the uniforms continued their slow charade and eventually released us into Gabon, with the bad news that we still had to report to the police station in the next town and we had to buy insurance and have the passports stamped. What a charade! We entered Bitam after a pleasant drive and spent the next hours being treated with efficient disdain at the police station, with great hospitality and kindness by the agent selling us the insurance document and with kindness by the two Nigerian women selling cold drinks, sweets and photocopies opposite the police station. After a visit to a supermarket, we drove to the immigration office on the corner, Luisa running in and emerging soon after that with stamped passports. By early lunchtime, we were on the road which runs parallel to the Equatorial Guinea frontier.

The first thing we noticed about Gabon is that the roads are excellent by West African standards, the rainforests are thick and healthy, and there are sections of road which wound around large lakes and would not have been out of place in Colombia or southern Brazil. It was easy going, the most relaxed travelling we had done in a very long time. There was only one problem with Gabon - the exploitation of wild animals. At the border police station, we had noticed a poster detailing the endangered and protected species advising that there would be strict fines and incarceration levied against those who hunted and killed these species. That had been a good sign, but it was soon apparent that it was a law regarded with levity. Animals hung from poles anchored in oil drums beside the road at each village. Sun Tailed Monkeys, Baboons, West African Pangolin, Mandrills, possums, anteaters and a variety of mammals which I cannot name. They hung beautiful and dead, waiting for the pot and we wondered how difficult it would be to clear a yard, build a fence and raise chickens. Certainly, any seed dropped on the ground would yield a fruit or vegetable (I suppose the trick would be to keep nature from consuming the crop before it can mature and reach the table) and with Gabon's excellent roads, it would not be too difficult to transport food and supplies. The problem is that hunting is essentially free, and locals cannot generally afford to shop as we do, they must hunt. Well, husbandry and agriculture have been achieved in places far less fertile, why not here? Perhaps because people who live in one or two villages their entire lives, do not see the long term disastrous effects of relying on wildlife for the table. Their ancestors have hunted for centuries before them and eating a monkey is as natural for the people of Gabon as it is for us to eat beef, ostrich or chicken. Perhaps they do not know that the population of Africa is exploding and that the population of wild animals is dwindling and one day the two will come head to head. But, those are our problems, not their problems, for now.

With night approaching, we entered a town built the Gabonese way - brick and mortar homes, well built, large and relatively modern. As soon as we stopped, I received a scheduled phone call from Scott Brady, and we chatted about a tyre review which I had written for the Overland Journal and needed to edit. We chatted about the review, travel and vehicles and Africa for a while and then I returned to the Defender to help set up the camp for the night and power up my laptop to edit the review and do some research. We had found that WiFi and internet connections were relatively easy to find and we often did not have a problem buying sim cards and accessing the internet and while I would prefer to travel as the old-timers did - on mud tracks, without online communities and resources, without the distraction of the "real" world, we would not be able to travel and live the way we do without the internet and a regular internet connection. I am willing to trade impossible freedom with possible opportunities. Writing has become such an important part of our journey, as it is our primary source of income. I write articles for publications and work on book projects and spend a lot of time ensuring that our social media exposure is what it should be, my challenge is not to become a writing machine but rather a better writer, quality beats quantity. And if you are reading this book, I thank you for choosing to be a part of our story as without readers there is no need to write.

Setting off the next morning after a bucket shower and a simple breakfast, we rejoined the wonderful paved road and enjoyed meandering across a country which is peaceful and beautiful. Isn't it amazing how much difference a border can make? Villages in Cameroon consisted mostly of brick homes, plastered often depending on the wealth of the village. In Gabon houses were often built of wood slats or planks, often with insufficient foundations, it was not uncommon to see leaning wood homes. Gabon was, by far, the most peaceful and friendly country we had travelled since Morocco, and this was welcome. We had now officially left West Africa and had entered Central Africa (though for the sake of simplicity we refer to this journey as the West African route) and, to be honest, we were running out of energy. The constant heat, traffic, police and military checkpoints, illness, disease, expense, mechanical problems, poverty and uncertainty, had taken its toll on us all. We were looking forward to Angola; we were looking forward to Namibia and an eventual return to Cape Town. Some enjoy the West African journey, who relish the wildness and adventure of it all, some have less responsibility and risk - as a working, travelling family, the West African journey is far tougher than any journey that we have ever undertaken, by multiples of 10. The Pan

American journey is a pleasure cruise by comparison and feared Central America is a stroll in the park, Venezuela and the Guyanas, and the crossing of the Amazon don't even break a West African sweat. Which is not to say that those routes are easy, not by any stretch of the imagination, but they are in comparison to the journey we found ourselves on.

The overland route across Western Africa is, arguably, the last great overland route. Yes, there are routes which are more remote, wilder, more extreme in terms of terrain, temperature and location. The Canning Stock Route in Australia is a good example of a great one-dimensional overland route which pales in comparison to the West Africa route. But, why is Western Africa such a challenge (and therefore incredibly rewarding)?
Bureaucracy

It becomes crystal clear as soon as you leave the Moroccan Western Sahara border and enter the no mans land to Mauritania that you are very, very far away from the peaceful and prosperous shores of Europe, a few days drive to the north. Burnt out vehicles are strewn across the landscape, a track weaves between them, there are landmines here, you may not leave the track. It is as if you are entering a post-apocalyptic world beyond the high gates which welcome you forebodingly to a country of sand and wind. Men in military uniforms and black full-face scarves point at a building, "stop there, go there". All we see is a white building, and once we enter, we find a forecourt full of men and a few closed doors, no signs. A metal door opens, a man escapes, men start to shout, we are pushed forward, "what's going on"? Behind the metal, door is the immigration room where a barefoot man dressed in a suit packs Euro notes into drawers overflowing with Euro notes and languidly, eventually issues visas. To enter Senegal from Mauritania, you most likely need to have a visa, and if you do not have a carnet for your vehicle (a carnet is essentially a passport for your vehicle), you will need to pay Euro 250 despite there being no law which supports that demand. In Dakar, you have to fight the flow of traffic to apply for the visa for Guinea Bissau where you will melt in the heat while applying for the visa for Cote d'Ivoire and Guinea Conakry. In Abidjan you will need to apply for the visa for Ghana, In Benin, you will apply for the visa for the Democratic Republic of Congo (even though there were some bikers the week before whose visas issued in Benin were refused), in Lagos you will camp in a construction yard for four days so that you can apply for the visa for Cameroon, and you will have to repeat the process of travel, pay and wait for Gabon, Angola, Congo, Namibia and South Africa (depending on your nationality). The average visa costs $50 (x 4 x 15 in our case), and that does not include the *expense and effort to travel to the cities and find accommodation while applying for the onward visa. And if just one of the visas is refused your entire journey can grind to a sudden and expensive halt. When asked why the visa for their country is so expensive, the official will usually answer "how much is a visa for me to enter Europe"? The system is reciprocal, you see, and tourism does not yet yield sufficient revenue to encourage tourism.*

(By contrast, we spent almost three years touring South America overland where visas are usually free, and borders are run quietly and efficiently).

A uniform is power, and there are border officials and policeman who run scams and prey on everyone who passes. But, it must be said that the corrupt officials constitute only 10% of the officials you will encounter on the road, but they have a huge impact. Don't get me started on the Nigerian visa and entry process, please - I would rather just forget.

Malaria and Bacteria and Ebola

The tiny Anopheles mosquito is a murderous little creature, and she preys on the young and pregnant women mostly. This vermin still kills almost a million people a year despite decades of attempts to eradicate the scourge, but there are expensive preventative regimes and less expensive treatments. When our daughter fell ill, we attended a basic but efficient pediatric hospital in the city of Enugu, Nigeria where she received affordable blood tests to confirm that she had malaria and treatment cost less than $10, which is OK when you earn more than a dollar a day. She recovered fully, but the reality is that she was infected with a potentially fatal disease.

Bacteria is virulent. A cyclist friend had to return to Europe from Senegal after a scratch on his shin became horribly infected, and you simply have to coat your hands with hand sanitiser before you can touch food or your mouth. Everything must be washed before being consumed, and the flu will attack you when you least need it, your energy will drain when you need every ounce of strength to continue, and the heat will keep you awake all night while your head pounds and a cough wracks your lungs. No matter how careful you are, you will invariably find yourself hovering over porcelain, in pain.

Infrastructure

Some roads are simply atrocious and the two annual wet seasons wreak havoc on the thin pavement which struggles to connect countries north to south, east to west and their neighbours. While there most definitely has been progress over the last few decades and there are new bridges where ferries once dominated, it can take entire days to travel short distances. Ghana, Gabon and South Africa have fantastic roads, the Ivory Coast is a joy to drive (mostly), and Nigeria will offer you a few wonderful roads and hundreds of kilometres of automotive hell. And while some cities, such as Dakar, are a nightmare to navigate and endure, there are other cities which are a pleasure. Abidjan is a wonderful city, and a great surprise and Accra has its moments.

Internet connections can be adequate or non-existent, and the entire region hums to the drone of generators. There are hardly any trains, trucks rule the roads and do so with impunity, and a road without a hundred military and police checkpoints are rare and suspicious (particularly between Morocco and Gabon). There are few municipal services and all trash, including plastic, is burnt in large, suffocating heaps rendering blue skies grey and acrid.

Terrain

You may be as surprised as we were to learn that West Africa is mostly quite flat and that Senegal is dry and dominated by grassland. It is only from the middle of Guinea Conakry that the famous rainforest appears and once the rainforest starts the terrain becomes difficult, particularly where roads are few and only partially paved. And we have the distinct impression that many West African countries do not have great relations with their neighbours and there is certainly not much trade. The border between Guinea Bissau to Guinea Conakry is located on a track of road which hardly qualifies as a road. It took three days of offroad driving to cross from central Nigeria into Cameroon as the southern Ekok border was closed due to the civil war in Cameroon. The terrain was mind-numbingly beautiful (very similar to central Colombia) but the mud thick and cloying. Yes, it is possible to drive the route in the dry with a 2x4 vehicle but once the rain starts you simply have to have a capable 4x4 if you are to avoid becoming stranded in the highlands. The terrain dries significantly south of the Congo River which forms the natural border between Angola and Congo, and Namibia is a land of sand, part of a desert and semi-desert ecosystem which stretches across Botswana and Northern South Africa as far as Zambia and Zimbabwe.

Civil War and Unrest

Mali and Burkina Faso offer a direct route to Benin or Niger and Nigeria, but Boko Haram and ISIS are disrupting those countries, attacking villages and kidnapping foreigners. Chad is a no go zone as is the Central African Republic and parts of the Democratic Republic of Congo. When armies and rebels and Islamists are not vying for control, tribal disputes lead to bloodshed and massacres. We did not sleep well in Nigeria - a shot rang out just after dark, and a man with an assault rifle entered the hotel compound and beat the staff with a rod (that is another story for another day). The following day we were escorted to a police station where we were instructed to sleep in our campers because the area is infamous for kidnappings. Cameroon suffers an ongoing civil war, and Angola is still recovering from a decade's long Cold War proxy conflict. Students march for democracy and human rights, governments control information and energy and the old guard will not go without a fight. The good news is that the terrible conflicts in Liberia and Sierra Leone and Cote d'Ivoire are a thing of the past. Of all the countries on the Western Africa route, it is the wealthiest, South Africa, which suffers the most violent and virulent crime and all other countries along this route are safe by comparison but, Nigeria is volatile). Crime is less of a concern than martial conflicts, and we had nothing stolen during our cautious journey.

Expense

Unless you live on a (local) diet of onion, potato, avocado, tomato and green pepper and travel on a diplomatic passport, Western Africa is very expensive. Visa costs are exorbitant, a decent hotel unaffordable and "western" food bitterly expensive. Boondocking and free camping is not a popular option, and most nights will likely be spent parked beside a hotel or restaurant and paying a room or full meal rate for the pleasure. Fuel costs roughly a dollar a litre and there are many toll booths collecting funds for roads which have already been paid for or will not be built for decades.

So why do it?

We do it because it is the last great overland route, it is a grand adventure, and it is the fire in which a man is forged. We met amazing people, were welcomed with respect and kindness, we witnessed great things and terrible things, and we are left with a knowledge which very few have. You simply do not know until you know. And there is one undeniable upside to taking on the worlds most difficult overland route - all other routes are "easy" by comparison. Currently, we are planning a journey from Cape Town, South Africa to Vladivostok, Russia and while we are not underestimating the longest possible overland route, we are not sweating bullets of anxiety. Western Africa gave me my first ever panic attack and most likely, my last".

But, when all is said and done, we were looking forward to getting back into familiar territory. If you had to ask me which is the best route across the west - north to south or south to north - I would say that the south to the north route would be best as you would be able to ease into the journey as opposed the birth by fire border crossing which is Mauritania. State of mind is incredibly important, and if you enjoy the beauties and pleasures of Southern Africa before heading into the belly of the beast, you will have time to relax into the journey and not rush for the finish line. We were rushing for the finish line for more good reasons than one alone.

In Benin, we had been issued a visa for the Democratic Republic of Congo (DRC) which was valid only from a specified date and only for eight days. Our time in Cameroon had left us with ten days to cross Gabon, The Republic of Congo (Congo), Cabinda in Angola (the "island of Angolan territory separate from the rest of Angola and protruding into the stomach of the DRC". We had to cross Cabinda in Angola on that exact date, and if we did not, we would be faced with few, very expensive alternatives. Either we would have to ship the Land Rover from Cabinda in Angola to mainland Angola (there are no ferries FFS), or we would have to try and drive back and around Congo and attempt to enter the DRC at another border crossing. To make matters worse, there had been recent instances of travellers with the identical visas issued in Benin, being denied entry to the DRC as the visa had not been issued in their country of residence. The rumour was that the consulate official in Benin was issuing the visas illegally and pocketing the money. He had seemed like a nice man, and he had assured us that we would have no problems with our visas. Dick (remember him) informed the West African Whatsapp group that he was in charge of the situation and that we should wait for him to give the go-ahead. We had put ourselves in Dick's hands once before, and we all know how that turned out. While in Cameroon, Luisa had appealed to the South African Consulate and, surprisingly, we were informed promptly that the consular general would look into the matter and provide feedback. We explained that we had been travelling for years and had not returned to South Africa for half a decade; therefore, we could not have applied for the visa in our home country, the consular assured us that he would do what he could. A few days later, we received an email from the consular general in which he shared the contact particulars of the Director-General of Immigration in Kinshasa.

Once we reached and crossed the DRC, we could relax again and enjoy the journey.

While driving down a beautiful rainforest fringed road, we came across two overlanders - a Canadian driving a South African Defender accompanied by a huge German Shepard and a Swiss man on a BMW motorcycle. We chatted for a while beside the road, while a local construction crew worked on the verge of the road - hard hats and modern machinery, not spades and picks and hoes. The Canadian, a charming man with a friendly face and casual demeanour, agreed with the solid Swiss that the road from Gabon to Angola was, "easy, no problems at all, very good roads, definitely, no problems at all, yeah, all smooth sailing from here". We believed them. Our spirits soared. The Land Rover had been experiencing a lot of mysterious electrical issues, and the gearbox was showing signs of imminent failure. At the same time, it was sad to think that the true adventure might be over. Africa is always waiting to surprise.

Oh, beautiful Gabon. Such beautiful people, sublime rainforest, great roads (I may have mentioned) and wonderful countryside. But the bushmeat trade was horribly depressing, and the logging trucks bearing ancient behemoth trees to the mill reminded us that the Garden of Eden would be strip-mined for a profit if fat cats an ocean away, could fatten themselves further. Those trees were fantastic, some so large that a truck could carry only one half of a single tree, the trunks almost three meters in diameter. Rounding a corner, we passed yet another logging truck and witnessed a large female Mandrill monkey hung by a leg from a pole, a bullet through her heart. We stopped for Luisa to photograph the animal (it seems only right to document such things) and while we waited, a group of children gathered near the Land Rover to shout happy hellos. A woman, alerted by the commotion, disappeared into her house and emerged with an infant Mandrill. She approached us with a large smile and held the petrified monkey up to me - his fluffy grey fur standing out against his body, large imploring beautiful and soulful brown eyes, mouth agape in screams, his legs bent and feet clinging to his tail as he would a thin branch, seeking comfort. His mother hung lifeless from the pole across the road. We were saddened deeply and faced with a dilemma. Should we buy the monkey and deliver him to a sanctuary? Purchasing wild animals was essentially illegal, and particularly so for foreigners, I believe. The authorities would not bat an eyelid if a Gabonese family approached a checkpoint with a young Mandrill on board but, I believe, we would have been in deep trouble. We also had no idea how to care for a wild animal. It was a tough moment for us, and we were tempted to rescue the orphaned simian but not at the risk of contributing directly to illegal wild animal trade, which may encourage targeting mothers with young. It was a tough decision, and we drove away saddened beyond mere words. That beautiful little monkey represented much that is wrong with our world, whereas we humans refuse the role of custodians and continue blindly to exploit the natural world.

It took a while for us to explain the situation to ourselves and the children and hardly any words were spoken as we continued to meander swiftly through Eden until we reached a moss-covered sign hanging askew beside the road - VOUZ FRANCHISSEZ L EQUATEUR (you cross the equator). Keelan took a photograph of me standing in front of the Land Rover, the girls in no mood for photographs. This was the sixth time that we had crossed the equator in our Land Rover, and we hope to cross it six times more. We know that we will cross it again in Kenya as we drive to Russia and then many times more when we return to South America to spend a decade exploring our favourite continent.

There were no charismatic men with buckets of water to demonstrate that at the equator, draining water will vortex counterclockwise in the Northern Hemisphere, clockwise in the Southern Hemisphere and straight down at the equator. There was no large sculpture replicating the earth or a nail through a board the sharp tip upon which you could balance an egg; there were no curio shops or tour groups or tour guides or restaurants, there was only the fallen sign and the rainforest and the road to bear witness to our achievement.

At the town of Ndiole, we encountered Pygmie workers at a local store where they were buying supplies, and we bought bread. Despite their diminutive stature, they carried themselves with dignity and were not intimidated by the size of their neighbours. If anything, it seemed as if their neighbours treated them with respect. Unfortunately, the story of the Pygmies is not a happy one. First, I am not sure if the word "Pygmie" is derogatory, but I am also not sure if the name "Central African Foragers" is any better, so we use the name Pygmie with respect. The Pygmies are diminutive people who number roughly 900,000 spread across Gabon, The Republic of Congo and The Central African Republic. They were displaced over centuries by the expansion of the Bantu people and are if left to choose, inhabitants of the rainforest. In Gabon, they are said to enjoy a degree of protection, but in The Congo their lives are desperate - they are enslaved by the Bantu people in what is referred to by the Bantu as a "time-honoured" tradition. I wonder if the enslaved agree. During the Ituri conflict from 1999 to 2003, Uganda backed rebel groups that were accused by the UN of enslaving Mbuti Pygmies, forcing them to prospect for minerals and hunt for food, those who returned from the hunt empty-handed, would themselves be slaughtered for the pot (their flesh is believed to confer magical powers). Pygmies are not considered full citizens in many African countries and are denied identification cards, health care, schooling and deeds to lands. Colonialists exported many Pygmie adults and children to carnivals and zoos in Europe and America, where many perished.

In that store in Ndiole, we said hello and left them alone. Such beauty and despair, living hand in hand.

Seventy kilometres south of the equator, we entered the city of Lambarene, located in the Central African Rainforest on the banks of the river Ogooue (which divides the city into three districts). We filled up with fuel at a clean and modern fuel station before driving on the N1 bridge across the river and past the Albert Schweitzer Hospital. Turning right off the road, we drove down into the parking area of a Hotel Bo Bebe, where we were greeted cooly. iOverlander information about the hotel stated "Very, very friendly owner who let us stay for free at the parking lot of his hotel. Hotel is situated on a nice street with several big supermarkets, a good bakery across the street with fresh bread in the morning, nice bars, restaurants and little shops. There is no noise in the night from the street. You can use the toilet and a bucket shower during the daytime. In the night the door closes. We stayed here for two nights and of course gave him some CFA for his kindness and hospitality".
The only problem with posts like that is that every penny-pinching overlander for the rest of time will show up expecting friendly and free, which is no way to run a business. We were quoted a big, fat fee for parking, took the hint, said thank you anyway and drove back across the river to the Soeurs de Conception Immaculee Catholic School, where we were greeted by a friendly nun and shown where we could park. The school is established in an immaculate set of buildings built in the French provence style with large wooden doors and windows, exposed clay brick and large cool verandas. We parked beside a cool green lawn and played with a puppy while Luisa tried to dry the camper as one of the onboard water tanks had leaked and flooded the vehicle. When Luisa cleans she does so with righteous fury, she will strike down with a great vengeance and furious anger those who attempt to distract her.

And you will know she is Luisa when she lays her vengeance upon you. Say "what" again. I dare you. I double dare you motherf@*ker.

As it was late in the afternoon, there were few school children still waiting to be collected, and we had the garden to ourselves until a young Japanese man joined us and set up his tent on the lawn. We had met him in Ivory Coat in the city of Man, where we had shared a meal. He had been a lot cleaner then, his white "tunic" had since taken on a red hue from the soil and sweat, but his smile was deep, and he retreated into his tent shortly after sunset, and we did not see him again. Yuki spoke very little English or French and communicated with smiles and gestures. He asked for a lift to Angola, but I am reluctant to take passengers, we have a dynamic, and we know what we are carrying, I will always help someone if there are few options, but Yuki had many options, particularly in Gabon. With the Land Rover clean and dry and the floorboards swelling, we had a pasta dinner and a shower and lay down for a cold river breeze evening, safe, secure and happy.

That morning we showered again (Hot water! Privacy!) and paid the nun for the camping and extra for the school as a donation before setting off across the river for a long, pleasant days drive to the border at Ndende, a few hundred kilometres south. It was a quiet day of relaxed driving through peaceful villages and towns. Gabon has the fourth-highest Gross Domestic Product per capita in Africa and a low population density. The country is rich in petroleum and foreign private investment, and while there remains a largely poor population, there seems to be upward mobility. At 4.30 pm, we arrived in Ndende and headed to the immigration office, which was located on a large freshly cut lawn. The doors were locked, and we were advised by locals walking the path in front of the building that the office closed at 4.00 pm and would reopen at 8.00 am. With a few hours of daylight to kill, I sat at one of two benches under a covered carport and worked on finishing the tyre review for The Overland Journal; it is official, we are digital nomads. After writing, and before the sunset, I gave the Land Rover her daily inspection and crawled under to check that everything was as it should be, topped up the coolant and searched for our evasive electrical gremlin. We decided to set up camp on the grass beside the immigration office, and I searched a wooded area behind the stand-alone immigration office for firewood and found a family living in a large room. I asked a teenage boy if I could buy some firewood or coal, he said he had none and offered to find some for me. I handed him some banknotes, and he returned an hour later with a small bag of coal. With the sun setting, Luisa and I chatted about the road ahead, what we would do when we reach Namibia, the food we would eat and the friends we would visit and the trails that we would drive. The night was cool, and though more than a few locals were using the track beside us, we never felt any threat or menace or danger. But it was a Saturday night, and the locals were partying like it was 1999, all night long.

We slept very little but at 8.00 am we were dressed and ready for the immigration procedure. The officials were friendly, polite and efficient and after having our passports and carnet stamped, we soon found ourselves on a long, straight road leading out of town. We bought provisions and had a chat with the Pakistani storekeeper before driving to a T-junction, turning right and discovering to our dismay that the paved road ended and was replaced by mud.

CONGO

The Congo also known as Congo-Brazzaville is one of the most urbanised countries in Africa. It is a country located on the west coast of Central Africa. It is bordered by Gabon, Cameroon, the Central African Republic, the Democratic Republic of the Congo along with the Angolan exclave of Cabinda to the South. The official language is French

Congo uses the Central African Franc
100 CFA = EU0.15/USD0.17

Most nationals from West Africa can obtain a visa on arrival; all other nationalities must apply for a visa before entry. The approximate cost will be EU130 for a one month visa or EU80 for a 15-day visa

Unleaded = EU0.95/USD1.02 per litre
Diesel = EU0.95/USD1.20 per litre

MTN
Airtel

Christianity is practised with a mix of Catholics, Awakening Lutherans and Protestants. France colonised the Congo

No specific insurance was requested

Police = 117
Ambulance = 118

Valid passport
Vehicle title papers
Carnet de Passage (recommended) but a TIP will be issued on arrival
Vaccination certificate for yellow fever
International Driver's licence (required)

The official language is French
Bonjour! – Hello
S'il vous plaît – Please

Au revoir! – Goodbye
Pardon – Sorry

allez-vous? – How are you?
Excusez-moi – Excuse me
Où est…? – Where is…?

ça va bien – it's going well
Plus lentement – More slowly
Merci beaucoup – Thanks a lot

Je ne comprends pas – I don't understand
C'est combien? – How much is it?

The food in The Congo has been influenced by the French, Asian and Arabs with staple foods such as cassava, potatoes and chicken

Lefini Reserve - great for safaris
The Lesio Louna Gorilla Reserve
Odzala National Park - to see primates whilst hiking
Tiger Fish Congo Camp - fishing expedition

Douli National Park - many marine animals, sea turtles, chimps and elephants

Lake Tele in the Epena District - a freshwater lake where the legend of Mokèlé-mbèmbé originates - a large reptilian creature

Summer - November to April - Low of 23C/73F and a high of 31C/88F

Winter - May to October - Low of 18C/64F and a high of 29C/84F

Pygmies still reside in the rainforests and may wander closer to the villages and towns but prefer to remain hunter-gatherers in the forests.

Oil accounts for almost 70% of Congo's GDP.

The endangered Bonobo monkey (our closest living relatives) can be found in the forests of the Congo Basin.

About 70 percent of the country's area is covered by rain forest

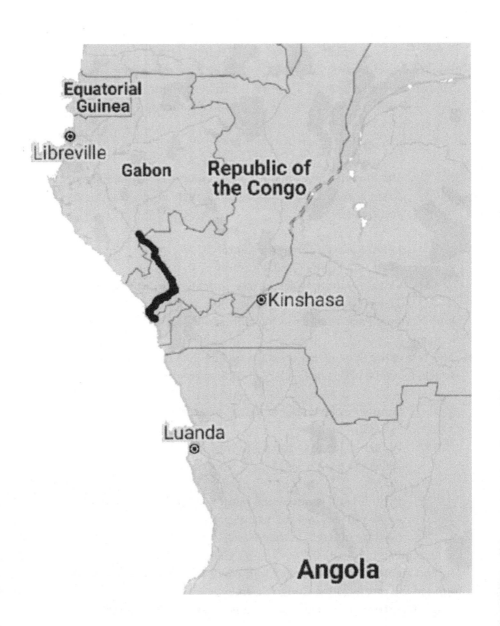

14

The Republic of Congo (not to be confused with The Democratic Republic of Congo)

"Ma, Jessica is not feeling well". We asked her if she had been drinking water and she promised that she had. She couldn't possibly have Malaria again, could she? I had finally recovered from the illness which had plagued me since Benin and Luisa and Keelan had both benefited from Gabonese civilisation. We gave Jessica some water, immune booster and paracetamol and continued along the track bouncing through deep muddy holes surrounded by tall, thick elephant grass. Occasionally a local on a motorcycle would appear and we would make way but usually, we had the road to ourselves. Two hours and 30 km's later, we arrived at a checkpoint where a young officer entered our passport details into yet another thick ledger and I took the opportunity to use the squat toilet above an abyss built on a rotting wood floor. I had images of plummeting through the floor into the devil's gloop. I held the walls tightly. When I returned, Luisa asked me to have a look at Jessica who sat quietly, as yellow as the walls of the office, her head slumped forward as she had almost fainted. "Jess! Are you OK?". She smiled back at us dimly, bravely, "Yes, I am fine, I think I have Malaria again". It was time to make a decision - should we head back and find a clinic or continue? The Canadian and Swiss had told us that the roads were good, surely after the border, the road would improve. We asked the Gabonese policeman, and he said the roads are not so good in The Congo, depends on the rain. We took Jessica back to the Landy and immediately started her on a course of Coartem, Luisa had stocked up on enough treatments to cure a few villages, but we had not been able to find test kits in Ndende as it was a Sunday and the test kits which we had bought in Nigeria had not been supplied with the vital flush solution. Driving gently so as not to rock the vehicle too much, we drove on towards the border and Jessica slept and the road deteriorated, we had to cross a river, mud flew from the tyres and eventually we reached the final Gabonese checkpoint around lunchtime. A few young uniforms sat joking under a tree, a small monkey played with a stone, a rope around his neck, another orphan.

The sky was blue and hot as we descended through the last checkpoint and drove across a river and up a severely eroded track to a boom and group of tin and mud buildings, The Congolese border. There, sat in the shade of a large avocado tree, we again met Yuki. A large, boisterous official searched the Land Rover and told us that we would have to wait a while as the customs officer was away having his lunch. I asked Yuki if he wanted a lift and he jumped in the Land Rover before I had a chance to change my mind. Luisa took care of the immigration process, and together, we bought fruit and snacks from a portly, laughing woman. The soil clung to everything, red and rich and staining. Our new friend, the customs official, arrived lazily and slowly completed the temporary import papers. It was a slow Sunday in the Congo. After a horrible drive, we arrived at a town called Doungilla, where we were told to report to the police for our passports to be inspected. Another official with perfect handwriting and a large ancient ledger took his time noting our details and then those of Yuki. He wanted to know why we were travelling together. While waiting at the police station, I studied graphic posters on the wall. Three dead bodies are lying in the road full of bullet holes, a man with a deep gash in his face and forearm, machete, a dead body tied to a tree, naked. The police had successfully broken up a criminal gang - judge, jury and executioner. We asked if there was a safe place to sleep in the town and we were told that there was not and we could not camp outside the police station, it was not safe. The police had a look in their eyes which I had seen in the eyes of men in Pretoria's maximum-security prison, eyes without a soul, but the uniforms were reversed.

With Jessica sleeping, we continued to drive and, despite the assurance of our Canadian/Swiss friends, the road did not improve. There is a lesson to be learned here. I am not saying that this was indeed the case, some roads are worse than others, and some peoples definition of "bad" is different to others, but if you ever meet overlanders heading the other way - be honest about the road conditions. Misleading bravado impresses no-one, and you might give advice which a family takes seriously and later finds themselves on a bad road with a sick child, a Japanese hitchhiker and a vehicle on the verge of a breakdown. A good road is a good road, and a bad road is a bad road, whether paved or unpaved, we all know the difference - a good road requires the use of 4th and 5th gear, a bad road requires only 1st, 2nd and 3rd (and low range). The only real exception is corrugated roads which are bad, but you can drive them in higher gears. Simple really. Bad roads can be great roads and lead to awesome places, and sometimes a bad road is just terrible.

The Land Rover was coughing and chugging and misfiring along the muddy roads and Congo is not Gabon - there is an atmosphere of danger, electricity in the air, drunken youths in football shirts blocking the roads, slapping the Land Rover as we passed, shouting, laughing and chasing us down the street. They were full of testosterone and pride and palm wine. "Stop! Stop!" We smiled and waved and rolled up our windows and pushed gently through, smiling and waving as each young bull tried to prove his courage. Village after village, mud houses and dirt floors and chickens and screaming children, were running after us with their hands outstretched. "Donnez-moi! Donnez-moi! (Give me! Give me)!". Did they imagine that we carried pallets of cash and footballs to dispense as we drove?

The Land Rover continued to cough and misfire and the dreaded check engine light illuminated as we spluttered along. If we stopped in a village, we would be swamped with locals, and we did not have the energy to deal with that scenario. Downhill the Landy would coast without a problem, but it was uphill that the engine struggled the most. The one reprieve was that it had not rained as the road would have been a quagmire when wet. Luisa searched the navigator and iOverlander app for a quiet place to stop, but every possible overnight spot we passed was exposed and therefore undesirable. As the sun began to set, we soldiered on, up and over and down endless hills through village after village, each poorer than the last. The road widened, and we could see evidence of road work, Luisa suggested that there might be an area to stop up ahead, and thankfully we pulled into an excavated area, the soil removed by heavy machinery. Invisible from the road, we parked the Land Rover and made the beds, getting Jessica comfortable before the work began. Yuki quickly set up his tent and disappeared into it before the sunset entirely. Keelan scavenged firewood and built a small fire, Luisa and I set up our tools and searched for the fault using the Nanocom diagnostic tool and visual inspection. The Nanocom had a few gobbledygook suggestions - Crank Position Open Load and Throw a Match in the Gas Tank. We had a suspicion that the problem was either oil entering the ECU via the loom (a common Td5 problem which we had not yet suffered) or the CPS (Crank Position Sensor) was faulty, or the wiring to the CPS was faulty. Working together, we first checked all of the fuses but found none blown. We then accessed the ECU and checked the red and black plugs for oil, but they were dry. By now it was dark, and we worked with head torches checking looms and wires and ground connections and cables and battery connections and then disconnected the battery. Our process of elimination led us to the CPS and Luisa found that one of the two thin wires was worn almost through. We disconnected the CPS and Luisa repaired the connection as best she could, kneeling on the hard metal wings, struggling to move her hands in the cramped space behind the engine and above the bell housing. After two hours, we were ready to test the new wiring, and I turned the key in the ignition. Nothing. Dead. Shit!

"Hey, the battery is still disconnected!"

"Dumbass!"

"You a dumbass!"

"Why didn't you check if the battery was connected?"

"I told you to check!"

"You disconnected it!"

"Dumbass!"

"A-hole!"

All day, every day.

I reconnected the positive battery terminal, but still, there was no power to the vehicle, no lights, nothing. Luisa removed and reconnected the crank sensor, and I turned the key, the engine started immediately and revved beautifully. Success! Hopefully. Only a long drive would determine whether we had solved our problem. But, that was tomorrows problem. We packed away the tools and tidied up, locked up and covered the windscreen so that no lights would be visible from the road where logging trucks occasionally rumbled past. The terrible roads are the saving grace for the rainforest. As soon as a paved road is built, the forest will be decimated on an industrial scale with likely little consideration for sustainability. I hope I am wrong, but the road is being built quickly, and by the time you drive that route it will be done.

Keelan had the campfire ready and cooked a delicious and tender coarse salt seasoned fillet, which we had been maturing since Cameroon. He had arranged a couple of jerrycans for us to sit on and produced two large, cold beers from the fridge (he could have unpacked our camping chairs, but we had to be ready to move quickly). What an adventure! It is when the going gets tough, that this family pulls together and shines brightest. We squabble daily; we have power struggles, mood swings and idiosyncrasies, we become infuriated with each other, and we have had moments when the whole grand adventure has come close to a sudden end. But, we live and travel together every day in an area not much larger than a king-size bed where we cook, eat, sleep, poop, work and relax. Together. Every day. 24 hours a day. All the silly stuff disappears when you are faced with a potentially life-changing situation, far from any assistance as we had proven before when we suffered the four-day breakdown in the remote Moroccan Rif mountains. We had pulled together again, and it was with an immense sense of satisfaction that I sat and enjoyed the flames of the fire, a long, cold draught of beer, a bite of the succulent perfectly cooked fillet, the conversation of my family. It had been one hell of a tough day on the road but, looking back now, I would love to be there again, right now, feeling that satisfaction, enjoying the brilliance of a life lived dangerously yet intelligently, of a family bonded and successful and full of love and strength.

Had we not been able to fix the Land Rover, we would have been in a very difficult position. It is possible that a truck could have towed us for the remaining 150 km of the dirt road but can you imagine the dust and the danger and discomfort. We might have waited a few days for another overlander to pass or we might have asked a passing villager to arrange a tow truck which would arrive days later and demand a fortune. We might be found by the unslaughtered gang of criminals and relieved of our possessions, dignity and the unimaginable. Yuki wasn't going to help us but might have hitchhiked to the next proper town and delivered a letter to the authorities. Or we might have continued working until eventually we found the problem and were able to do a repair in the field.

But all of that was tomorrows problem. Jessica had stabilised, her fever was down, and she felt better even though she hated drinking the pungent immune booster. She luckily had no difficulty swallowing her Coartem malaria pills. We killed the fire, checked on Yuki, brushed our teeth, locked up and lay down to a blissful sleep dreaming of good roads, friendly people, deep-fried food, salad, swimming pools, hot showers, ice-cream and cold drinks.

The confidence with which we went to sleep abandoned us when we awoke to a bright blue sky. There was a splotch of minty green toothpaste on the ground beside where we had parked, evidence of other travellers who had sought haven in this large pit. Little Yuki was packed and ready to leave, sitting on a rock, smiling serenely.

Jessica was smiling and had some colour back in her cheeks. I started the Land Rover. No problem. I drove her out and back onto the road. No Problem. We drove down a long hill, through a village and up a long hill. No problem. The Landy pulled beautifully, and fists were pumped. Good work, family. We stopped in the town of Kibangou, where a large blue administration building overlooked small stalls. We bought fruit, bread and cold drinks, chatted to the locals for a while and enjoyed the shade of an ancient tree. Leaving the town, we drove onto a large, elevated and unpaved road, prepared for paving.

We all shouted with joy as I changed from 3rd to 4th gear. Yay! No more swaying and braking and accelerating and swerving and swaying and accelerating and braking, stirring the gearbox like a thick stew. No more wading through muddy craters or being chased by hordes of kids (a pity, we loved those kids). With the Landy purring along at the ridiculous, reckless speed of 70 kph we rolled towards Dolisie, smiling, enjoying the wind in our hair and the relaxation which comes with a long, wide, safe road. There was not much traffic sharing the road, and we made good time. We rounded a corner and Keelan leaned forward in his seat. "Dad, that's tar". I squinted, and sure enough, the road turned light grey then black ahead of us. With a final jolt, the Landy bounced onto the paved and rolled silently as if flying on silk. No more squeaks or bangs and squeals, just rolling along as smooth as butter. There is a happiness and sadness at the end of an unpaved road, almost as if the adventure is over and life will now return to normal. Almost immediately we came to a stop at a toll booth and happily handed over a few dollars before stopping at the new, modern, South African style gas station where we soaked in the air conditioning and bought croissants, before relieving ourselves and washing our faces. Yuki disappeared for a while but soon reappeared with his serene smile. He had sat on the floor of the Landy eating bananas for the last few hours, Yuki loves bananas. He had slept most of yesterday and that morning and was covered in a fine layer of dust from lying at the back of the Defender along the long high-speed gravel road, our rear door seals failing to do their one job.

The wonderful paved road to Pointe Noir winds through the Bimonika Biosphere reserve, and we were determined to reach coastal Pointe-Noir before nightfall. Again, what a difference a paved road makes. Suddenly the Congo was no longer dangerous hard work, the villages gave way to developing towns, and the winding road continued to be smooth and quiet. Yes, Chinese investment in Africa has a lot of negative implications, a lot, but it is possible that the building of roads and bridges and investment in telecommunications will finally achieve what countless billions of dollars of aid have failed to achieve over the decades. As long as communities live isolated and far from opportunity, they will continue as they always have, but when a school bus can deliver and return students from school and produce can reach markets and travel is possible, progress will be inevitable. And, yes, progress is not always positive despite the verb (or is it a noun) being distinctly positive in nature, But paved roads bring information, opportunity, new ideas and investment. The Romans knew this and the developed world is built on a network of paved roads; what good is a modern port if resources cannot be distributed inland effectively? In the next decade, it may be possible to drive from Casablanca to Cape Town on tar and concrete entirely. For overlanders, that is both a blessing and a curse, but we will always have the opportunity to head off the beaten, beautifully paved road and explore further inland, reaching areas where few ever venture. The Pan Western African highway will resemble the Pan American highway, and no-one complains about the Andes mountain passes being beautifully paved. If Europe wants to curb illegal immigration, they should send road-building crews to Africa, if America wants to halt the spread of Islamic extremism, they should let the churches pay for newly paved roads across Mali, Burkina Faso, Mauritania, Nigeria and Senegal. If aid organisations want to end poverty and fight Malaria and save children, they should build roads. Asia and Africa were developing at a similar rate in the first half of the 20th century and faced similar challenges as colonialism failed and retreated, following the Second World War. Investment in the Asian Highway Network in the late 1950's achieved the goals of promoting domestic and international trade and certainly contributed to Asia becoming a powerful economic region, while Africa floundered under the rule of dictators and presidents for life, who built mansions and cathedrals and countless bizarre vanity projects instead of investing in roads, highways, paved towns and connected cities. Tourism and wildlife conservation go hand in hand and nature reserves which do not attract investment and income for the surrounding communities, will forever be a source of raw resources and bush meat. I do not know the answers and will not pretend that I do; I am not an economist, or a conservationist or a historian.

I am an uneducated bastard doing the best he can to understand the world we live in, but I can tell you one thing - wealthy countries have excellent road networks, and none would be wealthy without those roads. Imagine England with unpaved roads, or the USA, or Germany, or Japan. Unimaginable. So. Save a child? Build a road and save millions. End Poverty? Build a road network and uplift millions. Fight Malaria? Build a god damn road. And don't wait for the Chinese to build the roads from rainforest to port, mine to port, mill to port, build roads which serve the communities and they will be able to take care of themselves and, hopefully, protect their natural resources.

Here are some figures for you - a highway from Western Sahara to Angola would cost approximately $40 billion based on a cost of $4 million per kilometre and a distance of 10,000 kms. Total financial aid to Africa since the 1960s has been $1.5 trillion (according to economist Dambiso Moyo). If roads are the arteries of an economy, why have none of the geniuses at the World Economic Forum or the United Nations or World Aid etc., never figured out that the only way to end poverty and all the associated misery is to BUILD BLOODY ROADS. It's almost as if they want to fail. Aid is big business, after all.

Search the internet for aid agencies, and you will find hundreds with names like Aid for Africa, Action Africa, Africa Classroom Connection, Africa Development Corps, African Aid Organization, African Children's Haven, African Food and Peace Foundation, African Rural Development and Sustainability Organization. I am sure they are all doing the best they can to build schools and teach farmers, but "If you want to prosper, first build roads" - Chinese proverb. Hence the Chinese Belt and Road Initiative which aims to increase trade, travel and Chinese economic power. We will all just have to wait and see if the positive will outweigh the negative.

We arrived in bustling Pointe-Noir late in the afternoon, our navigation app guiding us into the city and through crowded, narrow streets where we had to negotiate the crowds of people and stalls. We encountered a detour and had to squeeze past a multitude of urban obstacles before emerging onto a road full of vehicles. Yuki asked to be dropped off near the hospital, and we fought towards the centre of the city. I misjudged the width of the Defender and smashed the side mirror of a parked van, but with no option to stop, I continued until the road widened and handed the driver of the van our last pile of CFA to pay for his shattered mirror. Luckily the driver had been in the parked vehicle and was able to follow us until we stopped. He was not happy but accepted the money and my apology and left while we released Yuki from the back of the Land Rover. Luisa guided us to a pleasant beachfront neighbourhood, and we parked in a parking area beside the sea. Vendors approached, and we asked if it was safe to park and they informed us that it was not but, there was a nearby restaurant called Brasserie de la Mer where overlanders had been allowed to park in exchange for buying dinner. It was Monday night, and the restaurant was closed, but we were lucky enough to meet the burly French owner Pascal, and he invited us to stay and to use the toilets and showers. Parked between the restaurant and another, we waited until the sunset before each enjoying a hot shower, our first since we had arrived in Gabon a few days before. The next day we would be in Cabinda, Angola and would soon face the last major hurdle of the Western Africa journey - The Democratic Republic of Congo.

15

Cabinda, Angola

After a morning shower, we thanked the night security guard and headed towards Cabinda, enjoying a relaxed drive along the coastal road. We stopped to withdraw dollars from an ATM (very important for travelling in Angola where a black market for dollars exists) and try to find a refill for our large gas can, but there was no way to refill, we could only purchase a replacement tank. I had a great chat with the female proprietor, while Luisa enjoyed the air-conditioned pharmacy, searching for Malaria test kits. Jessica had almost fully recovered and was sleeping off the remnants of the infection, she had slept an average of 18 hours every day for the last four days, and she has the ability to sleep through anything.

It was a great morning drive, meandering parallel to the beach under palm trees, a cool breeze blowing off the ocean and the radio playing Portuguese music.

The border crossing was unremarkable, and we soon found ourselves driving through a fantastic wetland, occasionally stopping for a police or military checkpoint but otherwise progressing unhindered. We drove into Cabinda, admiring the infrastructure, sports grounds and apartment buildings and supermarkets. We tried in vain to find a gas company to fill our Moroccan gas can and eventually resigned ourselves to the fact that we would have to braai every night. Oh well. Cabinda is a city on the move, a city with trains and ports and an economy based on the oil trade. If Cabinda, formerly known as Portuguese Congo, was connected to northern Angola, The Democratic Republic of Congo (DRC) would not have access to the ocean. If it did connect to the north of Angola, our lives would have been much easier as we have had to pay for and stress over a visa which may not be honoured. Likewise, if there was a ferry running from Cabinda to northern Angola, we would simply have been able to skip the DRC and take the ferry, even though we absolutely despise ferries, particularly ocean-going ferries where inclement weather could result in a tragedy (at least you have a chance to swim across even a wide river). A ferry was built in Singapore for the Cabinda - Luanda journey, but the ferry will only be operational once the construction of the Cabinda and Soyo (Zaire Province) maritime passenger and cargo terminals are completed. And I believe the road south from Soyo needs some work.

We drove to the Angola / DRC border and arrived shortly before 4.30 pm.

With no guarantee that we would be able to cross, we approached the border and were relieved to find a relatively modern compound of immigration and customs buildings, immigration to the right, customs to the left beside the boom. A friendly soldier directed us to the immigration building and to a window in a wall beside a sunburned verandah where we sat and sweltered and waited to be assisted. A window slid open, and a hand of long red nails appeared. Passaporte por favor. In our broken Brazilian Portuguese we greeted the plump lady attached to the hand and explained that we were South African and we had been travelling for many years, that we had not returned to South Africa for many years and that our valid DRC visa had been issued in Benin. The plump ladies red lips called the head of immigration, and a tall, intelligent man approached, listened to our explanation and advised that he would have to cross into the DRC and secure permission from the DRC immigration head for us to enter. We informed the officer that we had procured confirmation from the Director of Immigration in Kinshasa in the DRC and provided printed emails with the various communications between Luisa and the Director. He thanked us and asked us to wait a moment. A moment became an hour and as the sun began to set the official returned with our passports and told us that there should not be a problem, but we were unable to cross that evening as the customs office was closing and would not have time to process our documents. I think he was doing us a favour, in retrospect. We were told that we could park the Land Rover on a stretch of dry lawn beside the immigration building, within the tall fenced perimeter where we would be safe. We drove the Land Rover back to the compound entrance and parked where instructed. The evening was hot and dry, and we settled in nervously, hoping that the next day would be without stress and that we would finally be able to cross the border which had caused us so much stress for so long. If we could not cross into DRC, we would be left with only very expensive options.

Across the road from the compound, a small, busy and noisy pub sold beer and snacks and Luisa and I wandered over to by cold drinks for the kids and soothing beers for ourselves. As in Venezuela, Angolans are fans of small, potent, ice-cold beers (200ml) and we bought a few to help settle the nerves and pass the time. As the sky darkened, the border grew quieter, and soon we were alone with only a few uniforms patrolling the perimeter and a few taxis waiting for last-minute clients. The heat intensified with the last rays of sunlight, Luisa made tuna mayonnaise sandwiches, and I sucked on a cold beer, Keelan and Jessica kept themselves busy reading and playing games on their phones. The night was long and hot, and the next morning we were awake and ready with the sunrise. We filtered some water and prepared the Land Rover for the drive, asked the cleaner if we could use the bathroom and returned to the immigration office refreshed and ready to roll. The Angolan immigration officer stamped us out of Cabinda, and we drove to the boom adjacent to the air-conditioned customs office and waited for an hour for the customs people to complete our carnet. Ahead the DRC border bustled, and it was clear to all with eyes to see that the DRC was three decades behind Angola.

Men pushed carts of produce along dusty streets between old, dilapidated buildings. Goats wandered aimlessly, and there was an atmosphere which we observed from the bubble of modernity, a reality which we enjoyed realising that this imaginary line had eventually become as tangible as night and day. Upon Luisa's return, an old Angolan border guard eventually motioned for us to approach the boom. He then checked all of our paperwork and wished us a pleasant journey and good luck. We drove off the paved road and onto the yellow dirt of the DRC. Another old official waved us over to the immigration building to the left of the road and made us park exactly where he wanted us to and how he wanted us to, facing away from the building and within mm's of imaginary lines. We locked the Land Rover and approached the derelict immigration office, the moment of truth.

We were told to sit and wait for the immigration chief to review our passports. A man with a beard and a belly stood by and joked with his colleagues who did not seem to notice that he had the voice of a woman, no breasts to speak of and was wearing an elaborate purple dress and white pumps, a matching white purse draped over his/her arm. She joked, and they laughed, and we noticed another woman with a beard standing nearby. We would later observe that many older women in the DRC wear beards, and apparently it is during menopause that a woman's body creates elevated levels of testosterone which leads to the beards. Also, apparently, Congolese men find a bearded woman attractive and special as "not every woman can grow a beard". Each to his own, I suppose. The mind wanders when the ass sits long on a wooden bench. An official beckoned and told us that we should follow him through the busy building, a tall, young official grinning and struggling to take his eyes off Jessica as we passed. "Tss! She is fifteen", he smiled at me nonchalantly.

We were shown to another wooden bench and waited a while for our names to be called, two officials poring over our passports for an eternity as we stood waiting to be processed. Words were exchanged, the boss was called, he looked over the passports, looked at us. "You are South African?" Yes. "Welcome". The passports were stamped (hallelujah!) and we were instructed to follow another official to an office where we sat and chatted to the immigration chief about South Africa, while he noted our passport details in his own ledger. He had been to Johannesburg once and was amazed how busy and modern the city is, but he complained that it was very dangerous and he did not feel safe. He preferred Cape Town and was duly impressed when we told him that we had lived in Cape Town, the greatest city on earth. We asked him about the DRC, and he told us that the country had problems, but they were working to solve those problems, one day it would all be so much better. He welcomed us to the DRC and wished us a safe journey. With that, we left and exchanged low-level fist pumps - we were in!

With Jessica and Keelan waiting in the Land Rover (windows open please!) Luisa took care of the customs procedure - stamp, stamp, stamp and scribble in the carnet de passage - while I located the ATM and extracted $300 US for Angola, keeping a close eye on whoever was keeping a close eye on me. I returned to the Defender as Luisa walked out of the immigration office. Success! Now, let's cross the DRC.

+

THE DRC

The DRC, also known as Congo-Kinshasa, is the largest and most populous country in Central Africa. It was named after the Congo River which flows through the country and which is the world's deepest river (with measured depths exceeding 220m). The DRC was formerly called Zaire between 1971 and 1997 and has a population of over 84 million. The Eastern DRC has been the scene of ongoing military conflict in Kivu, since 2015

The DRC uses the Congolese Franc
100 CFA = EU0.15/USD0.1
You can withdraw USD or EU's at select ATM's

Most nationalities must apply for a visa before entry and will cost an approximate EU80 for eight days

Unleaded = EU1.20/USD1.30 per litre
Diesel = EU1.20/USD1.30 per litre

Vodacom
Orange
Tigo
Airtel

Christianity is the main religious group.

Comesa insurance will be sufficient

Police = 117
Ambulance = 118

Valid passport
Vehicle title papers
Carnet de Passage
Vaccination certificate for yellow fever
International Driver's licence

The official language is French

Bonjour! – Hello

S'il vous plaît – Please

allez-vous? – How are you?

Au revoir! – Goodbye

Pardon – Sorry

ça va bien – it's going well

Plus lentement – More slowly

Excusez-moi – Excuse me

Où est...? – Where is...?

Merci beaucoup – Thanks a lot

Je ne comprends pas – I don't understand

C'est combien? – How much is it?

It is costly to eat out in the DRC and even purchasing food can be more expensive than Europe. Still, you can find some chicken or fish with cassava leaves along with tilapia dishes in the small local restaurants. Tubes such as cassava and potatoes are vital in every meal

Virunga National Park - home to the critically endangered mountain gorillas

Mount Nyiragongo - Volcano with a red lake

Equatorial - hot, humid and rainy, all year round

Tropical - Dry season - December to March and June to September with a low of 19C/66F and a high of 33C/91F

Rainy - April and May / October and November with a low of 19C/66F and a high of 31C/88F

Despite its poverty and history of conflict, the DRC boasts a space program. Previously privately funded but now backed by the government, it strives on becoming a full-fledged space program.

The DRC was once the personal property of Leopold II of Belgium, and he ruled the country like a psychopath on crack, enslaving the people and bearing personal responsibility for the death of millions.

The coast is a meagre strip of 23 mi/37km, but more than half the country is covered by dense tropical rainforest.

Nyiragongo Volcano is a great hiking challenge with a five-hour climb to the top to view the world's largest lava lake.

The DRC loves being creative with their postage stamps with Mick Jagger, Freddie Mercury, Tin Tin, Rudyard Kipling and The Beatles featured on their stamps

16

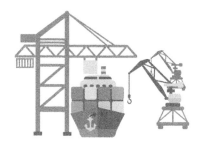

The Democratic Republic of Congo

The DRC, formerly Zaire and the Belgian Congo before that and the Congo Free State before that, is a massive country; the second-largest in Africa after Algeria. If we had the inclination and permission, we could drive from the Atlantic across the DRC to Tanzania and the Indian ocean, but that is a journey for the extremist. Plagued by colonialism and then war and now war and Ebola and bad government, the DRC has incredible natural wealth and a population of 84 million, making it the largest officially Francophone country in the world. Good old King Leopold II of Belgium treated the country as his own private possession, but he had little love for the country, seeking only to exploit the hell out of it. He built railways to extract resources, rubber mostly and had his corporations enslaved and terrorised the population, removing hands (if impossible) rubber quotas were not met. The British became aware of the atrocities perpetrated by the Belgians and the British consul at the Congo was instructed to investigate. The subsequent report, known as the Casement Report, confirmed the allegations of humanitarian abuses. The Belgian Parliament forced Leopold to set up an independent inquisition, and the Casement Report findings were confirmed, concluding that the DRC population had been reduced by half under the "leadership" of Leopold through murder and disease. In 1908, control of the country was removed from Leopold by the Belgian Parliament and renamed the Belgian Congo with independence finally being granted in 1960. There are, of course, detractors who insist that the accusation of holocaust and slavery are fabrications. The reality is that this is a country with massive potential and equally incredible problems.

Leaving the border, Luisa suggested that her research had found that there were a lot of informal tollgates manning the countries roads and that we could expect to pay up to $50 per toll. We were determined not to be victims. The iOverlander map showed that there was an alternate route around the main "toll" road and as we left the border, we saw other than the main route, only one filthy track which led to what looked like a rubbish dump. Locals waved and pointed at the track, but I was reluctant to drive down the narrow track. It was only once we had travelled a while down the unpaved main road that we realised that that track must have been to escape route. We had a look at the map and decided that we would return to the border and take the track which indeed led to a dump of sorts, but tracks were leading out into a field surrounded by palm trees. The track was used mostly by locals on motorcycles, and it branched off in many directions, we drove the wrong track and had to return through deep sand to the track and continue all the while trying to figure out if we were heading the right way. One track led us to a farmhouse under construction, another led to a thorny bush field, and another led to a village where the road seemed to terminate, and to which we returned to after taking the wrong track to the unfinished farmhouse. In the village, we encountered an old man sitting in the shade of one of many palm trees. Using sign language, we waved and asked which way we should go. He pointed to his right, and a man emerged from a hut carrying a machete, surely for farming purposes but we took that as a sign to keep moving. The track out of the village crossed a small stream with steep banks, and we soon found ourselves driving surrounded by tall grass towards the palm trees. Occasionally the dual-track would become a single track, and we were forced to plough through the long grass only to emerge in a deep mud hole. This could not be the correct route? Our near useless navigation app indicated that we were driving in the right direction and we began to wonder whether we should have just negotiated a toll instead of bundu bashing into the country. Eventually, the track joined another, regularly used by four-wheeled vehicles and we emerged in a village where children laughed and chased the Land Rover, the elders pointing to the direction in which we should be travelling. The track was thick sand, and we motored along choosing the correct "line", up and over large banks, through river beds feeling like true adventurers. And then a heavily loaded Peugeot sedan car barreled towards us. Yes the suspension had been lifted, and the driver was driving like a maniac to maintain momentum, but once again we were astounded at what can be achieved with a sedan driven un-lovingly. The first breakneck Peugeot was followed by another, and we soon found ourselves peering around each corner eager to avoid a head-on collision with a low flying French city car. Dot Bekker (the Zimbabwean lady returning from years in the UK) had driven the same route in her 2x4 Ford van, and I tip my hat to her. Yes, she was in convoy with Bruce, an American driving a huge American 4x4, and she did not know what she was getting herself into, but she did it. The winding sand track led to a river (with a bridge) where a woman washed clothing in the shade of a hundred swaying palms and a tall white block building waited to be a hotel. Beside the white building the road climbed up, and we realised that we were exiting a fertile valley and entering a dry plateau where tall, grey grass blew in the wind. We had been driving this trail for two hours, and there was no end in sight. We must have taken a wrong turn. Eventually, we reached an area where small natural gas rigs burned brightly in large clearings, with no crew in sight. We considered calling it an early day and camping near the gas rigs but realised that that would not be popular with the local authorities. Not too long after that, we emerged from the track onto an unpaved corrugated road which shook the joy out of us for the next 120km. The road was a nightmare to drive, and the dust covered everything in sight, the palm trees, plants and grass brown with dirt. Rounding a corner, we came upon the skeleton of a truck burned out, black and rusting, the frame blocked the road, surrounded by dust and framed by a deep yellow light. This road kills. We were close to the ocean, but the dust and dirt sucked the moisture from the air, it was a long, long drive until eventually we reached a bridge and came upon the first of the infamous toll booms. I was not in the mood for a song and dance after the terrible roads. A young, smiling man approached the Defender, sniffing for dollars.

"Bonjour monsieur, ici vous devez payer la taxe de circulation".
"Sorry, no French". My voice cracking, caked in dust.
"Here you must pay the road tax".
"Road tax for what? That road is terrible".
"Yes, but you must pay so that we can build the new road".
"We won't benefit from your new road".
"What? No, you must pay. $50".
"Speak to my wife".
"Haha, you are the man, I must speak to the man".
"Speak to my wife".

The young man laughed at me as he walked away, "Haha, speak to my wife, speak to my wife!". He would not be laughing for long. Luisa took a $10 note (a ridiculous amount to pay in itself) and walked down a steep bank to a collection of wooden huts where she would be issued with a receipt.

"$31".
"I paid $30 at the border, but the receipt flew out the window".

The head honcho did not speak English, but the grinning young man did. He translated, and the head honcho shook his head.

"$31.00"
"No"
"You must pay!"
"No"

The grin and the Honcho looked at each other surprised.

"$31.00!"
"No, why must I pay, the road is terrible, and I already paid at the border. I only have $10. I paid all my money at the border".

"$31.00"
"$10.00"
"$31.00!"
"$10.00!"

"You must pay!". As predicted, they were no longer smiling.
"No, I don't have to, but I will give you $10. Phone the border, they will tell you that we paid". Luisa had overheard Honcho saying that he did not have the border toll gate Honcho's phone number, her French comprehension had improved significantly. Corrupt police and immigration officials are met with polite defiance; extortionate toll collectors are met only with defiance. Voices were now being raised, and Luisa stood in mothers pose, hands on hips, chin thrust forward. They had met the Ginger Ninja.

Honcho straightened his back and scowled, "We have the authority of the transport ministry of the Democratic Republic of Congo, and we are mandated to collect funds for the use and improvement of our roads, and you have used our roads. The fees are not decided by us but are the fees set forth by the transport ministry, and you will be in contravention of the law if you refuse to pay the fee as stipulated!".

"No. $10".

They were not smiling. The kids and I watched all of this play out as locals arrived, paid a few bucks and carried on with their journey under the watchful gaze of old policemen who had seen it all before a million times.

"You must pay! OK, you can pay $20.".

"No. $10. I had $50, and then I paid $30 for the toll at the border and spent $10 on Malaria medicine for my daughter, and all I have left is $10 ".

"Where are you from!" Honcho was exasperated with this woman.
"We are from South Africa".
"Aaahh". A smile broke across his face. "I understand now; you are an African too!".

"Yes". Luisa handed him the $10 note and asked for the receipt. The Honcho shook his head and smiled in resignation. The grinning young man who was no longer grinning wrote out the receipt and handed it to Luisa, looking hurt.
Luisa took the receipt and prepared to leave, but Honcho wanted to chat, the ice had been broken. Luisa chatted with him for a while, telling him where we had been and where we were going, and they shared a laugh, the formalities done and forgotten. Luisa returned, and the boom was lifted, as we drove under the boom I slowed and made eye contact with the grinning young man who no longer grinned at me.

"I see you have met my wife!" "Goodbye". I waved gloating. Luisa 100 - Corruption 0.

A few hundred meters later, the road improved, and with it, life improved exponentially. To live beside a good paved road is to be potentially wealthy, to live beside an unpaved track is to be forever poor. The afternoon was spent trying to reach Matadi before dark, cruising along paved roads where Chinese foreman harassed African labour, occasionally stopping to gift bubble gum to policemen and enjoying the beauty of the country which we now "sped" across. Muanda to Nzali to Boma to Kinzao to Matadi along the N1. Black tar snaking between ancient and modern villages, past a factory, a farm, a school. Beautiful black tar delivering the country to eventual modernity, improving lives and making our own lives so much better. The road snaked between rocky green hills and, with the sun setting, we dropped down to the incredible Matadi bridge. The Matadi bridge is a 520m long suspension dual-use road, and rail bridge across the mighty Congo river paid for and built by the Japanese. It was completed in 1984 and was the longest suspension bridge in Africa until the inauguration of the Maputo Katembe bridge in Maputo, Mozambique. The city itself is located among stone hills on the left bank of the mighty Congo River and is the DRC's chief seaport, 148 km's inland and 8 km's below the last navigable point of the Congo before the impassable upstream rapids. Almost all of the DRC's exports and imports pass through Matadi, and we had been invited to stay at the home of an ex-French Paratrooper by the name of Philippe. We paid $6 to cross the bridge which the Japanese paid for and rolled into choked and bustling Matadi city low on fuel and supplies. We stopped at a gas station and tried to send a message to Philippe but could not as we did not have a DRC sim card. Luckily Philippe had provided GPS co-ordinates in an earlier message, and after filling the fuel tank with enough expensive fuel to get us to Angola, we forced our way back into the congested traffic and made 50m progress in 15 minutes, heading uphill, clutch in, clutch out, clutch in, clutch out. Luisa jumped out the Land Rover and shopped for groceries while we inched forward and returned a while later to find we had hardly moved. She had bought ice-cold drinks, and we sipped the sweet icy fizz while we waited to move a few cm's closer to our objective. After a lifetime, we reach our turnoff, and I felt the Defenders clutch slip, not fully engaging. As a precaution, I selected low-range (more power equals fewer gear changes) and followed Luisa's directions, but instead of finding ourselves at a home, we found ourselves parked between a factory and a bar on a very, very dark dirt road, we had reached our destination. I parked at the entrance to the factory and a night watchman approached. I asked where Philippe's house was, and the man had no idea, there were no houses here. Another local approached, and we asked if he could phone Philippe and let him know where we were. It was a stressful situation, parked in the dark industrial area of an unknown city. The local managed to get hold of Philippe and inform him where we were waiting for him. We were told to wait, and twenty minutes later, a new Toyota Hilux pulled into the dark street, and a muscular, confident man emerged. He introduced himself, paid the locals a hand full of cash and led us back to the main road. I warned him that we were having problems with the clutch and asked him to go slow as we would be in low range. "Ah, Defender", he said with a knowing smile. We followed him back to the now less congested road and drove up the side of a mountain, up, up, up. We made a few turns and climbed up another side street and came to the gate of an impressive residence. We had to do an Austin Powers 21 point turn to get into the driveway and pulled up beside the house where an armed guard stood at his station in the garage. The house was old and exquisite, built in the '70s to accommodate captains of industry or the holder of high office. We dragged ourselves from the Land Rover, hot and tired after a very long day on the road. We were greeted by Philippe's wife, Anette and were offered a cold beer which we enjoyed at the bar while the family took turns showering, Jessica first and begged not to take forever as we were surely stinking up the house and Jessica is well known to take hour showers. One by one, we entered and emerged from the shower refreshed in clean clothing and smelling fantastic. It is amazing how strong the smell of soap can be when you have not showered for days. After the stress of the border crossing and the terrible roads, the near mechanical failure and getting lost in the city, we were relieved and extremely grateful that Philippe had invited us and fed us cold drinks and a French three-course meal. After dinner, Philippe produced a bottle of Jack Daniels, and after a second glass with ice, I asked if we could stay two nights, we would cook dinner the second night, and we had a lot of washing to do. Philippe agreed, and we chatted about his work in Matadi and his career in the French Army. He is not the kind of man who has fear. I asked about the armed guard, and he told how two armed men had broken into the house while Annette was in France, stripped him naked and beat him, demanding that he open the safe, he told them that he was not stupid enough to keep cash in the house, told them where his wallet and the electronics were and told them to get out of his house, He told the story without drama, he had faced much worse in his life as a combatant who had served France in many conflicts. The DRC is dangerous and expensive, but the pay is good, and Philippe was head of a team of 500, taking care of shipping to and from the country. His plan was to retire in five years and then build his Defender in France and travel the world. He asked many questions, and we answered as best we could before the night came to an end. Luisa and I climbed into a king-size bed in an air-conditioned room and slept like babies. The next day we swam in the pool overlooking the smoky city and rolling hills, worked and cleaned the Land Rover, washed clothing and worked on articles and projects, answered emails, checked finances and planned the route forward. In the afternoon, after a lunch of chicken and chips and salad, Philippe's driver came to take Luisa and Keelan to the supermarket for Luisa to buy the ingredients for the South African stew Luisa was cooking for dinner. That night I had a sip of wine while

Philippe and Jessica drank a few glasses each with dinner. We chatted until late and went to bed, smiling again. The Angolan border was only 2 km's from Philippe's house, but he advised us that the border was very corrupt and the road on the Angolan side very, very bad and very, very busy. We said our goodbyes before going to bed and thanked Philippe and Annette for being such wonderful hosts and for allowing us the opportunity to be clean and happy and human again. Philippe's driver returned in the morning to take us to a bank where we could draw more dollars for Angola, and after saying goodbye to Annette, we packed the now clean and shiny Land Rover and set off to the alternate border crossing 82 km's to the east. Leaving the city was difficult as we fought traffic, pedestrians, carts, motorcycles and trucks, many trucks, on the cities cramped, suffocating roads. The trucks were a huge problem as they had to negotiate their way through the city to reach and leave the port. We were lucky to leave the city on paved roads. The country, which is the 11th largest country in the world and roughly four times the size of France, has only 2,250 km's of "highway" and only half of that is in good condition. Transportation across the country is a nightmare and waterways are more commonly used than roads. To be a truck driver in the DRC is to serve a sentence in purgatory, a hell of its own.

Approaching the turn off to the border on the N1 Luisa informed us that the toll gate just before the border would be very, very expensive but, there was a track we could drive to avoid the toll gate.

"Are you sure".
"Of course"!
"The last toll gate detour was a bloody nightmare".
"Look, it's here on iOverlander".
"What could go wrong"?

We pulled off the N1 at the beginning of the track and were stopped by two friendly chaps who said they were policemen.

"This route is closed". Cop one
"Yes, it is very, very bad". Cop two
"Thank you very much. But, is it closed or very bad?" Overlander one
"Where is the road to the border?" Overlander two
"It is very bad". Cop one
"There is a new road to the border". Cop two

"How far?" Overlander one

"Not far". Cop one

"500 km". Cop two

"What!?" Overlander one and two together

"Screw that; we will take the very bad road". Overlander one (Luisa, in case you were wondering)

"Are you sure?" Overlander two, Cop one and Cop two

"Yes, what could go wrong?".

And so we drove forward and found ourselves driving through savannah with grass three meters tall and on fire, the sky grey as we pushed through a single track which became a double muddy track and then single track again. Seeds filling the air and the Land Rover, smoke blowing across the track from invisible fires. What the hell were we doing? Risking it all to save $10? But, it's on iOverlander, what could go wrong? After half an hour, we emerged from the savannah into a small village where locals stood dumbfounded and waved inquiringly. Crazy Europeans - they drive all the way from Europe in their fancy machine and then drive through a burning field to save $10. I don't think they are very smart. It was then that we realised that Cop Two had said 500km but had meant 500m.

It's true; we are not very smart.

We re-entered the burning savannah and emerged eventually near a small river and surprised a policeman who was taking a break behind the toll booth compound.

"Where are you coming from?" called out the policeman on a break.

"From the savannah. It is on fire. We are not very clever!" Overlander two called back.

"Where are you going?" The policeman on a break.

"To Angola. Is this the right way?"

"You are crazy. Yes, drive up to the road and stop at the boom". The policeman on a break.

"Is that the toll boom?"

"Yes, it is. All that work for nothing. You are not very clever". The policeman on a break observed.

"Please tell them that we did not use the road and therefore should not have to pay the road tax".

It is a sickness.

I drove the Land Rover up a bank and emerged a few meters before the toll booth. Oh, how they laughed and laughed. Luisa became tight lip defiant, and I asked the booth operator to let us through as we had clearly not used the road. They must have pitied us because they managed to stop laughing long enough to lift the boom and way us through. "You are not very clever!" It is true, but we saved ten bucks!

The road was unpaved and corrugated but flat and not on fire, as we made our way to the border, which was the most chaotic we had ever encountered. Trucks, donkeys, motorbikes, trailers and hand carts all piled meters high and way over capacity, choked the dirt road as vendors shouted, and money changers swamped, and pedestrians swarmed through the colourful chaos. A no-mans-land between the borders, served as a market for Angolan products and every day thousands of Democratic Congolese (as opposed to Republican Congolese) fought for a few dollars profit. We stopped at customs, and Luisa disappeared into the chaos before emerging to take our documentation to a customs officer whose little office overflowed with files and a large, old desk. With customs out of the way, we made our way through the chaos, often hooting, being confident, moving forward slowly, allowing the cart workers to get out of the way before moving forward. What a tough life these guys have. Out of the dust and mayhem, rose a new white building which was not yet in use and around which we had to drive through a field of trucks and across a road and into another fenced field, the entrance limited by large, heavy rocks. The immigration hut was populated by tough-looking uniforms and aviator sunglasses relaxing on the patio, legs up. Now and then a uniform would be offended by the sight of a civilian and would jump up and shout orders. Luisa walked into all that without a moment's hesitation, while I stood outside the Land Rover, watching her disappear into the dark building. I used to be responsible for all the customs and immigration procedures, but, for some reason, Luisa has assumed that role, and it is her role entirely. For half an hour she worked her magic while we waited, the kids relaxing as best they could in the Land Rover, and I was negotiating quietly with money changers and watching people go by, hard-shelled. Jessica had broken a golden rule of border crossings and emerged from the Land Rover, when called by Luisa, wearing her pretty little pink dress, you know, the one with the plunging neckline and ten fingers above the knee. Jaws hit the floor when she emerged, and the mirrored aviator glasses misted up. I had noticed that she was wearing the little pink number that morning and had asked her to change as we were crossing a border that day. She said she would change her clothing "later", but later had not come. I was furious, and Keelan and I formed walls around her, shielding her from sight. In Europe or North America or Asia or South America, that style of dress would not get a second look, but in Africa, it is considered immodest and provocative for a girl to show a lot of leg, even if she is fourteen. Unfortunately, Luisa, the anarchic-feminist, does not help me to enforce this rule and we find ourselves in a situation where, instead of distracting attention, we have every hot-blooded eye in the Congo on us. Did I mention that I was furious?

Keelan is luckily very sensible and aware of his surroundings (unlike Jessica), and he made sure that he kept her out of sight (with my long-sleeved Craghoppers shirt wrapped around her legs) while the immigration official stamped us out of the country. Back in the Land Rover, we closed the windows and blinds, and Jessica apologetically changed into more suitable attire.

We drove out of the dusty compound and made our way through the chaos to the boom and entered the Angolan immigration compound, which was quiet and air-conditioned and efficient. We parked the Defender beside an abandoned Porsche Cayenne and went through the motions, speaking our terrible Portuguese.

Camping at a police station, Nigeria

Lovely Pia, a friendly, courageous and talented woman

Gorgeous highlands of Nigeria

The trail from Nigeria to Cameroon through the Gashaka Gumti National Park

Our first night in Cameroon

The chief of local village visiting us after camping on the roadside for the evening

There are several checkpoints along the way, at this one, the police officer was friendly

Sickly, malaria ridden Jessica. She suffered Malaria twice in three months

Perfectly tarred roads, Gabon

Crossing the Equator, Gabon

Baby Mandrill for sale as bushmeat / pet, Gabon

Crossing the mighty Congo River

Burnt out truck, DRC

The chaotic DRC/Angola border crossing

ANGOLA

Angola is the world's 23rd largest country, twice the size of Texas and the 7th largest in Africa. Angola is located in the southern hemisphere and overlooks the Atlantic Ocean, and the climate is tempered by a cool sea current along the coast and by the altitude of the plateau which is found in the interior. The result is a sub-tropical climate, almost everywhere

Angola uses the Kwanza
1 Kwanza (AOA) = EU0.092/USD0.10
The Dollar can be traded on the Black Market at a rate mentioned on www.kinguilahoje.com. "Cash is King" in Angola

Most nationalities receive a 30-day visa on arrival with permission granted online, and most Southern African citizens are visa-free. The visa fee will be an approximate EU100

Unleaded = EU0.26/USD0.29 per litre
Diesel = EU0.22/USD0.24 per litre

Unitel
Movicel

The culture of Angola is predominantly Portuguese, and the culture of the indigenous ethnic groups of Angola are mostly of Bantu culture.
The majority of the population is Christian with more than half practising Catholicism and the remaining religions originating from Protestants

No insurance was requested

Police = 113
Ambulance = 112/116

Passport with visa (if required)
Vehicle title papers
Carnet de Passage - recommended

The official language is Portuguese
Good morning - Bom dia (till noon)
Good afternoon - Boa Tarde (till sunset)
Good evening - Boa Noite (after sunset)

How are you? - Como voce esta?   Fine, thank you - Bem, Obrigado
My name is - Meu nome e   Please - Por favor
Thank you - Obrigado   Sorry - Desculpa
Yes - Sim   No - Não
Excuse me - Com licenca   Goodbye - Ciao
Do you speak English - Voce fala Ingles

Eating out can be expensive, but purchasing food from the local supermercados is cheap, and you can buy a lot of South African products on the shelves. Seafood with cassava is available at most roadside restaurants or stalls

Ruacana Falls - largest waterfall in Africa
Parque Nacional de Kissama - one day adventure to spot elephants, giraffes and zebras under towering baobab trees
The Tundavala Fissure - breathtaking gorge
Dala Waterfalls - 60m high waterfall
The Maiombe Forest - The second-largest evergreen forest in Africa
The Iona National Park - a vast national park with lagoons, plains, shifting dunes with rough mountains and cliffs

Rainy season - Nov to April - Low of 22C/72F and a high of 30C/86F
Dry season - May to October - Low of 17C/63F and a high of 27C/81F. Angola has a rainy and dry season but no real winter

When Angola gained independence in 1975, it was the last country in Africa to gain independence from Portugal.
Luanda is known as the "Paris of Africa", due to the city's sophisticated culture and atmosphere.
Angola is the second-largest oil and diamond producer in sub-Saharan Africa

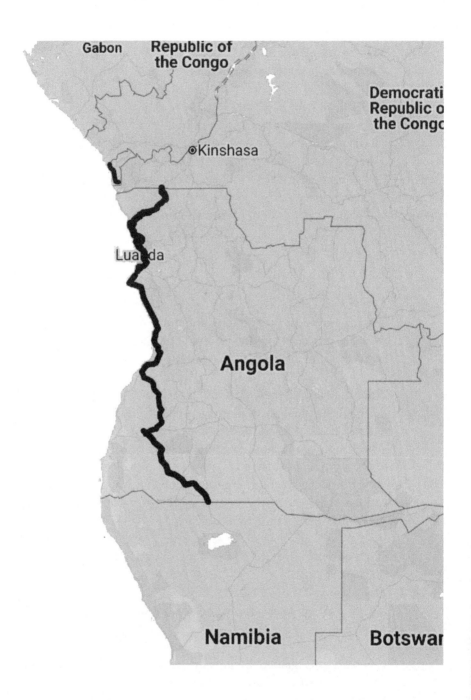

17

Angola, The Real Angola!

Ten minutes later we were in Angola, the real Angola, the Angola where roads were good and infrastructure good, where we did not need a visa and where the smooth sailing down to South Africa began! We were elated. It had been a hard, long, expensive and dangerous slog and now we were mere weeks away from returning to our home country South Africa, a country which Jessica and I had not returned to for seven years and Keelan and Luisa had not returned to for half a decade. We were in Angola! A country with great roads and good food and cheap fuel and friendly people. There was just one small glitch - Angola is also a country where my countrymen and women had been at war for most of the '70s and 80's. You might not have heard much about the conflict, if not, here is the South African Border War (aka the Namibian War of Independence, aka the Angolan Bush War) in a simple little acronym heavy nutshell…

After World War 1 South West Africa, a German colony was handed to South Africa to administrate temporarily under a League of Nations mandate type C. South Africa took to the task with great enthusiasm, too much enthusiasm actually, and decided that South West Africa should indeed become the fifth province of South Africa. After the Second World War, the Cold War heated up, and international liberation movements found financial and material support hand in hand with some good old fashioned Marxist-Leninism ideology supplied by the Soviets, Chinese and Cubans. The North-West African liberation movement, SWAPO (South West African People's Organisation), military wing PLAN (People's Liberation Army of Namibia) fought the South African Defense Force on Angolan soil. In the South African corner, we had the puppet Transitional Government of South West Africa, Portugal (until 1975), UNITA (from 1975) the FNLA the CIA and the KKK. In the SWAPO corner, you will find the MPLA (FAPLA), Cuba, ANC (MK), SWANU and loving support for the proletariat from the Soviet Union, East Germany, China, North Korea, Egypt, Ghana, Nigeria, Algeria, Libya and Tanzania. It was a giant shit flavoured acronym sandwich which included the Angolan Civil War. Yummy.

Apartheid South Africa was fighting for political survival and to avoid being completely surrounded by blerrie Commies and the Cold War, superpowers were fighting for world dominance, Portugal was fighting to retain Angola (and Mozambique) the ANC was fighting to end Apartheid, and nobody knows what the hell Algeria was fighting for.

South Africa, not unlike the USA in Vietnam, won the battle but lost the war but, while the Americans eventually prevailed and won the Cold War, the South Africans ultimately lost white minority rule because the Cold War ended (the West no longer needed the right-wing ally in the far south). The "old" South Africans are very proud of the achievements of the Apartheid and the South African Defense Force who developed their own world-class weapons of war (guns, tanks, fighter aircraft, armoured personnel carriers (APC's), etc.) and in two decades suffered less than 2500 casualties while inflicting almost 16,000 combat casualties all while being outnumbered 3 to 1.

Africa is very proud of the freedom fighters because they eventually defeated the white giant and liberated Namibia and South Africa in the process.

And that, my dear friends, is an only slightly abbreviated history of the Angolan Bush War.

For the last two decades, Angola has fought to recover from the long-lasting effects of the war and large areas of the south have long been designated no go areas due to the proliferation of land mines and unexploded ordinance. The north suffered far less during the war, and we were now driving through pleasant villages and towns with an infrastructure to rival that of the more impoverished regions of northern Brazil or South Africa. We entered the town of M'banza Kongo running low on fuel; unfortunately, we were unable to pay for fuel with dollars. The decision was made to drive into the town and try to find someone to buy our dollars at a reasonable rate. With the "empty" icon burning up the dashboard, we drove down a long road and turned left at a T-Junction, navigating by instinct towards a supermarket listed on our navigation app. The Mercado Nosso Supermarket had yellow branding and a large, spiked red metal fence. Located beside a large, dusty traffic circle adorned with a large statue of muscular workers. The parking lot was empty, and as we sat trying to figure out where to sell our dollars, a white Japanese 4x4 pulled up next to the Land Rover. A tall, bald man looked the Defender over for a moment and engaged me in a conversation, in Portuguese.

After explaining who we were and where we had been, I asked the friendly man if he knew where we could change dollars. He asked how much we wanted to change, and I suggested $300. He checked the exchange rate on the internet page Kinguila Hoje and asked if 400 Kwanza per dollar was fair, I said yes, he told me to wait five minutes and returned with 120,000 Kwanza. Suddenly every purchase became 30% cheaper, and Angola was affordable. We thanked our new friend and entered the Supermarket, hungry and ready to spend. We found many South African and Portuguese products and stocked up on essentials and a few luxuries before heading out to find a store where we could purchase an Angolan SIM card and then seek a place to sleep for the night. It was a Sunday evening, and the sun was preparing to illuminate elsewhere, the store did not sell SIM cards, but the padaria (bakery) had fresh rolls, steaming and delicious.

We had satisfied a few essential needs but still had to find a good place to sleep for the night; the Hotel Estrela do Congo receptionist was well dressed and trained. We asked if we could pay to sleep in the parking lot and she at first did not understand the request, then called to ask her manager. When we explained further that we did not want to pay $250 for a room, her manager said no, and we stepped onto the lovely clean pavement and had a look around. Across the road from the hotel, a long clay brick wall surround a church and tall oak trees. With now grumpy Luisa waiting with Keelan and Jessica, I crossed the road and entered the church compound, luckily meeting a nun en-route from the church to the clerical barracks. I greeted in Portuguese, explained who we were and that we were driving from Europe to South Africa before asking if we could park on the grounds for the night and leave first thing in the morning. The nun told me that it was not her decision to make, but if we were willing to wait for the head priest to return we could ask him, she showed me where to park behind the tall, white wall within the barracks and I returned to grumpy Luisa with the semi-good news. The only problem was that if the priest said we could not overnight, we would be out on the street after dark with very little diesel in the tank. Luisa remained irritated as I drove the Defender into the Igreja Ieba (church Ieba) grounds, past a crowd of young worshippers and into the barracks where we parked beside the wall and waited for the priest to return. The town had surprised us with its European architecture, clean, orderly streets and calm, safe atmosphere. A band practised on a stage set up on the other side of the barrack wall and we kept ourselves busy tidying the Land Rover and preparing for the evening. The head priest, a friendly portly man, arrived well after dark, driving a white Land Cruiser. I introduced myself, and we chatted a while. Of course, we could stay the evening; the church has an obligation to care for travellers. There was a bathroom which we could use, and we should just ask if we needed anything. The priest helped me to correct a few mistakes which I was making, ruining the Portuguese language with Spanish words and incorrect tenses, a young priest kept himself busy unloading the Land Cruiser and the head priest excused himself, there would be a concert that night, and he had to make preparations. With the worshippers going about their business, we settled in and had a glass of wine before going to sleep, a deep, welcome sleep.

The night was cool, and we awoke early, thanked the priest and made a donation before heading out to the outskirts of town where we were finally able to fill the fuel tank with cheap Angolan diesel. We had a relatively long drive ahead of us. We were heading to Luanda, and we were not in a huge hurry, the manic and stressful days behind us and now only the demanding and challenging tasking of keeping the wheels rolling remained, our eternal struggle if it is was easy too many would be doing it. We made our way down to the coast surprised by how dry and arid coastal Angola is. I had always imagined Angola to be similar to Mozambique in terms of climate and vegetation, and the Caprivi strip (a long finger of Namibia protruding into Botswana to the Zambian border) had been mostly green and lush when we had driven there nine years before. We soon learned that Angola, and southern Angola in particular, is facing the worst drought in decades. Baobabs stood tall and unmolested, but all other vegetation seemed to be decimated by villagers seeking fuel for their cooking fires and, of course, some areas were worse than others. The roads were quiet, and drivers drove fast, often exceeding 120 kph, the fastest speeds we had experienced since Senegal. Driving parallel to the mighty Atlantic Ocean, we made our way down the EN100 and entered Luanda at sunset. The outskirts of the city were unimpressive but industrial at least, the highway wide and unmarked, the lack of lanes leading to a strange movement of traffic which broke away as we headed further into the city, towards the harbour and the Yacht Club which was said to be very welcoming to overlanders. The city streets were quiet and only slightly confusing as we made our way, the glow plug lights flashing and our fuel low. At the Yacht Club gate, we were welcomed by the guard and told that we could park anywhere, we chose to settle in by the shore, near some yachts being repaired in dry dock. The city lights welcomed us as wealthy locals visited the restaurants nearby. We took a while to explore our surroundings and had a simple dinner of french fries and a few cold Cuca beers before going to sleep.

We awoke to a hot morning and introduced ourselves to the Yacht Club staff and handed our passports in to be recorded before Ricardo, the groundskeeper, gave us a quick tour of the facilities, showed us the games room where we could sit and work and the bathrooms which were clean, modern and welcoming. We enjoyed our first shower since Matadi, and it was one of the best showers we had experienced in a very long time. Clean and smelling soapy, we sat down to work in the games room, the kids making use of the gym equipment and us all taking the time to stand in front of the floor to ceiling mirrors, admiring the slim bodies which Western Africa had bestowed upon us gracelessly. We had all lost a lot of weight due to the heat, illness, Malaria and a poor diet. I was reminded of an article I had written a year before:

"Recently I was sharing a cold beverage and stories with a new adventurer friend in Bavaria. Carsten has travelled the world for decades, is wiry, muscular and speaks with the gravelly voice of a man who has rolled his own cigarettes for thirty years. Carsten complained that he struggled to gain weight as he does not like food and has to remind himself to eat. In our image-obsessed society, we tend to regard thin as the holy grail and deride those few lucky souls who complain that they struggle to put on weight (yeah right, whatever, shut up, eat a burger). I was hardly sympathetic to Carstens weight dilemma until he explained to me why he needs to put on weight - he regularly travels to remote parts of this planet. It was then that I remembered my experience in Africa.

Before overlanding saved my life, I was big fat. By big fat I mean 6'5" tall, two cases of beer a week, never missed a meal fat, not Gilbert Grapes mama. But, being big may very well have saved my life when a microscopic little devil attacked.

During an overland journey in Mozambique almost a decade ago, I contracted a viral infection while staying at a coastal lodge run by bitter Zimbabweans, far from a hospital, doctor or pharmacy. I found myself too weak to leave the lodge, and the medicine in our first aid kit proved entirely ineffective. The combination of a head-splitting earache, extreme nausea and diarrhoea rendered me immobile for two weeks, a period during which I survived on custard and pain killers and lost an incredible thirty pounds! It took a month to recover fully, and I believe that a healthy heart and an ample waistline saved my life. The healthy heart is a result of years of surfing, hiking, powerlifting, genetics and a relatively healthy diet of meat and two veg and the ample waistline? Well, South Africa is famous for its excellent food and drink. I believe it is the extra body fat which was the most effective in allowing my body to fight the virus. A luxury which thin Carsten does not enjoy.

Had I been Instagram thin when that virus assaulted my body, I would most certainly have been in a more precarious position. Because I was carrying an extra 40 pounds, my body was able to use that unloved fat as energy to fuel itself while fighting the powerful virus. Without the extra mass, my body would have begun to cannibalise the important stuff, feeding on muscle and vital organs which would have invariably led to kidney failure and, possibly, death. Yes, it is incredibly important to carry a well-stocked first-aid kit which contains antibiotics and specific medicines which you are most likely to need in the countries to which you are travelling. And doing a first aid course before you leave home can only be a good idea. But, as I did, you might find yourself in a situation when your body has to rely on itself to fight illness and heal.

Now, I am not suggesting that you should Chris Farley before heading out onto the road, but it would be a good idea perhaps to pad your body a bit. Remember, you will be losing weight in those first few months on the road, and it is in those months that you will be encountering new bugs, bacteria and diseases like Malaria and possibly the Zika virus, depending on where you will be exploring. It is worth mentioning that during our overland journey across East Africa every member of my family suffered mild to severe gastrointestinal infections and our son Keelan had a high fever every night for months - a condition which we treated with Voltaren suppositories until we eventually found a decent hospital in Malawi.

We all know that the BMI (Body Mass Index) was invented by the diet industry to make you feel short and fat and the only people who really achieve the ideal BMI are movie stars, models and my friend Carsten. So, could a higher end of the scale BMI indeed be an advantage in some extreme situations?

To confirm my theory, I shared this story with a nutritionist and asked for a professional opinion;

" I think your situation was definitely unique. Your trips are much different than most. If you're embarking on an adventure where your food would be in limited supply (climbing Mt. Everest or hiking for months on end), I would highly recommend building a good base of fat before heading out. This is due to excessive calorie burn. An individual can only carry so much food with them at one time while being physically active. The fat itself will fuel the body in the absence of food.

In your case, this (being overweight) was a significant benefit. Contracting such a bug would make it difficult to eat or keep things down. You're absolutely right that the extra weight probably kept you going. Without that, your body would have converted muscle and then organs into fuel to help sustain you. But the body goes to fat first. So having an extra 40 lbs definitely helped. I don't know that I would recommend this approach for driving adventures when food isn't sparse, but if food supplies are limited or unknown, then yes I would. Sunny Brigham, MS, CNS".

May I suggest a few extra slices of pie before you head out into the developing world? An extra ten pounds will provide a buffer and may buy you the few days you need before you can find quality health care.

Many of you may be asking, was the journey worth the risk? Yes, absolutely it was. We had the time of our lives once the health issues were dealt with (have a look at those images!) and learned a lot about travelling in developing nations, working together as a family, taking care of each other and persevering through hardship.

(A final note it is important to read the fine print on your life insurance and death policies before travelling abroad. There are some countries which are excluded from the broad-based policies (mostly West Africa), and there will be no payout to your loved ones if you meet your end in any of the excluded countries)".

All of our extended Southern Hemisphere journeys have to lead to significant weight loss. East Africa, Western Africa and South America all took their toll on us but, it is very important to note, we did not suffer illness in South America, but our diet was healthy, and we drove long distances and often skipped meals. Now, standing in front of the mirror in Angola, we were pleased that we had lost weight but not exactly excited by how we had lost the weight, as every gram had been extracted at a cost. We looked forward to a good steak in Namibia, a cold beer, boerewors and Simba chips. It was only a matter of weeks, and we would drop into Namibia, a full circle around the Atlantic via the Pacific and the Northern Sea. Back to a land where our second language was spoken as a first language by many and where we would be able to measure the change which a decade brings. We were not going to be hanging around in Angola for too long.

The Yacht Club found us busy for a few days, but we needed to get moving, lest we fall into the overlanders trap and find ourselves outstaying our welcome in an expensive city with weeks flowing by. The night before we left, we had a visit from a young British family who had driven an ancient Land Rover across Africa. The Kempson family work and live in Luanda and are very well settled in. We shared a few beers, and some takeaways, Andrew leaving to take the family home and returning to spend some time together before we moved on. There are some people who you meet and have an almost instant affinity with and the Kempsons who would make great travel partners with our friends the Fuchs, from Germany. Andrew gave us some great ideas for travelling in Angola and explained a lot of the ins and outs of living as an ex-pat in a relatively poor oil-rich country. It has its challenges, but some people thrive on challenge, I believe the Kempsons' are those people. All too soon we had to say good night but not after finishing the selection of Angolan beers which Andrew had brought for us to sample and swig.

Angola has an oil-based economy, much like Venezuela and suffers the same economic swings as the oil price yo-yo's every time Israel sneezes or Russia steps out of line. The dollar has an official and a black market rate, which we were sure to take advantage of on a micro level, exchanging and spending less than $1000 during our time there. The ruling, mostly Creole, Angolan elite prosper wildly by taking advantage of the black market rate and the oil economy as do the ruling Chavistas in poor, wealthy Venezuela. The parallels between the two oil-rich countries are difficult to ignore; both have a background in socialism - which makes complete sense, if you wanted to control vast reserves of oil would you not want the oil companies to be owned by your state so that you could funnel billions away from public expenditure and into you and your cronies offshore bank accounts? Angola was a communist country from independence until 1992 when it became inconvenient to be communist. Isn't it funny how ex-communist revolutionaries tend to become billionaires when they come to power? The veteran ANC politicians and freedom fighters once screamed for equality and majority rule, their heads full of the rhetoric of Marxist-Leninism and dream of a classless state, but over 25 years of ruling South Africa, they have all become elitist fat cats with very, very expensive tastes. Angola could be the Switzerland of Africa with Venezuela filling that role in South America.

Here are some Angola statistics courtesy of the BBC:

The third-largest economy in Africa, with a GDP of $121bn in 2013.

China's principal trading partner in Africa, and the USA's second.

It is classed as a "Low Human Development" country, coming 149/187 in the UN's Human Development Index for 2014.

Child and maternal mortality rates are among the highest in the world - about one child in five doesn't survive to the age of five, maternal mortality is 610 per 100,000 live births (UNICEF).

Luanda: Most Expensive City in the World for Expatriates (Mercer Cost of Living Survey, 2014).

$32 billion went missing from Angola's oil accounts between 2007 and 2010 (IMF).

98% of bridges (more than 300), 80% of factories and schools, 60% of hospitals and most of the roads destroyed in the civil war (Economist Intelligence Unit).

63.7% of Angola's population is under 25 years old (Unicef).

Our camp at the Yacht Club is the epicentre of the elite's playground, and we were reminded daily of the income inequality as powerboats and yachts surrounded us. Despite the economic issues, the country is a pleasure to travel overland, particularly compared to her northern neighbours.

We had our second vehicular accident of the journey (the first being the smashed side mirror in Pointe Noir) as we left Luanda on a beautiful, cool and sunny morning. A large American pick up truck merged into our lane beside the Land Rover and did not stop, despite me hooting persistently. The pick up knocked its large chrome side mirror against the side of the camper, backed off and then raced ahead to cut us off, hit the brakes and forced us to stop in the middle of the two-lane road. I jumped out and headed for the drivers' door of the pick-up. An elderly man threw open the door of the pick-up and stood on the chrome rock sliders.

He shouted at me in Portuguese. I shouted back. It was clear who was in the wrong. He mumbled something and inspected the mirror for damage. He glared at me, and I glared back. He mumbled something in Portuguese, and I responded in Afrikaans, we told each other how much we loved each other, how we could not live another day without each other, we spoke words of passion and parted in sweet sorrow. What an arsehole.

We stopped at a Shoprite store on the way out of Luanda but had a problem as we were out of local currency. I told Luisa not to worry about it and Keelan, and I walked around the glass and steel open-plan mall looking for a high-end clothing store or jeweller. In Venezuela, we had learned that the black market resides behinds the doors of retailers selling imported goods. I spotted a large fragrance store, and we approached the ladies working inside, apologised for our terrible Portuguese and asked where we could exchange dollars. They did not hesitate and wrote down the exchange rate, I multiplied that by 100, and they agreed. One of the two ladies took my $100 note and walked out the door, hopefully, to be seen again. Keelan and I had a look at the fragrances and watches and more fragrances and then again at the watches, had a chat about fragrant watches, watched the time go by and kept an eye on the door. Twenty minutes later, the lady returned and handed me 40,000 Kwanza. I offered her a few thousand as a thank you, and she waved me away. By the time we returned to Luisa in the grocery store, she had become quite concerned and was not amused when I pretended to have failed - she knows me by now. Secure in the knowledge that we could pay for our groceries; we bought South African style meat pies and Coca Cola, meat for the braai, vegetables, salad and bread and a large container of water.

Heading south along the EN100, the wind blew, and the land became drier with every hour. The Defender was grinding into fourth gear but cruising well along the dusty, paved roads beside the Atlantic ocean. We stopped to admire the Mirador de la Louna cliffs and have a lunch break of cheese and crackers, breaking the monotony of sardine sandwiches which had become our staple diet. That evening we pulled into a gas station at the entrance to the town Chongoroi, opposite a police station. With the sun low, we asked the security guard if we could park for the night and he told us that it would not be a problem. We settled in for an evening of breakfast for dinner and salad and a Batman movie after watching the world pass by for a while. Just before 10 pm, the computer died (our solar system had not been working as it should) we turned off the lights and settled into bed. A knock on the side of the camper, there stood the security guard, dressed in jeans and a Michael Jackson jacket of red leatherette, with hanging belts and studded shoulders.

"Mwara tam dun wara tun, do lantu dantu pinto mino cama wara pama na". A flat, fast monotone.

"Sorry, I don't understand, please speak Portuguese".

"Nara pam tanda nara wam, pum ta dom do mamparwara tam da nara da".

"Que?".

We had spoken to each other in Portuguese earlier, but now the young man had forgotten how to speak the colonial language, instead standing a meter from the open window, telling me the story of his life, or asking for something, in a language far from my comprehension.

"Mara nam pum a tam wara num tee warata, kape de kapa de korra, korra".

In Portuguese, I apologised for not understanding him and asked if we could speak again in the morning. He went silent, stood there for a minute and eventually left.

At 5 am, there was a knock again on the side of the camper, beside my dreaming head. Knock, knock, knock, knock, knock, knock, knock, knock, knock.

"What!?"

"Mwara tam dun wara tun, do lantu dantu pinto mino cama wara pama na". He picked up where he left off the night before.

"Sorry, I don't understand, please speak Portuguese".

"Nara pam tanda nara wam, pum ta dom mamparwara tam poephol da nara da".

"Que?"

Luisa. "What does he want".

Me. "I have no idea; I think he is nuts. Grab some cash out the wallet".

Luisa, looking bewildered. "Where is the wallet?"

Me. "What do you mean, it should be in the same place we put it every night?"

Keelan. "It's probably under my bed, next to the computers".

Jessica. "Nn gggggg, mmm gggggg". Snoring gently.

Security guard. "Kahana num pahana haka manana pa ka bafana manju ka pana hey".

Me. "What, speak Portuguese please!"

Luisa, on her knees digging under Keelan's elevated bed. "I can't find the bloody wallet!"

Keelan. "It must be there, Ma; we always put it there".

Jessica. "Nn gggggg, mmm gggggg!", snoring loudly.

Me, searching the countertop. "C'mon guys; we put it is the same place every night! Wait, what's this in the sink? Ah, found it. Who the hell put the wallet in the bloody sink?"

Luisa. "Well, you were the last one to use it!"

Me. "No I wasn't, you went to the store across the road!"

Luisa. "Agh, whatever. How much are you going to give him?"

Me. "Smallest note is 1000".

Luisa. "What!? Are you mad?"

Me. "It's only three bucks!"

Security guard. "Mampara manana wamwama mampara we".

Keelan. "Just get rid of him please!"

I hand the 1,000 Kwanza note out the window, and the security guard takes it quickly.

Me, in Portuguese. "Ok, thank you very much, goodbye".

He. "Obrigado, boa viagem". (Thank you, good travels) !

Before we had a chance to leave the King of Pop returned to replay the entire fiasco, but we were not in the mood for his moon dance and hit the road with the sun rising and after topping up the tank and the jerry cans; as we had heard fuel becomes scarce near the Namibian border. It was great to get an early start, and we drove at a serene pace towards Lubango and the Serra da Leba, the beautiful mountain range outside the city. We had planned to free camp near the Serra da Lebba summit but had recently heard of an overlander, who had been attacked as he had camped there. Two men armed with blades approached the young German, who was travelling alone and tied him up before ransacking the vehicle. The robbery took a few hours, but eventually, the victim was released. He reported the assault to the police, but it was apparent that he should not hope for any swift justice.

The drive up the Serra da Lebba pass was quite beautiful. We had been looking forward to taking photos of the pass and the view but were disappointed to find the sky grey with dust and smoke, and the view from the summit obscured. As we parked to explore the summit, two Mumuhuila (Mwila, Mumuila) girls approached us, asking for money. They were bare-chested with red oncula paste caked into their hair and thick rings of mud and grass around their necks, accompanied by colourful necklaces and bright print skirts. The red mud plaits which resemble large dreadlocks are called nontombi and have a precise meaning as does the jewellery which the woman wear. There are a number of tribes associated with the Mumuhuila, each having their own specific variant of a similar culture and, most importantly, most reject the modern lifestyle and cling to their ancient culture. The Mumuhuila are a Bantu people who are believed to have migrated south from the Congo in the 17th century and established their home near Lubango, which was to be a predominately European populated city during Portuguese rule, as the Mumuhuila refused to live in the city, choosing instead to pursue their hunter, gatherer lifestyle. We had seen these proud people first as we had driven towards the city, and we found them quite fascinating. Luisa gave them some cans of food and some cash, and in exchange, they posed for some photographs with grey stone and a grey sky as a background. We had been disappointed to have met young Mumuhuila boys begging outside a supermarket in Lubango (Luisa never misses an opportunity to wander aisles of produce, her hunter-gatherer instincts still quite alive and kicking). We left the girls and walked/hiked around the summit viewing area before returning to the Land Rover and cruising back down the mountain pass and heading south towards Namibia.

We realised that we were re-entering the world of off-road overlanding as we passed many well equipped off-road vehicles. South Western Africa is similar to Australia in many ways, as the great outdoors is the destination primarily. To overland here is to drive far into the desert, far from society and civilisation and into the old world, where tracks are simple, risks are high as is the reward. We had reached the point that we were transiting, as that is the primary philosophy of overlanding Western Africa, the challenge is to make it through each country, to negotiate the bureaucracy and survive the perils. Angola and Namibia are another world and demand a different concept of overland travel; it is in these countries that a person can seek a unique experience and get very far from the beaten track, similar to the Australian Outback experience, I assume (as we have yet to explore Australia). The hinterland of Angola and Namibia demands preparation and resourcefulness, toughness and a vehicle which is mechanically sound and ready to take on the great wilderness. Our vehicle was limping. The poor Land Rover had worked so hard over the last few years and months, and we were suffering problems with the electrical system (headlights and hazard lights fusing constantly, illuminating glow plug lights, an occasional misfire, occasional non-starting, etc.) the gearbox was grinding and getting worse, we suffered a leaking main fuel tank, our solar system had failed, and the fan bearing needed replacing. We worked often to replace and repair the Land Rover and keep her moving predictably forward, but we had a horrible idea that there would be some serious work required in the near future. Unfortunately, the problems we were experiencing might ruin the plans which we had made to explore some of the most challenging and remote regions of Angola and Namibia. There was a chance that we may be able to nurse the old Defender deep into the desert, but we would need her to work hard and return us to safety. I needed to make a call.

We drove a quiet road from Lubango to Xangongo, the landscape dry and ancient, thin cattle hoofing wet but nearly empty water holes, large trees providing precious shade above desert scrub. At Xangongo, we left the main road and headed into the town, chasing a rumour of a free camp beneath giant baobab trees. We stopped, parked beside a small store on a quiet boulevard. Three beautiful girls approached the store dressed in traditional Mumuhuila skirts and necklaces but without the red clay dreadlocks and mud neck tyres. They looked nervous and shy, conspicuous of their bare breasts and the unwanted attention of the group of young men in tracksuits who loitered outside the store, leering. One of the larger boys herded the girls towards the Land Rover, and it was apparent that these girls were not traditional Mumuhuila, their faces and skin clean, moist and lighter than those of a people who spent all day under the sun. Perhaps they were en-route to a ceremony or a celebration. I greeted the girls but ignored the leering boy behind them; I kept eye contact with them, asking if they were well. Treating the girls with respect helped them to regain their confidence and dignity, and they shirked the bully behind them and broke small, polite smiles. Inside the store, I found eggs, bread, cold drinks and some snacks, enough to tide us over until the crossing into Namibia the next day.

Luisa steered us down a bumpy dirt road which led south from the town and the boulevard; we passed houses and a dry dirt football field, a farmstead or two, a field full of angular steel and onto a deep sand track between large hedges. We emerged from the hedges into a large, flat expanse where gigantic baobabs stood like ancient parched giants, waiting for relief. Baobabs are synonymous with Africa, and we had seen these giants across both the East and West Coasts of Africa. Only now, the baobabs were squat and wide, very wide and very tall. Closer to the tropics the baobabs have tall, moist, smooth and relatively slender trunks with the "upside-down" root branches reaching to embrace the sky. The desert baobab does not have the luxury of daily rain, and while gigantic, they are fragile. The baobab tree is much like the human body, as it is composed of 70% water and a long sustained drought can be fatal.

There are nine species of baobab, and they are found in Africa, Madagascar and Australia. Unfortunately, many baobabs have died in Southern Africa over the last twenty years, fatalities which scientists attribute to global warming. We were often surprised to find the baobab the only tree left standing in many communities where homes are heated and food cooked with coal or wood, perhaps the wood does not burn well unless left to dry for half a decade. The baobab tree is known as the tree of life, with good reason. It can provide shelter, clothing, food, and water for the animal and human inhabitants of the African Savannah regions. The cork-like bark and huge stem are fire resistant and are used for making cloth and rope.

Our shelter that evening was a baobab 25m tall with a 6m diameter. The tree had served the community for hundreds of years, and there were signs of the everyday life which the shade of a large tree attracts. Dung beetles rolled the dung of goats who had taken a break in the shade, a makeshift bench had been made by a shepherd, the folds of the trunk housed insects and colonies and careless travellers had carved their names into the ancient bark. We made a small fire and watched the night come to life, bats swooping, the moon and stars coming into focus as the sunset. We might have had a cold beer or two. Beer is my lubricant.

"Overlander Lubricant

It has been a long, hot and difficult day. The rig has been behaving badly, the last of twenty checkpoints involved a locked and loaded Kalashnikov, your convoy partner has been very hard work, and there is a difficult multi-day remote mountain pass ahead. It is at times like these that all an overlander needs is a campfire, Santos and Johnny's Sleep Walk on repeat and an ice-cold, refreshing beer.

Beer is to this overlander what engine oil is to his Land Rover. Yes, I know, beer is the working man's beverage, but that is exactly what I am and some days on the road are hard work! Anyone who reads my books will know that often stories of life on the road end with the sentence, "We pulled into camp, made a campfire and enjoyed a cold beer". I will not apologise, that is the reality. Our journey around the globe has in some ways been a grand brewery tour as we have savoured brews from Cape Town to Kilimanjaro, Ushuaia to Bogota, Panama to Alaska, Florida to the United Kingdom, France to Turkey, Portugal to Namibia. Some days we will have a cold brew with dinner or a few ales around the campfire or a rip-roaring bonfire hootenanny with overlander friends in a remote paradise. Cold, delicious, refreshing, liberating and usually cheap, beer is globally as ubiquitous as Coca Cola (except in many Muslim countries), and you can usually find a six-pack of the local brew in a small store days away from civilisation, thankfully. Everyone loves beer.

Beer in moderation is good for you, good for your heart and is a source of nutrition. While on the road we cook soups, stews and soften meat with beer, we cook chicken on the fire upright with a can of beer nestled between the ribs. Historically we collectively fed our children beer to help them grow big and strong (it worked) and beer has been central to our culture since we were Neolithic. It is safe to say that the golden brew has played a significant role in our history as a species and is a cornerstone of our civilisation, some archaeologists suggest that the urge for alcoholic beverages is what motivated humans beings to focus on agriculture as opposed to being nomadic hunter/gatherers. And if it was good enough for Cleopatra, Alexander the Great and the Vikings then, bloody hell, it's good enough for us!

Beer travels well. A case of large cans can usually be found in our camper; we often slip four cans into the fridge before hitting the road in the morning knowing that they may be called upon at sundown to provide relaxing relief after sun, sweat, dust and adventure. Is there anything more rewarding than grilling some meat over a fire, your best friend at your side and a cold brew to share? No, for us, there is not. A good evening will end with a shot of whisky, and a shot of coffee as the fire turns to coals, and the world's problems have been solved. Sometimes the stress of the day, the problems of the future and the doubt burning in your chest can be extinguished with a Yuengling lager, or a Helltown Hefeweizen or a dripping Quilmes. When you forget to focus on the problem you might find a creative solution, sometimes a bit of Dutch courage makes the journey easier, sometimes the stars shine brighter, the fire burns warmer and the conversation flows better when you are relaxed. The trick is not to overindulge, drunk is never a good look (ask the Alexander as mentioned earlier the Great), and you become a liability to yourself and others when you are not in control or able to react to situations.

Here are some tips gleaned from years from travelling with liquid friends:

- Pack cans rather than bottles, they pack easier and are less prone to breakage but, be sure to store the cans where they cannot be punctured, They are not as robust as they used to be,
- It is advisable to wash the can before drinking if you want to avoid a bad belly in developing countries,

- The less ingredients, the purer the beer and the better it is for you. Coors Light is not a great beer, Perlenbacher is as it is made to the Reinheitsgebot, the German purity laws. According to the Reinheitsgebot beer should only be made with four ingredients, namely barley, hops, water and yeast. Beers containing rice and corn syrup are a poor substitute for the real thing (but if you have no other option, what can a man do?)
- Microbreweries are springing up everywhere, perhaps carry a Growler and make brewery tours part of the itinerary,
- Snack on olives, gherkins, nuts and jalapenos while enjoying a day time brew,
- In many countries drinking in public is frowned upon or even illegal, be sure not to run foul of the law,
- A fold-up cooler bag helps to keep the beer cold if you do not have a fridge or it is full of pesky food, ice is usually available from gas stations in warmer countries around the world,
- If you are trying to keep the weight off drink less beers with a higher alcohol content,
- A shandy (beer mixed with Sprite or lemonade) quenches a thirst like nothing on earth, besides water of course,
- Plastic cups ruin beer; you can always find space in the rig for a well-packed beer mug or glass,
- Never, ever leave home without a beer koozie or two,
- Don't drink and drive, clean up after yourself, keep the music level down, know when to stop drinking and always have a spare beer in case a friend pops around".

The nights were becoming colder as we approached Namibia and the full extent of the mild Southern Hemisphere winter. And what a relief it was to be cool, even cold, after all those months of exhausting heat, those many long nights of sweating and struggling to sleep as mosquitoes buzzed around the Land Rover trying to find a way in, the mosquito netting stifling whatever breeze we may have enjoyed. Our bodies had absorbed so much heat over those long months, that it took a few weeks for us to feel cold enough to pull on socks and jackets, instead of enjoying the feeling of the skin cool to the touch, of a body dry without the drench of sweat, bodies clean without a layer of red dust clinging to moist skin. Luisa always loved the heat, 30c was a perfect temperature for her, but she had lost her love for the constant, oppressive heat. At least when you are cold, you are able to dress warmly and enjoy the comfort of blankets and warm boots and jackets. Heat can be as inescapable as extreme cold, particularly when you live outside in the elements.

Luisa took photographs of the stars, while I studied the flames of the fire, mesmerised, peaceful, relieved and alone. The next day we would be back in familiar territory, as close to "home" as we had been for a very, very long time. Staring at the fire, cold brew in hand, I thought about the last year, of the sacrifices which we had made, the adventures we had, the dangers we had faced and the people we had met. We had done so well to get this far south, and we had achieved what few families had, with limited resources. Our children were no longer children; they had left Southern Africa as children and were returning as young adults. We had all changed so much; we had grown and evolved; we would soon come face to face with our former selves.

That morning we awoke to the bleats of goat and the laughter of young children. While we prepared for the day, two young ladies walked past the Land Rover and disappeared into the bush for a few moments and reappeared with wet faces and containers full of water; there must have been a well; well hidden. We chatted to them for a while before taking a walk around the enormous baobabs which surrounded us. We did not need to fill our water tanks as we had made a habit of filling the jerry cans and filling the Lifesaver water filter jerry can at every opportunity and were well stocked. The Lifesaver jerry had become an indispensable part of our journey and had liberated us from the reliance on bottled water. That morning we decanted a few litres, washed our heads and faces, brushed our teeth and packed up after a quick breakfast of fruit and yoghurt. The kids joked and posed for photographs beside the baobab, hanging onto each other, in front of the Land Rover, smiling and laughing and happy. The pressure was off, and we were all feeling happier and healthier than we had been in quite a while, at least since Morocco.

We drove back towards the town, eager to rejoin the main road and enter Namibia. As we passed a field of shrubs Keelan, who was sitting upfront with me, spotted an angular wreck, two, three, four, five angular wrecks. "Dad, those are tanks, stop!". Keelan has been fascinated by aeroplanes and tanks and military vehicles in general since he was a boy playing Call of Duty and Medal of Honor and other military "video" games. It is one of the positives of his career as a gamer; the other is that he has become part of a community of like-minded souls spread across the globe. He knows more about tanks and aircraft than I will ever know about Land Rovers and he has been known to give lectures about Soviet and German capabilities during World War Two, the evolution of fighter jets and the origins and evolution of the battle tank. He will study anything with tracks and is an amateur expert in the field of tracked vehicle suspension. And his lectures are not just the ramblings of an enthusiast - he researches the individual engineers and designers who have contributed most to the field and understands how their contributions gave birth to the modern machinery employed by the modern military. Unfortunately, Angola has yet to open their military museum, and we were lucky to find a field of history rusting slowly in the dry desert air.

We hopped out of the Land Rover and crossed the dusty, corrugated road to study the wreckage of a war in which we had a personal connection. I thought that the wrecks might have been South African, but Keelan knew better. "Dad, I think these are Soviet, I am pretty sure of it. Wow, Dad, this is an APC, and this is an amphibious tank, and this is a half-track. Oh. My. God!".

After a bit of research, we discovered that the disabled wrecks were Soviet BTR 152 Half Tracks, BTR 60 APC or Infantry Fighting Vehicle and PT 76 Amphibious Light Tanks. There were about twenty vehicles in total, strewn across the field most bearing deep, structurally destructive cuts from a blow torch. The mystery is whether the Soviet vehicles were disabled by the Angolans, South West Africans or Soviets during or after the war. There had been an assault on Xangongo by the South African Defense Force (SADF) in 1981, as there were SWAPO (PLAN) training and logistics bases there. The SADF had scored a decisive blow to their enemies in the attack and suffered ten casualties vs 1000 enemy KIA, but these figures are contested.

We clambered over tons of heavy of rust coloured steel which were slowly becoming one with the earth, trees growing defiantly through gun turrets, the wind and sand doing their best to absorb man's machinery of death. This was a graveyard filled with the memory; ghosts of young men sent to fight and risk death in a Cold War conflict, most of them could not have understood. I had not understood the conflict as a teenager, and it was always on my mind as my final years of high school approached. Chances were excellent that my friends and I would have been conscripted, trained and sent to fight at the border, young dumb and full of silly ideas. The South Africans who did fight in this conflict suffered few casualties, but there were many who returned Bos Befok ("Bush Fucked"), suffering from PTSD and there were those few who loved the conflict. I had a school mate, a kid who was always oddly fascinated with death, who returned from the Namibia/Angola border (he had dropped out of school at the age of 18 to join the military) even stranger than when he had left. Steven, tall and thirsty for Brandy and Coca-Cola, chatted to me one evening at a house party at a friends house on Earls Avenue, Linden, West of Johannesburg. It was the early 90's, and Steven was on leave for a few weeks from the border, where the South Africans were still trying to their best to keep militants out of Namibia. We chatted about Steven's new car, the friends we had in common and his girlfriend. Steven pulled a small photo album out of his pocket and flipped through - the new car, his girlfriend sitting on the car, his girlfriend in the passenger seat, he and his buddies in uniform, a dead man hanging from a fence, another dead man in the foetal position dressed in blue jeans and a dirty black jacket lying in a pool of blood, his dog, a plate of grilled meat, he and his assault rifle, two dead men lying in the dirt stripped almost naked. Steven had permission to carry a concealed firearm, he lifted his shirt and showed me the polished blue-black metal glinting in a waistband holster. Steven smiled a crooked smile and had another long sip of his Brandy and Coke, lit a cigarette and started chatting about his girlfriend again. Another friend returned from the border traumatised by the things he had seen, done and experienced, but the solution was hardly ever therapy, rather self-medication. In the late Nineties, we lived on a farm owned by the family of a man who was in every way a regular guy, but he suffered from nightmares and addiction; he constantly drank to deal with his memories. I always regretted not learning the skills and discipline of a soldier, but I am glad that I did not have to go to war, that I did not have to kill and watch my friends die.

The bush war was low intensity, and South Africa never declared war on Angola, the statistics are relatively unimpressive when compared with similar cold war conflicts, i.e. the Vietnam War. During the 23-year border war, approximately 2,500 South African soldiers died compared to more than 16,000 Namibian and Cuban combatants casualties. By comparison, more than 58,000 Americans lost their lives in Vietnam while killing short of a million enemy, with the help of their allies and over a 19 year period. On paper, the Americans and South Africans both won their respective wars against communist imperialism and expansionism but, while the USA eventually rose triumphant from the Cold War, it was the success of the West and the crumbling of the Soviet Union which led directly to the downfall of the Apartheid Government and White political domination in South Africa and South-West Africa. The Central and Eastern European revolutions of 1989, culminated in the fall of the Berlin Wall on the 9th November 1989 and Namibia held democratic election between the 9th and 11th November of that same year. Negotiations which led to the first universally democratic elections in South Africa, began in 1990 after the release of Nelson Mandela on the 11th February, after 27 years in prison. It is obvious to me that had the Soviet Union not fallen, and until the end of the Cold War, South Africa would have retained reticent support from the West; Apartheid would have continued, and South-West Africa would most likely have remained under South African control. SWAPO (and the PLAN) was founded with the aim of attaining the independence of Namibia and thus is part of the African Nationalist movement. Pre-independence SWAPO harboured a socialist Marxist-Leninist ideology, which was abandoned when independence was achieved, SWAPO became the ruling party and adopted a capitalist ideology. The African National Congress (ANC) followed suit in South Africa. Communism and specifically communist support was convenient for liberation movements in Africa, but ultimately, the global experiment was not sustainable and was soon cast aside by liberation movements. In 1990 the Angolan ruling party, the MPLA, abandoned it's Marxist ideology and declared social democracy to be its new platform. Unfortunately, the Angolan Civil War continued until 2002 when UNITA's, Jonas Savimbi was eventually killed in a government strike, and a cease-fire declared. The war had taken a massive toll on Angola, and the country struggled to recover from destroyed infrastructure, internally displaced persons, famine, drought, unemployment, and an exodus from rural areas. It is estimated that militant forces had laid 15 million landmines until 2002. Since 2018, 1,100 people have been killed by landmines and abandoned ordinance, and it is wise not to stray far from the beaten track.

The ghosts of the conflict haunted me, as Keelan searched the Soviet wreckage for clues and explained to me how the crew would have operated the machinery and guns. He was beaming with enthusiasm, clambering from one vehicle to another. We left eventually, to the girls' relief, and rejoined the road to the border; passing thin, thirsty livestock and villagers, empty watering holes and dry brush. We were driving the EN120 road and shortly before Ondjiva, Keelan spotted something interesting next to the road. It was a T54 Medium/Main Battle Tank! The tank squatted disabled beside the road, one track lying limp in the dirt, the barrel at a 45-degree angle aiming at long-gone enemies in the sky. The round turret bore white graffiti, "Brigadeiro 29, 09, 015 JP", which referred either to a delicious Brazilian confection or a specific brigade commander, which is more likely. Keelan wasted no time climbing into the old tank and found that the machine gun turret still rotated smoothly. It was not apparent whether the tank had been disabled on purpose either by the South African or by retreating troops or if it had merely broken down, perhaps it had hit a mine, hence the one failed track. Keelan would have lost his mind if there had been a hole blasted in the side. There was something nostalgic about the old tank lying there, waiting for a thousand years to reduce it to nothing, perhaps I was reminded of the footage from the border war that I had seen as a youngster, perhaps I was reminded of stories told by veterans. I had read many books about the war and had seen many photographs of the destruction; it was surreal to be standing on one of the imported casualties, bringing to reality the television footage from my youth. I had dressed in military fatigues until I realised that I was an outsider in my own country and always would be, but I never lost that fascination with the military and that interest had passed down to my son, who sat astride the 20-foot barrel and grinned, he had been waiting for this day for a long time.

In Ondjiva, we traded dollars with a very large and friendly man and filled the fuel tanks with cheap Angolan fuel before heading to the Namibian border, excited!

GRAEME BELL

NAMIBIA

Namibia derives its name from the Namib desert, one of the oldest deserts in the world. Namibia is the second least densely populated country in the world and the driest country in Sub-Saharan Africa. Namibia is bordered by South Africa, Zambia, Angola and Botswana with less than 200 metres of the Zambezi River dividing Zimbabwe and Namibia.

 Namibia uses the Namibian Dollar as well as the South African Rand and is pegged 1:1 to the Rand
10 Namibian Dollar (NAD) = EU0.57/USD0.66

 Most European and Southern African citizens will receive a 90-day visa on arrival. Other nationalities must apply at their local Namibian Consulate. The visa fee will be an approximate EU70

 Unleaded = EU0.85/USD0.90 per litre
Diesel = EU0.82/USD0.90 per litre

 MTC Namibia
TN Mobile

 Christianity is the majority religious group with Catholic, Protestant, Methodist along with several other denominations. Germany colonised the country until after WW1

 The local road tax fund covers you for your duration in Namibia

 Ambulance = 21-1111

 Passport with visa (if a visa is required)
Vehicle title papers
Drivers Licence

The official languages are English and Afrikaans

Namibia has some excellent seafood restaurants along the coast and several game lodges where wild meat can be hunted for and prepared. Supermarkets are generally reasonably priced while stocking excellent, predominantly South African produce

Deadvlei and Sossusvlei - Salt and clay pan with its dead marsh
Dune 7 - the highest dune in Namibia at over 383 metres
Fish River Canyon - the largest canyon in Africa
Meet the Himba People
Spitzkoppe - a group of granite peaks standing at 1728 metres tall
Skeleton Coast - 500km long coastal stretch
Kolmanskop Ghost Town - a ghost town in the Namib Desert
Etosha National Park
Messum Crater - a 130 million-year-old crater

Winter - June to September - Low of 6C/43F with a high of 18C/64F
Summer - December to March - Low of 20C/68F with a high of 35C/95F

Etosha National Park, "place of emptiness, is one of the largest parks in the world.
Beer in Namibia is made in accordance with The Reinheitsgebot, the 1516 German purity law and the oldest law in the world that's still in force.
The San peoples or Bushmen are the world's oldest surviving hunter-gatherers and believed to be the most genetically diverse group of people. Their knowledge of the plant species and animal tracks are what makes them great foragers and hunters.
The Hoba meteorite is the world's biggest known meteorite weighing over 60 tonnes.
Namibia is the first country ever to incorporate environmental protection into its constitution

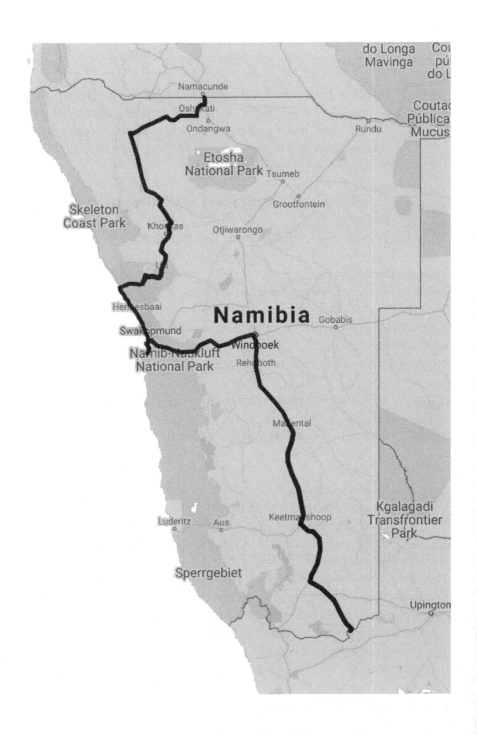

18

Namibia, Almost Home

The wind blew pale dust across the road as we approached the border and a sign which read "You are entering Namibia, drive safely, keep left", and another which read, "Welcome to Oshikango Border Post". It did not take long to stamp out of Angola, but it took a while to stamp into Namibia. The immigration official, a bored, bejewelled and grumpy woman, issued the kids and me with three-month visas but Luisa had written two weeks on her immigration form and was granted only two weeks. I sent her back to the official to ask for the full three months, the official complained and berated Luisa for five minutes, Luisa struggled to bite her tongue while I fumed quietly. We were expecting, for some reason, a warm welcome, but the chubby woman was saying that we had to leave Namibia, return to Angola and re-enter Namibia in order for the visa to be reissued. We appealed to her and apologised for making a mistake and only once we had bent back far enough for our heads to touch our heels, did the official relent begrudgingly and reissue the visa. That put a damper on our celebrations. We left the border and drove into Namibia, irritated instead of relieved or excited.

Soon enough, we began to relax as Luisa searched for a treat for us all. In the Maroela Mall in Oshakati, there was a branch of the South African Spur Restaurant chain which we had eaten at often many years before. We did not tell the kids where we were going, and their eyes lit up like Christmas morning when they saw the sign for the Silver Lake Spur. We parked the Land Rover and entered the restaurant, Keelan was going to have a kilogram of ribs, Luisa would devour a milkshake and study the menu for an hour, I had my heart set on a bacon, cheese and guacamole burger and Jessica was torn between the macaroni and cheese or a burger. Eventually, we all ordered milkshakes and our meal of choice and tucked into the large servings with relish, enjoying flavours which we had not experienced for so many years. It was like eating in a time capsule; the decor was as it had been, the menu almost unchanged, the patrons large bellied and casually boisterous. Full and satisfied, we visited the Shoprite supermarket and stocked up on all the South African food, which we had not found in Nigeria or Ghana. With the sun setting, I paid the car guard a $20 Namibian tip and asked him if we could park around the corner and spend the night (the Namibian dollar is pegged to the South African Rand, and it is not uncommon to pay with Rands and receive Namibian dollars as change, or vice versa, a remnant of South African occupation). He showed us into the service area of the mall and told us that we could park there if we left early in the morning. We had no problem with that and moved the Land Rover through the large security gates and parked beside the service entrance and settled in with full bellies and heavy eyelids.

This was the second time that we had travelled to northern Namibia, the first at the end of the Cape Town to Kilimanjaro journey and we had driven from Zambia across the Caprivi Strip. Namibia is utterly peaceful; there is a tranquillity in the dry air, and life seems to flow one day into another without drama. The country is half the size of Alaska and one and a half times the size of France but has a population of just over 2,500,000, that is just three people per square kilometre as opposed to 122 people per square kilometre in France. The roads are long, straight and empty of traffic, the towns are quiet, rural and laid back and it is not uncommon to see farmers and Herero people going about their business. The Herero suffered greatly under German colonisation, as colonists clashed with the tribes of Namibia over land and cattle, the Europeans employing superior firepower and tactics to defeat any resistance and establish dominance. Despite the conflict with the Germans, the Herero adopted European missionary style dress, and the woman are particularly noticeable dressed in colourful floor-length dresses with puffy sleeves, locally known as ohorokova, and horizontal horned headdress known as otjikaiva. Generally, it is the older women who dress in this style on a daily basis, while younger women will dress up only for special occasions. The Herero are a Bantu people who migrated across from East Africa in the 17th and 18th century and settled in Namibia where they now make up 7% of the population. They live in a part of the world in which only the toughest can survive, water is rare, temperatures can soar and drop drastically in a single day and wildlife remains wild not too far from the built-up areas. To the east is the Kalahari desert and the Okavango Swamps, to the west the Kaokaveld and Skeleton Coast and to the SouthSouth the famous Etosha National Park. We headed west in the direction of Opuwo hoping to find a place to camp for a few days and decide the route, there is an infamous pass in the north-west known as Van Zyl's pass and we were going to do some research and evaluate whether we should attempt the difficult pass. Luisa found a campsite called Omakange, and we drove there along arrow-straight roads verged by white sand and stone, fences and bush. The road signs advised that the speed limit was 100 kph and warned us of buck and elephants, but we saw only ostrich and donkeys that day. The camp was neat and basic with a large and simple ablution block, plans for a swimming pool and a bar. We parked the Land Rover in the shade of a tree and set up camp close to a braai area. While I set up the camping chairs and chopped wood, Keelan connected our extension cable to the electrical grid, and Luisa tidied the camper and made the beds. We then enjoyed hot showers and fresh clothing. I sat in the shade of a kiaat tree, studied my National Geographic Adventure Atlas and waited for the sun to set before I could crack a cold beer and start the fire. The maps showed that we were not too far from the kick-off point to the circular route of the Kunene Region and Kaokoveld, we had the fuel capacity to do the entire route without problems, and we could carry enough water and food. Logistically we would have no problems doing the route, and it would, without doubt, be a highlight of the Western Africa route, as we would have the opportunity to see wild animals in their natural habitat and to interact with the Himba people, red mud-caked and semi-nomadic. It would be an excellent opportunity to get photographs and videos of one of the most secluded areas in Africa and to see what few have seen before independently. We had only one concern - the Defender was still giving us problems, our electrical gremlins had grown more wicked, and the gearbox was playing up more than often, now that we were on the open road driving at highway speeds. Luisa joined me as the fire crackled and sparks rose into the purple sky. What should we do? If we suffered a breakdown in the middle of the Namibian bush, we would have a tough time recovering ourselves, and the guide books recommended that the trail was long and difficult and it is recommended that those doing so should have vehicles in excellent mechanical condition and should travel in convoy, if possible. The solution was to try and find the Gremlin and kill him, simple, no? The gearbox worked fine in lower gears and gave no problems at all in low range; I was confident that the box itself would not implode and leave us stranded. It was decided that we would work on the Landy the next day and see if we could find the Gremlin, we had not been able to find him before, and we were worried that there might be a few Gremlins. With the decision made to delay a final decision on the route, we relaxed and grilled a few excellent steaks and thin boerewors, washed down with Windhoek Lager and a bottle of fine South African red wine for Luisa. We chatted about how relieved we were to have made it to Namibia and discussed the route SouthSouth. We had travelled across Namibia ten years before, and we had loved it, but there were signs that the country was a lot more expensive than it had been before and our research had found that we could pay up to R600 per night to camp, the equivalent of USD 40 in May 2019. That was beyond our budget. We could free camp, but then we would have to head far off the beaten track into areas where wild camping was allowed. These were good problems to have. I suggested that we spend the next two months exploring Namibia, but Luisa told me that I was crazy, that we were getting low on funds, we had to get some work done, publish articles and finish the Europe Overland book. Besides, she wanted to see her family and our friends; it had been more than five years since she had seen them and they would not be happy if she waited another few months to visit them. And, didn't I want to get back to Cape Town and explore the places which we had loved and had not been to for so long? She had a point.

The next morning we awoke and had a hot shower before getting all the tools out, removing the bonnet and front seats and spent the next few hours hunting the elusive Gremlin. We removed the headlights and followed the wiring back across the loom, we removed all the electrical tape from the visible loom in the engine bay and inspected each wire as best we could, we traced the loom back over the bell housing and along the side of the gearbox and over to the ECU under the seat where each fuse and wire was inspected and checked with a multi-meter. The headlights seemed to fail whenever we hit a bump, the indicators worked intermittently, and the "hazards" emergency lights sometimes failed independently and sometimes along with the indicators. Together Luisa and I traced the loom through the chassis to the rear lights and inspected each wire, I crawled under the Land Rover and checked all of the earth points, removing, cleaning and tightening each earth. We ran the Land Rover with the Nanocom connected to the ECU and searched for faults, after removing and replacing both batteries. It took us most of the day, and there were a million little jobs done including replacing the gearbox oil, topping up the engine and transfer box oils and checking all the fluids and filters. Dusty and dirty, we took the Land Rover for a test drive, and to our dismay, the gearbox was still grinding into fifth, and the Gremlin was still alive and well, toying with the electrics. To say that we were frustrated was an understatement!

That night I made another a campfire, and we sat down to discuss our options. While the electrical problems were mostly inconvenient, there was a good chance that the situation could worsen and while the gearbox was fine in most gears, that too could change. Would it be responsible to head out into the wild knowing that we had these problems? Probably not. But, the problem remained that we really wanted to go out and explore the area, to experience great solitude in beautiful places, to listen to the wind blow and find wild animals in their natural habitat. Perhaps there was another option? Perhaps we should continue to head south and look for opportunities to explore areas which were less extreme but nonetheless rewarding? We would have to see how the Land Rover performed over the next few days, but the decision was made to skip the Van Zyl's pass and the Kunene Region. One day we will return and explore the area.

Luisa sat in the cool darkness and searched the iOverlander app for the next stop. There was a camp called Oppie Koppie (On the Hill) which was close to the Etosha National Park gate and which, apparently, offered free camping to foreign vehicles. We were not sure if this included South Africans, but the reviews were good enough that we decided that it would be a bad idea not to at least head there and see for ourselves. The next morning we paid the friendly camp owner and packed the Land Rover before driving to the gas station a few hundred meters down the road; which we had walked to the day before to buy some cold drinks and fresh bread, the chubby Afrikaans owners wife friendly and helpful until we had to return a cellular SIM card. She then turned sour. We topped up the diesel tank and hit the road, signs warning of elephant and kudu, the sky blue, the sandy verge white and bright. It was not a long drive, and by early afternoon we arrived at the small town of Kamanjab, where we were greeted by a Spar supermarket, a gas station, Himba women selling trinkets and local labourers surrounded by bustling tourists, tour group leaders and game viewing vehicles. Kamanjab is located close to the southwestern gate of the world-famous Etosha National Park, the entrance is known as the Galton gate which you may unfortunately only use if you have a booking at one of the ever full western Etosha campsites. We don't usually know where we will be a week in advance, which makes bookings difficult indeed. We can be very organised and disciplined when we need to be but a camp booking a month in advance, while we were toiling across Nigeria would have been ambitious indeed. While driving to Kamanjab, the Landy had been playing up again, and we made the decision that we would get down to South Africa at a gentle but determined pace while making a detour through the desert to the coast. Besides, it was the holiday season and Etosha was fully booked and full of local and foreign tourists, we agreed that we would do our best to return to Namibia once we had repaired the Land Rover in Cape Town. We had no real plan after we returned to South Africa, but we all knew that a trip to Namibia is never wasted.

With a fridge full of cold drinks and braaivleis (meat for the BBQ), we drove through the little dusty village and to the large gates of the Oppi Koppi Lodge. We parked the Land Rover beside a row of white 4x4's and entered the reception/bar/restaurant area to be greeted by the most beautiful bar that we had seen in many years. Polished glasses hung from a thatched circular "Lapa", above a solid wooden bar which invited you to sit and soak in a cold beer with cheerful Afrikaans music floating out of large speakers. Rugby flags adorned the walls, and a thousand Jagermeister ornamental bottles spoke of many nights of laughter and revelry, enjoyed by locals and international tourists. We were welcomed by well trained and friendly staff, who informed us that as international overlanders we were welcome to camp for free for a few nights and encouraged to buy a meal or a few beers at the bar. Music to our ears. The road to the campsite snaked past large, immaculate cottages and we arrived at the camp, astonished to find an immaculate camp. Each campsite has its own covered area with a sink, picnic table, light, electricity and braai. Beside the camp, a flock of ostrich stomped and pecked at the ground and a short walk from the campsite we found large, clean ablutions with hot showers. After the "camps" of Western Africa, this campsite was, without doubt, Five Stars and the kind of place where we could happily find ourselves "stuck" for a few weeks. Aside from a rotund South African family camped at the opposite end of the large camp area, we had the place to ourselves and settled in happily. As dusk approached, we walked down to the bar and had a few large, ice-cold Windhoek beers served in frosty, chilled glasses. The slender, pretty barmaids knew their jobs well, and they were fiendishly efficient - as you sipped your last of the refreshing golden refreshment, they would approach, smiling, another ice-cold beer and another frosty clean glass in hand. Yes, please! At the centre of the bar stood a Jaegermeester dispenser and I convinced Luisa that we should at least have one shot, which is served ice cold and is known to locals as the Namibian Cabernet. OK, fine, just one. Well, one became three and day became night, and our voices rose with laughter. An elderly Australian touring Namibia in a rental VW Polo sedan struck up a conversation with Keelan, a group of young women ordered glasses of house wine, a farmer in a two-tone farmers shirt asked for another double brandy and coke, and the music became slowly louder and more cheerful. This bar was dangerous. The owners knew what they were doing and, as a barman of a few years, I recognised a well-oiled drinking machine when I saw it. A well-run bar will invite you with a comfortable and efficient atmosphere, free bowls of salted nuts will get the thirst going, a few TV's silently playing sport helps you to relax, the music creating the atmosphere. You might have a budget when entering the bar, but the goal of the server is to encourage you along efficiently until the budget is doubled, tripled and then forgotten. My advice to Keelan is to never to take a bank card to a bar, take only the maximum amount of money which you would like to spend and enough to pay for a cab or a midnight snack hidden in another pocket. The Oppi Koppi bar is known as a bush pub in Southern Africa, and there is nothing quite like a bush pub anywhere else on the planet. We had not realised it but, man, we had missed a good bush pub experience. I stood from my comfortable bar stool and made my way to the men's toilet where a poster of a beautiful girl adorned the wall with a sign beneath which warned that if you touched the poster girls nipples, you would have to buy the entire bar a shot of Jaegermeister, apparently an alarm would sound in the bar if you could not resist. I resisted.

Luisa, realising that a few beers could become a very expensive night, soon urged us away from the bar and we returned to our camp in good spirits to find that the staff had delivered a stack of Namibian hardwood for the campfire. Oppi Koppi Rest Camp alone is worth the trip to Namibia and winter is the perfect time to visit the dry, arid country. The days are warm with clear blue skies and the nights are cool (if not cold) and full of stars, inviting you to sit beside the campfire and relax, reflect and breathe the fresh air. Namibian hardwood is the perfect fuel for a fire, as it burns hot and slow, producing perfect, fragrant coals for grilling thick steaks and boerewors, providing heat in the camp long after the meat is grilled and devoured, washed down with yet another ice-cold Windhoek lager.

I called it a night not long after 11 pm and climbed into the Land Rover to sleep deeply dreaming of Namibia. Luisa decided to stay up a while longer to clean up and enjoy one last glass of red wine as the fire died. Before joining us in the camper, she went to the loo to brush her teeth and prepare for bed. On the way back to the Landy, she heard a rustling noise and, to her horror, came face to face with a three-metre tall ostrich, prehistoric and excited. Luisa, not known to be cool under fire, panicked and made a run for the camper, the ostrich on her heels, red hair billowing, screams piercing the night, her butt tucked in, running straight-backed, not an athletic run, more a frantic, arm-flailing dash. The demonic bird, razor-sharp teeth, breathing fire and slicing the ground with it's murderous, dissecting talons, jogged behind Luisa perplexed and then disappeared menacingly into the shadows. Frightened, but well aware of her civic responsibility, Luisa woke the kids and spent five minutes extracting their expert advice and then ran alone to the main gate but found no security on duty, knocked on every wooden door in every square wall until she eventually roused the rest camp owner dressed in comfortable puppy pyjamas. "Quick, come, there is an ostrich lose! It chased me!". The lovely European lady looked at Luisa for a moment, trying to understand the emergency. "An ostrich, loose, it chased me!", Luisa explained further. The camp owner responded sympathetically, "It's *only* an ostrich!".

The next morning, while I cooked eggs and bacon, Luisa retold the story and thanked me for sleeping through the entire attack. I apologised and, unforgiven, we pored over the African Adventure Atlas maps as we ate breakfast. We felt confident enough to take the Land Rover into remote but relatively popular areas and made the decision to head to southern Damaraland and the Messum Crater en-route to the Atlantic coast. Yes, the roads were long and unpaved, and there was a chance that we might suffer a significant breakdown, but there would surely be other explorers in the area, and if we had to, we could hitch a ride to the nearest town to find parts or supplies. Namibia is a very safe country, particularly in the north and far from urban centres. Hell, we couldn't come to Namibia and not explore the desert! We relaxed and planned the route back to South Africa, cleaned the camper, enjoyed afternoon naps and walks into town, exploring the area around the rest camp and Kamanjab, simply enjoying life. After a last relaxing evening, we said goodbye to the camp staff, who took photos of us for their overlanders logbook and drove out of the town and onto a long gravel road called the C35 towards the Messum Crater. It was a long dusty day, as we passed small towns and huge expanses of open land, eventually passing the town of Uis and beyond that the D2342 road to the crater. The C35 was a high-speed gravel road, maintained and with limited corrugations, sporting sign warnings of elephant and kudu. The D2342 was terribly corrugated, shaking the Land Rover violently as we struggled to find the correct speed to minimise the vibrations. Often driving at a higher speed will allow the tyres to skim over the top of the corrugation peaks but this is often dangerous as you have limited traction, many an inexperienced driver has found themselves upside down in a ditch when driving too fast on a gravel road. We have years of experience driving gravel roads, but the road to the crater was no ordinary gravel road. Eventually, we gave up trying to drift at speed over the corrugations and accepted that we were in for a long, bouncy and dusty drive. Occasionally, an alternative track would appear beside the dark brown road, and we would veer off onto the track enjoying a few minutes of smoother driving before being forced to rejoin the main road. This was one of the worst roads we had driven since leaving Morocco, most West African roads are terrible, but they are not corrugated by heavy, high-speed traffic, rather merely poorly built and never maintained. It did not help that we were visiting the crater at the tail end of the holiday season after the roads last grading and after many vehicles. Fifteen kilometres felt like fifty, but eventually, we came upon a rocky trail which Luisa insisted was the turn off to the crater. There were no signs, no tourist infrastructure, only a pile of rocks packed beside other piles of rocks. I know better than to argue with Luisa, who is petrified of large birds but not her large husband, and obediently I steered the shaken Land Rover onto the track and followed the tracks of those before us. The great news was that the track was in much better condition than the road had been and we were able to relax and enjoy the scenery, the Brandberg mountain range to the north and a surprisingly large array of Welwitschia, a broad-leafed, tap-rooted plant which is endemic to the Namib desert. The Namib desert is thought to be the oldest and driest desert in the world, at approximately 80 million years old and rivalled only by the Atacama Desert in Chile. In 2013, we had driven our Defender (then still boasting a rooftop tent and four doors) to the Atacama, and while there are comparisons with the Namib in terms of age and exsiccation, the two deserts are quite different. The Atacama boasts pink salt lakes and volcanoes, is located in the Andes mountain range, is at an average altitude of 3,000m and reaches up beyond 4,000m; the most common wildlife is the flamingo and the vicugna (cousin to the llama). The Namib, by contrast, is mostly just above sea level (so you can actually breath real, thick, beautiful air), has many rivers and boasts leopard, baboon, elephant, hyena, kudu, springbok, steenbok and zebra to name a few. If we were lucky, we might come across desert elephant or the rare desert lion but judging from the number of tyre tracks such an encounter would not be likely. If you had to ask which desert we prefer, we would not be able to say, both had their unique attractions, but the Namib is in Namibia, which is a huge plus. Unfortunately, not all visitors to the desert follow the spoken rules that you should not make new tracks and that you must never drive over plants, some idiots drove directly over the Welwitschia, too self-absorbed to make an effort to slow down and swerve and suffer a moment of discomfort to avoid damaging a plant which survives under such extreme circumstances. Those kind of people are no doubt the kind who will blast music in a campsite until 3 am, burn copious amounts of wood and use all the water available while leaving the fire pit full of cigarette butts and beer cans. We continued onwards and began to discuss where we would sleep as the sun was setting, we weren't worried though, we could sleep anywhere we chose to, as long as we were not making new tracks.

We were soon approaching the crater which Lonely Planet describes as, "one of Damaraland's most remote natural attractions. The highly mysterious-looking Messum Crater is comprised of two concentric circles of hills created by a collapsed volcano in the Goboboseb Mountains. The crater measures more than 20km in diameter, creating a vast lost world that you may have all to yourself".

We were certainly alone as we dropped down into a dry river bed which snaked around large rocky outcrops. We would engage low range often to make our way through the thick sand and were soon engulfed by dusk's shadow, I flicked on the headlights, but there was no light from the LED bulbs, we also discovered that we had no hazards and no indicators. Brilliant. With the last of the daylight retreating, we climbed the eastern rim of the crater and found a level place to park, overlooking the crater itself and the rocky bluffs through which we had just driven. The sunset over the crater was spectacular, and we quickly threw on our hiking boots and grabbed the camera, then climbed to the highest point of the rocky ridge on which we had parked. Golden swords of light fought the darkness across the flat expanse of the crater, the elevated centre of the ancient volcano; a silent, deserted and crumbled Mount Doom, red light glinting off the rust-red rocks, the crater floor flat and crossed by two tracks, both leading towards the ocean. There was to be no moon that night as we sat quietly and watched the universe come to life just for us, putting on a spectacular show of light and promising questions for which we will most certainly never know the answers. But, we can guess, and we can ask, sometimes the answer to one question is another question, sometimes we realise how small and insignificant we are, the humbling reminder is liberating - we are from the earth and of the earth, and all that we will leave behind is what we can contribute through our lives and to others lives. That should be good enough for us; it is enough for me.

There was no fire lit that night, and we were sure to use the porta-potty under the soft glare of the campers lights - there were rumoured to be lions in the area, and none of us were willing to suffer the indignity of being eaten with our pants down. But, the chances of being attacked by a lion, or any other creature, was slim indeed. We were alone on Mars, and there were no trees or tall grass to provide cover. There were almost no plants at all except for the toughest, tenacious Welwitschia, a juvenile bottle tree and a few blades of dry grass. But, there were signs of life on the rim of the crater - buck droppings, lizard tracks and the old chirp of an insect. There were no flies or mosquitoes or any other parasite which are far too common in areas populated by animals and human beings. We slept warm and comfortable protected by the rim of the crater from an Atlantic wind which howled throughout the night. It is second nature for us to seek refuge from the wind when camping and we knew when arriving at the crater that we would be in for a windy night, we also know that wind direction often changes as the sun sets and we waited until the night wind blew before we selected our final camp spot for the night, which turned out to be a few meters forward of where we had stopped.

At dawn, Luisa crawled out of her warm cocoon and slipped on her winter clothing and headed out with the cameras to record the sunrise. It was bitterly cold, the middle of winter, and the wind did it's best to cut to the bone, but we wear Craghoppers gear mostly, as the threads are packed with heating, cooling and drying technology and cold wind cannot penetrate a good winter jacket. I soon followed Luisa with a flask of tea and together we moved quietly along the crater rim, Luisa taking the photos, climbing up, over and down the rocky face to get the perfect angle. The sun rose slowly, edging out the grey, bringing the desert to life in shades of yellow, orange and red, we waited patiently. Any outdoorsman will know the relief and life which the sun brings with it, imagine a sky filled with cloud and ash, the dinosaurs froze while starving. There is no wonder that ancient man worshipped the sun if you must have a God to worship; it makes sense to pay respects to the force, which gives us all life. We watched enviously as the heat banished the cold and wind, good vs evil, and eventually, the light reached the rocks on which we stood, crept forward and warmed us. West Africa had been too hot, and the sun shone too bright, for too long, there was no escaping the heat, even at night when the earth radiated hot. We appreciated the cold, and we loved the heat in winter Namibia where the balance of both is near perfect.

Returning to the Land Rover, we woke the kids and made a quick breakfast of yoghurt and fruit before setting off to explore the area again, looking for lizards and hoping to come across a snake or two sunning on the rocks. As the day warmed, we removed layers, and after a morning refresh, we started the Landy and drove her down the steep track which led into the crater, Keelan filming our descent and then running down the track to join us. Keelan is a large lad, and he always loved running, before he was a teenager he would run everywhere. We worried that he might trip and hurt himself or slam the camera and tripod against the rocks, but he is sure-footed and made it back to the Landy with a broad smile on his face. We followed the track as it cut across a swath of the crater, the sand deep enough to require low range fourth gear, one of my favourite gears. A light twinkled in the distance and then another. A group of white Land Cruisers were heading towards us from the coastal entrance to the crater, and we slowed down to wave to them as they passed. Not one of the occupants waved back, unsurprisingly. Alone we continued through the crater, enjoying the crunch of the tyres through sand and rock, Luisa trying her best to find the correct route back to the coastal road. After a few kilometres of the flat crater floor, we emerged into a gulley, following the bed of an ancient river. At times the sand was deep enough to present a fun challenge, and the scenery did not disappoint, we were surrounded by tall eroded walls carved into surreal shapes by 80 million years of lava, wind and water, ice and scathing sun. It certainly puts life into perspective to wander through a part of the world where ancient nature reminds us of the miracle of our existence, of all the wonders which combined to create a world which most of us inhabit without the awe, love and respect which our earth deserves. Human beings are a minute in time; the earth may eventually shrug us off and continue evolving for a billion years until the sun is too close, too far or too weak. Then the planet will be dark, cold and wet, our skeletons dust, our great structures eroded to nubs. What a privilege to live in a time when all human efforts have combined to create the conditions which allow us to explore and learn and experience all the wonders that the world has to offer. Is this the golden age of travel? It may well be.

Some of us were born in the wrong decade; some of us were born in the wrong century. If you had asked me years ago which period in history I would have liked to inhabit, my knee jerk response would definitely be the Viking Age. But then I would think for a while and realise that, had I been born then, chances were very good that I would not have made it to adulthood, that adulthood would be cut short by war or disease and there were no chocolate bars in ancient Norway. To be anyone but royalty in Europe up until the 1900s was a black tooth servitude and in ancient times, mass slaughter, rape and pillage were par for the course, blood flowed, you were either master or servant, and that status could change at any time.

After a bit of thought, the 1950s seem like a fantastic era to be born in the Western World. The recent war had accelerated technology, Land Rover had recently developed the Series One, and there were a gazillion surplus Willy Jeeps floating around the planet, some brand new, in boxes small enough to air freight across continents. Drug cartels did not exist; a man could go far with good manners and a bit of ingenuity; the world was free of plastic, the beaches clean, the fish plentiful and massive and lions still prowled across Africa from north to SouthSouth, east to west.

But. There were still tribes of cannibals in the Fifties and if they didn't get you, Malaria would (I am obviously thinking trans-Africa or trans-Latin America, not trans-Minnesota), those prowling lions loved soft, slow human flesh as much as the best cannibal and there were mighty rivers full of crocs, without ferries or bridges and jungles of mud would suck the joy out of your soul, while parasites suck the blood out of your body. Hell, even the USA did not have paved roads connecting all corners.

Fast forward to the future and, well, the future is uncertain. What we do know is that the population of the planet has exploded and resources are not equally shared, there are governments run by criminals, infrastructure inequalities, pollution, climate change and technology which is evolving at the most rapid rate in our short history. What does all this mean for overland travel? I am not sure. I cannot predict what electric vehicles and artificial intelligence will mean for you and I and our beloved internal combustion engines. Your guess is as good as mine. Which brings us to the now, the last decade and the next decade. Pandemics aside, we are living in a peaceful and prosperous time, we have freedom of communication and movement to a degree. It is possible to travel the world in a VW Beetle, to be a digital nomad, to access resources which our overlanding ancestors could not even conceive of (the Internet! Google Earth!) and we have access to parts of this gorgeous planet which were once the reserve of the hardy few. Think about it. A not too far above average retired couple can pack up their comfortable lives and spend a few years driving the Pan American highway, or they can drive around Australia, or cross Eurasia from Calais to Vladivostok; a man like me can travel the planet while raising children and enjoying access to an income. This is a privilege unique to our times. But, there are still parts of this world which offer the wild adventure of the past; you can still explore muddy jungles and savanna where lion and elephant roam free, you can escape to a land before time, virtually untouched by humanity and I am sure you could still be a cannibal's dinner if you try hard enough. Malaria itself was the bane of our collective existence but is now treatable and eradicated in many countries.

I guess, if you had to ask me again which era I would like to live, I would say this one, this magical moment in history where man has achieved unprecedented peace and success and opportunity. What makes *this* the great golden age of overland travel is that overland travel is accessible to many, not just the well-financed and adventurous few, you can choose how much adventure you wish to endure, and you can enjoy the wonders of the world without fear of death, disease and ruin. Well, that might still happen but is avoidable. This is the golden age of overland travel, and the opportunity is yours to get out there and explore, challenge yourself, learn and grow and evolve. There has never been a better time.

The Messum Crater is timeless and exploring with an old, well-loved Land Rover is to step back in time, it could be 1982 or 2030, such is the beauty and charm of the original Defender and the remote solitude of the ancient Namib desert.

While researching for this book, I came across the story of Des and Jen Bartlett, an Australian couple who made Namibia their home. Des started his career as a wildlife photographer and filmmaker in Kenya in the 50's where he was sent on a six-month assignment and did not leave for ten years except to marry Jen in London where she was competing in the Wimbledon tennis tournament and to return to Australia for the birth of their only child. After making an Emmy award-winning wildlife documentary in Canada, titled Flight of the Snow Geese, the family flew to Namibia to document the Lions of Namibia for six months and stayed in Namibia for over 30 years. Their documentary, Survivors of the Skeleton Coast, won them their second Emmy and I am sure the other 19 documentaries made by the couple were equally excellent. But what stands out in the Survivors documentary, is that the filmmakers themselves are as impressive as the desert lions, elephants and giraffe which they film. The Bartlett's spent most of their time alone together, sometimes staying in their basic remote coastal cottage but mostly camping in the desert with an old Chevrolet 4x4 and a Series 3 Land Rover. They did not have a tent but slept on a groundsheet exposed to the elements (and once had a lion stop three feet short of their bed). They had a pet mongoose called Suri who followed them wherever they went, eating anything with a pulse (the scene in the Survivors documentary of Suri trying to hunt baby ostrich is hilarious) and they had a deep love for the animals which they filmed. They also proved that where there is a will, there is a way. Having learned to pilot in Canada for the Snow Geese documentary, they had two microlight aircrafts stripped down and sent from Pennsylvania to Namibia, where they took to the skies and tracked herds from above. They lived simple, hardy lives and invested heavily in the tools of their craft, they worked together towards a shared passion and raised a daughter, while living cheek by jowl with the wild. What we would give to spend an evening with them, learning. While we are not award-winning, we have parallel lives; our passion is exploration, theirs was wildlife. Des Bartlett died in 2009 at the age of 82. I spoke to my friend Daryl Balfour, a world-renowned wildlife photographer, and he told me that he had the opportunity to work with the couple after Des crashed his microlight and ruined his legs. In the Survivors documentary, Des described how he would overload and fly his microlight "like a cowboy", and sure enough it was a flying accident which, supposedly, drew the curtain on his career.

What is difficult for some to understand is how a small family can choose to live such isolated, uncomfortable lives in one of the harshest environments known to man. Passion is the only answer. The Bartlett's not only documented the animals of Namibia, but they also broke new ground, and their studies brought to light the fascinating lives of these desert dwellers and directly contributed to vastly improved preservation, conservation and understanding.

We used to believe that you have to be wealthy to travel the way we do. We now know that you need to make sacrifices, work hard and smart and be 100% focused. There were times on the road when we were in trouble, with no fuel and countries to cross, but then we would get a payment for an article, or a book sale and we could keep rolling on. We have four self-published books, work with a few great companies, have the respect of the overlanding community and are planning to continue touring as long as our health permits. We understand how passion can change a person's life for the better.

Our journey out of the crater continued along out of the river bed and onto a corrugated plain and came across a rusted old sign with arrows pointing in either direction, bearing the legend "Moer Toe", which means "stuffed up", or "destroyed". It was difficult to find a path across the large, flat expanse which was not either strewn with rocks or heavily corrugated and we bounced and vibrated along for a few kilometres until the track led to a gorge bordered by walls, eroded by ancient floods to expose layers of geological history, one wall cream coloured and dotted with volcanic rocks, reminding us of tin roof ice cream, the other wall red dirt serrated "teeth" above cream coloured rock. It was here that we startled herds of springbok and impala, who were puzzled by our presence and bounded up steep banks to escape us. Now, if only we could find those elusive elephants. We stopped to take some photos and to check the Land Rover, severe corrugations can shake a vehicle apart, but we had no problems other than a side indicator light which had fallen out of the left fender. We had indeed built a stout truck! After a bite to eat and an exploration of the rocks, we headed back out of the gorge and emerged onto the wide, heavily corrugated road which we had left the day before to enter the crater but was now called the D2303. Ahead of us lay the Atlantic Ocean and the Skeleton Coast, a bank of fog lay across the horizon, waiting to engulf us. The desert undulated, and the road rose and fell, as we tried to maintain a comfortable speed and drive on the least offensive sections of road. The desert flattened as we approached the coast, and by the time we reached the C34 coastal road, the world was cold, grey and moist. The fog is the only real source of moisture on the Skeleton Coast, but there are few plants, no grass, only sand and more sand, similar to the coastal stretch along the Pacific coast of Chile (home to the Atacama Desert) and Peru. Sand dunes bore the tracks of recreational vehicles, and we passed isolated communities, fishermen, shipwrecks and white bakkies (pick-up trucks) doing what white bakkies do. The section of road to Henties Baai was pressed stone, not yet tarred, but flat and comfortable to drive and we made it to the small, quiet town in time for lunch. We had all been craving fish and chips and stopped at a small take-out across the road from a large and well-stocked Spar supermarket. We sat alone at the counter and chatted to the cook as he prepared our battered hake and crispy french fries. The portions were massive, and we each had twice what we could eat served on sheets of white paper, the fish was fresh, flaky and delicious, the chips large, golden and perfect and we devoured the meal which was better than any fish 'n chips which we had eaten in England. Lemon squeezed over the fish, dipped in tartar sauce, a cold Coca-Cola shared from a glass bottle, sprinkles of salt and pepper, some tomato sauce (ketchup) and sighs of satisfaction. The cook watched us eat with a bemused look on his face; he did not know that he was a master of his craft and that we had waited years to eat this meal. After paying, we stepped out into the cool air and met a German by the name of Michiel; he had travelled down the West African route ahead of us and had taken the route to Cameroon which Dick had refused to drive (despite leading us to the route). Michiel explained that the route was tough and the river crossing stressful, but he did not have any real problems and did not get stuck or need any help. We were not happy that we had to take the longer route through the Gashaka Gumti National Park but, in retrospect, I am glad we did, as the route was a highlight of the journey. Michiel was delayed and staying in a local campsite, he invited us to join him for the night, but we had plans to meet an old friend in Walvis Bay, 100km south. We chatted a while longer, and I was struck by how lonely it must be to travel alone. Travelling with a family and keeping three other people happy is not always easy, but you get to share the highs and the lows, the sights and the sounds, the long days and nights. We said our goodbyes and drove to the edge of town where we filled the fuel tank and scoured the area for a specific 50amp fuse, pink, in a square plastic box with two blades, which were screwed into a fuse panel. Without this fuse, we had no lights, and the fuse kept blowing. We had managed to swop one over from an unused circuit, but that too had blown, what we really needed to do was find the short circuit, but that had proven almost impossible. It was a Saturday afternoon, and I crossed the wide, quiet road to a mechanics workshop which was shutting down for the weekend, the young mechanics chatting and joking, looking forward to an afternoon braai, rugby match, a few beers and a few rum or brandy with coke and ice, maybe a slice of lemon if the wife was a larnie. The young men were of different races but spoke to each other without reservation, the way it should be and was not a generation before. I asked the old man if he had the pink fuses and he dug around for a moment in a box. He had none. OK, so no lights then, and no indicators, I would just have to imagine that we were driving a BMW and all would be fine. Luckily, there were few turns on the coastal road to Walvis Bay, and we arrived at the city after a slow drive through Swakopmund. The German history of this area is alive and on display in Swakopmund, the architecture is German, the bookstores German, the road names German, the butcheries, apartment complexes, business names - German. Those of you who have read We Will Be Free will remember our description of the town when we visited in 2010. There had been a lot of development, and new upmarket housing estates stood where once there had only been sand and wind, it is imaginable that one day Swakopmund and Walvis Bay will join and become a small megalopolis in the desert. We had a few hours of daylight, as we had left the crater early in the morning, the roads are straight and quiet and time likes to stand still in Namibia. Luisa messaged our friend Anthea, a professional hunter, and asked if we could pop into her house after we visited and climbed Dune 7. Dune 7 is the tallest dune in Namibia at 388m high. We parked in the recreation area where the locals sat in groups drinking and listening to music, a transgender couple came over and asked us for cigarettes and a beer, families, raced each other up the side of the dune, most running out of steam 30m up the steep, red, soft face. Keelan ran to the dune and ploughed his way up, followed by Jessica and I. The problem with climbing a sand dune is that every step slides a bit back, the sand sucks in your feet, and you find yourself on your hands and knees panting and overheating. We learned that the trick is not to look up, fight forward until you can't go any further, stop, take a break, enjoy the scenery and keep going. Keelan summited, caught his breath and ran back down. Jessica fought the dune every step of the way and begged to be allowed to give up. "Eyes down! Just keep going! You can do this!". She fought on and soon we were both sat at the top with the sun on our backs, the wind blowing sand into our hair and ears as we sat and looked around, waving to Luisa and Keelan, looking out over the desert and then back to the sea and the small city. It took a while for our bodies to cool and our heart rates to normalise. The dune is tall, very tall but there is no way that it is 383m tall, as tall as the Empire State Building, I don't care what the internet insists. Apparently, the dune is 570m above sea level, and the sea is a short, flat drive away. Impossible! Jessica and I ran down the dune and rejoined Luisa and Keelan who were chatting to some locals, we put our shoes back on and drove back to Walvis Bay, stopping at the large, impressive mall to buy some food and drinks for the braai we would soon enjoy with Anthea, who lived in a neat white house in the suburbs. We had first met Anthea in 2007 when she had travelled to Cape Town and had stayed in our home for a few days. She was friends with our friends Johan and Charlene, and when we looped back to Namibia, we had spent a few nights at her game farm outside Gobabis, close to the Botswana border. As a professional hunter, she and her family worked hard to maintain herds of wild game and to attract hunters from around the world. We did not hunt when at her farm, there was no need to, they had East European clients at the time, and the fridges were full of game, but we did enjoy some target shooting. In the years since that first visit, there had been some upheavals in the family, the business had suffered some challenges, and Anthea gave birth to two beautiful daughters. We sat around the braai, built into the living room wall, and caught up after a good hot shower. As a woman who spends a lot of time working with rough and ready hunters, Anthea is no wilting flower, and she told us stories about her time in the bush and brought us up to speed with all that was happening in Namibia and with mutual friends. I went to bed early and woke up to find that my relatively new phone had its screen cracked by a clumsy wine bottle, well, someone had too much fun, I won't tell you who.

As I was the first to wake, I cleaned the kitchen, did the dishes and prepared a large, hearty breakfast of spicy tomato and onion relish, crispy bacon, mushrooms, toast and wors and steak grilled the night before and reheated, sliced in a pan of hot butter. We had to be careful not to replace all the fat which we had lost in West Africa, but we know by now that our collective weight fluctuates as we travel, times of plenty prepare us for the tough times on the road. The smell of cooking bacon brought the people out of their slumber one by one, and after a lazy meal, we packed some goodies in Anthea's white pick up (you can have any colour car you want in Namibia and South Africa, so long as that colour is white, only gangsters and hairdressers drive colourful vehicles) and set out for the beach. We drove through the quiet Sunday morning, past the container terminal and turned onto the Pelican Point sand spit where a salt extraction company processes 70 million tons of seawater to extract 500,000 tons of high-quality salt annually. Square, watery pits of pink, attract flamingos in their thousands and the adjacent deep water harbour, the only such harbour in Namibia, has been attracting ships since 1485. A safe harbour is especially attractive on a coastline with over 1,000 shipwrecks. Anthea's husband Mark then drove the Hilux onto the spit and drove a kilometre along the sand until finding a good place to stop, where the kids could play in the sand, and we could walk their energetic dog. We then sat on the sand and enjoyed the cool misty beach; I took some photographs of a decaying predator, the children played until hunger knocked. We then drove to the waterfront to enjoy delicious calamari. It was good to be with friends, doing normal things, and already we felt that the journey had drawn to a close but, as you may now know, our journey does not end.

The next day we drove to Windhoek, surprised to find that there is no direct tarred road, well, there is an indirect tarred road, but Anthea had advised that we should take the shorter route, and we were happy that we did. At first, the road was straight and boring, but soon enough, we entered the mountains, and the scenery became much more interesting and engaging. We found ourselves on the C28, a road listed on the website Dangerous Roads as one of the least travelled roads in the world. The road is 317 km from Walvis Bay to Windhoek, and we had made the rookie mistake of not filling the tank before leaving Walvis Bay. As the tank was three-quarters full and we expected to find a fuel station en-route. We had not done our homework, we had let our guard down, and we had dropped the ball. But, sometimes the best adventures are unplanned. The C28 took us up into the Khomas Hochland mountains via the Bosua Pass, a pass deemed too steep for trailers and caravans, and we often stopped to enjoy the views out across the Namib Naukluft National Park. We passed very few vehicles that day and very few people at all. At times we spotted a sign to a farm of a 4x4 camp, signs of an old homestead, a hardy farmer. Only once we descended the Windhoek side of the pass, did we realise that we would not be able to reach Windhoek that night as our fuel was running low and the fuses had blown again, meaning that we had no headlights and no indicators? Part of the road was severely corrugated and quite grim, but as the sun-kissed the horizon, we entered an undulating plain where game roamed behind tall fences - giraffe, impala, kudu. I made a call as the sky turned purple and visibility was reduced, the suns golden rays disappearing behind a distant red koppie, it was time to find a place to stop for the night. On we drove, trying to maintain a balance of speed and fuel efficiency, vibrating across the corrugated, wide and dusty road.

At last, Luisa spotted a bank beside the road, exposed but relatively level. We pulled into the area and looked for signs that people had camped here before and found a small fire pit and a beer can. Often locals will know where they can overnight, and the evidence is not difficult to find. We would not be making a campfire, the surrounding grass was tall, dry and yellow and it would not take much to spark a conflagration which would have the local farmers string us up from a tree, figuratively. It was to be a cool, dull and quiet evening. I stood outside and watched the stars fight through the light; occasionally a white pick up would blast by, leaving us to breath the dust, occasionally farm labourers would rattle past in ancient vehicles held together with baling wire, hopes and dreams. No-one stopped to ask us what we were doing, no-one hooted or waved or paid us too much attention, which is exactly the amount of attention we enjoy.

The following morning we rose cool and quiet. A giraffe stood close by and studied us, his tongue long and languid as we brushed our teeth and prepared for the final push to Windhoek. I syphoned a few precious litres of diesel into the main fuel tank, we brushed our teeth and enjoyed the warm winter sun on our faces before starting the Land Rover and driving back onto the long, straight dirt road. It was a pleasant morning, cruising along surrounded by the pristine Namibian bush, cool air blowing in through my open window, the family relaxed and happy, listening to a radio station playing mellow music. It did not quite make sense that the navigator showed that Windhoek was less than 15km's away, yet we were still driving on a dirt road. Rounding a corner and after climbing a hill, we came to a halt at a surprising police checkpoint. We had not expected to see another checkpoint until we left South Africa and entered Mozambique. Luckily the policeman on duty was Namibian and not an unfortunate transplant from Guinea Bissau or Nigeria. He did not ask what we had brought for him, he did not insist on inspecting each passport, and he did not demand that the vehicle be opened for a search. He did not flirt with Jessica, he did not have a colleague join him for an exhausting game of good cop, bad cop and he did not demand that we pay USD 50 for the privilege of driving an unpaved road. He smiled, asked for my driver's license, asked where we had come from and wished us a safe and pleasant journey. Well done Namibia, very well done.

We entered Windhoek without working indicators and made our way along wide, quiet boulevards to the first gas station on the map. The city was mid-winter, dry and dusty as we made our way under the Western Bypass and stopped at a red light. Diagonal to us, four lanes and a traffic island apart sat Japanese Yuki who we had dropped off in Point Noir. "Yuki!". He was heading out of Windhoek, towards the coastline, hitchhiking and wearing his stained tunic and carrying his faded light green backpack. What a lonely, magical and liberating existence. We did not have much which we could say to each other, and we waved him goodbye and good luck.

We rolled into the gas station on fumes and happily filled the tank and bought cold drinks, hot meat pies and a large bottle of cold water. Our British Zimbabwean friend Dot, who we had met our first day in Morocco, was house-sitting for friends in a nearby suburb and invited us to stay a night. We drove first to the local supermarket and stocked up before making our way to a neighbourhood of high walls, spiked fences and large dogs. Dot's friends were German Namibians, and I felt like I was walking into my grandmothers home after driving up the steep driveway and parking the Landy under a carport beside a dusty sedan. Dot's vehicle was at the mechanic waiting for some much-needed spares and repairs. We had lunch and caught up, Dot and Luisa chatting about the various travellers on the West Africa route and I complimented Dot on her accomplishment, driving a 2x4 van across such terrible roads. Dot suggested that I should publish a how-to book, I told her that I had, Dot told me that Luisa should have written it because "No-one wants a man telling them how to do something", I responded that Luisa had co-authored the book. We smiled at each other and paused to sip a cold drink. The braai burned slowly, and a large white parrot chased Luisa around the patio. The next morning Luisa and I headed into Windhoek to buy replacement fuses and searched for an auto electrician who could help us fix the Landy, but all the workshops were busy, and we had no plans to hang around Windhoek any longer, we had already visited the quiet city back in 2010 and had plans to move on. The following morning we left after saying goodbye to Dot and having a young Rottweiler drag us around the neighbourhood.

We followed the B1 towards a town called Keetmanshoop. Some might say that driving a significant road in Namibia is boring; it was not dull, rather peaceful. You can drive mostly at 120kph, and there is not much traffic once you leave Windhoek and the eternal Sunday afternoon. The gearbox was now being even more problematic, getting into fourth was now becoming more difficult, and she was still grinding into 2nd gear. Despite those problems, we were able to cruise along at a decent speed, Luisa and Jessica lazing in the back while Keelan and I listened to music and chatted about tanks, wars, robotics, computers, and his plans for the future. Keelan had been offered a job by our friend Bill in Canada. Bill ran a company working on the oil fields, and the job paid very well, Keelan would, however, have to complete his schooling (high school certificate), obtain a light truck drivers license and do a few rope access and first aid courses.

Keelan felt that this would be an excellent start for him as he could get in a couple of years work experience, earn and save and then be able to make a decision what he would do for the rest of his life, as a career. He had plans of one day buying a large piece of land, building a huge warehouse with a workshop and living quarters. There he would build fantastic creations which could fly or cover any terrain. We have a similar end goal. If money was no option, he would build that dream, and it would not only satisfy him, but it would allow him to grow and progress, unleashing his ideas and creativity. If Keelan had to happen upon a million dollars, he would not change, he would not buy stupid luxury items and waste the money on drink and women, he would invest that money into finding the limits of his skill and creativity. If he could find a good life, work, gamer balance. We encourage him to study engineering, and the hope was that after working he would be able to help pay towards the cost of his study in Europe, where he is able to study at high quality, low tuition institutions. He has already seen much of the world, and he has seen enough of it to know where he can live and prosper and make his dreams come true. Our job is to support him and to help him achieve those dreams, and his job is to apply himself to the hard task of doing what is difficult but right, not what is easy.

We drove past Keetmanshoop, past two gas stations and stopped at a guest lodge with a campsite who asked us to pay a silly amount of money for a nights camping. Luisa checked the internet, and just down the road there was a place called Trupen Garden Accommodation and Camping, perhaps we would have better luck there? We drove into Trupen and were greeted by a kind elderly lady whose eyes had lived a full and eventful life. The camping was not expensive at all, and we were surprised when our host offered us a large bag of free wood and a pack of beef sosaties! The camp area has two stands, side by side and separated by an ablution block with a private bathroom and a large wash-up area. Perfect. We settled in for two days before heading to the border. We had relaxed a bit and washed West Africa out of our skin; it was time to return to South Africa!

Mumuhuila girls in Angola

Disabled and abandoned USSR T54 Main Battle Tank being explored by Keelan

Overlanding Namibia

Exploring the Messum Crater, Namibia

Home at last! The gorgeous Cape Peninsula

SOUTH AFRICA

South Africa is situated at the most Southern tip of Africa, hence the name, South Africa. The Indian and the Atlantic Ocean meet off the Southern Cape coast. The country is bordered by Namibia, Zimbabwe, Mozambique, Botswana and Eswatini and surrounds the enclaved Lesotho

South Africa uses the South African Rand
10 Rand Dollar (ZAR) = EU0.57/USD0.66

Most worldwide citizens will receive a 90-day visa on arrival. Other nationalities must apply at their local South African Consulate. The visa fee will be an approximate EU35

Unleaded = EU0.85/USD0.93 per litre
Diesel = EU0.87/USD0.90 per litre

MTN
Vodacom
Telkom
Cell C

Christianity, Islam, Judaism and other Africa religions are practised in South Africa

No insurance was requested and is not compulsory, although recommended with cover for 3rd party, fire and theft

Police = 10111
Ambulance = 112

Passport with visa (if required)
Vehicle title papers
Drivers Licence

South Africa has 11 official languages
Howzit - how is it? (generally a rhetorical question)

Koppie - a small hill (can also mean a cup)
robot - traffic light
just now - sometime soon (from Afrikaans "net-nou")
now now - sooner than just now! (from Afrikaans "nou-nou", pronounced no-no)
braai - barbecue

 South Africa has a large variety of foods and restaurants from traditional serving potjiekos, braai, bunny chow, sheep head to 5 starred restaurants serving European/Asian/African food.
Supermarkets are generally reasonably priced and are sometimes priced the same as the USA or Europe

 Notable National Parks:
Kruger National Park
Kgalagadi Transfrontier Park
Addo Elephant National Park
Pilanesberg National Park
Cradle of Mankind
Robben Island - Prison where Nelson Mandela was housed
Drakensberg Peak - the Great Escarpment between South Africa & Lesotho
Table Mountain - a flat-topped mountain in Cape Town
Cape Agulhas - the most Southern point on the African continent
The wine region in Western Cape
The Cape Peninsula

 Winter - June to September - Low of 6C/43F to a high of 18C/64F
Summer - December to March - Low of 20C/68F to a high of 35C/95F

 The first successful human heart transplant was performed by Christiaan Barnard in 1967.
South Africa has abundant minerals such as diamonds, gold, iron ore and platinum.
The earliest human fossils were found at The Cradle of Humankind, just North West of Johannesburg.
The Kruger National Park is one of Africa's largest game reserves with an abundance of wildlife

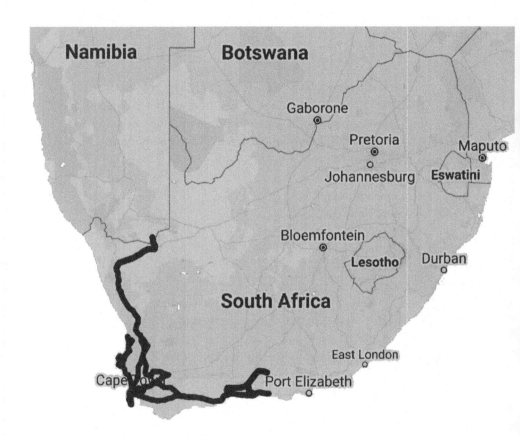

19

A massive circle, South Africa

It had been almost a decade since we had left our home country and I had sorted some shit out in my mind. That clarity was half the unspoken goal of my quarter of the journey. I wanted to return to South Africa wizened by the long, tough road, the mountains we had climbed. Instead, I found myself walking the middle road - a political centrist, mildly pantheist, middleweight, culturally ambivalent and suffering from a very average case of cognitive dissonance. Maybe that is what wisdom is; maybe it is a quiet confidence, belief in one's self and the knowledge that there really are no answers to all of life's big questions, there is only the right way and the wrong way, good and bad. I suppose the path to happiness is an often un-walked trail of forgiveness, forgiving not only those who "trespass against us" but also in learning to forgive oneself. Life had not been hard before we had left South Africa to explore the world, but it had been difficult. There were all the usual problems of modern life thrown in with the unrelenting problems of the past, of things, said and done, of unfulfilled dreams, of opportunities lost, hearts broken, relationships ruined and a dread of the future. I often wonder who we would meet if we had to bump into the family which stayed, which did not leave to travel the world together, the family who we would have become in a parallel universe. I am sure we would have been just fine; we are good people at our core and what better can a person be but "good". I would rather be good than wealthy, beautiful or powerful because being good is a gift which gives and cannot usually be taken away by circumstance or time.

But we would certainly be different. We would certainly be jealous of the other families wealth and possessions, their new cars and comfortable home, motorbikes and kayaks, jet skis and lounge suites, flat screens and wine cellar, wardrobes and shoe collection, bank accounts and security. And they would be jealous of our lifestyle and courage, our stories and experiences, our books and contacts, our minimalism, freedom and inner peace. If you compare the two lists, it will soon become apparent to you which family appeals the most and which is most like the you you want to be. If Luisa and I had to settle down in a few years, it would not be with the need for all the wonderful, shiny and expensive things for which most of us trade our time and labour. We would need a relatively spacious but simple home, a workshop to repair, prepare and create, a kitchen to fill with love and a patio from where we could watch the sunset over hills of green, edible green. We are in many ways, still the people who left, but we are fundamentally different. The beauty of trying, adventurous, self-sufficient travel, is that you learn your strengths and weaknesses, you confront your demons, and you slay them lest they slay you. If we had known how difficult the journey was to become at times, we would certainly not have had the courage to leave, but we dealt with each setback, each temporary bankruptcy, each danger and every challenge with determination, we had thrown ourselves at the mercy of the universe, and we remembered that no matter what life throws at you, you can overcome it with the right attitude and by doing the right things. Being selfish was never an option, and it is when people are selfish that the cracks become chasms which threaten to swallow you whole. I think that now would be a perfect time to declare, once and for all, that I have no intention of ever becoming a motivational speaker or a lifestyle coach, I still have too many questions of my own to be able to stand on a stage and declare that I have all the answers and doing this or that, or this will forever change your life. Be kind, do good every day, take only what you need, trust the universe and yourself, treat others like you want to be treated, everything in moderation, be brave, be smart and don't be an asshole. There, are you motivated? Good, my work here is done.

We left our camp outside Keetmanshoop, where I had chased a near-naked Luisa around the stroke of midnight, after a few good days. The kind lady who ran the establishment had quizzed us about our lives and seen us off with a warm hug. She had made a choice in life, she could have been bitter and resentful, but she was not. We had made the decision to cross into South Africa at the small Onseepkans border, as opposed to the much larger Vioolsdrif and the reason was simple. We are outlaws, in some ways, and we sometimes bend the laws to suit ourselves, faking insurance documents to get into French Guyana or driving for four years with an expired drivers license or rebuilding a vehicle, converting from a pick-up into a camper without gaining permission from an authority and with the certainty that the end result will, in fact, be roadworthy. The camper had so far driven on four continents. Across extreme terrain and was, without doubt, very well built and incredibly strong. The simple reason why we had not made an effort to have the conversion signed off by a designated engineer and the vehicle re-registered as a camper was a) where the hell were we supposed to do that? and b) we had found a loophole in the South African traffic law. Essentially the law states that a rebuilt vehicle which does not exceed the stated Gross Vehicle Mass (GVM) and has not had alterations to the brakes or suspension does not require re-registration. Of course, there are many different opinions as to the concise translation and legality of this clause, particularly in respect to other contradictory clauses and amendments (which we had not found, but our area of expertise was immigration law, not traffic law) but, the reality is, that we have no intention of ever selling the vehicle and have proven, beyond any possible doubt, that the camper is not only roadworthy but also incredibly capable.

Nevertheless, we are not immune from paranoia, and we agreed that it would be better to cross back into the country where the vehicle is registered through a small, sleepy, Sunday afternoon border where a few friendly chaps had just finished a vast Sunday lunch and were counting the seconds until they could return home for a cold beer and a long sleep. Could you imagine, travelling as far as we had and then having the Landy impounded at the South African border? A nightmare, a very expensive nightmare. We had the carnet though, and the hope was that a simple stamp, stamp, stamp without an inspection would free us to continue on our merry way.

The road to the border was dirt and corrugated and void of all traffic. We stopped at a small town called Karasburg and convinced a closing takeaway joint to microwave a couple of plates of Russians and chips (Russians are red South African style sausages) before making the final push to the border which lay in a dry wetland on the banks of the once-mighty Orange River. We parked beside the Namibian immigration office and stamped out of that amazing country before crossing a bridge and approaching the South African border boom. A policeman emerged eventually from the prefabricated buildings built beside a small compound and invited us to do exactly as instructed. We put on our happy border faces and soon had the policeman smiling and joking. He flirted shamelessly with Jessica as we walked to the immigration building, had our passports languidly checked and stamped and then joked with the policeman who had enjoyed a large lunch and who flipped through the carnet with interest. We told him a bit of our story and asked if there was a camp nearby and happily retrieved our paperwork and drove out of the compound and back onto South Africa soil.

We are home!

After so many years, we were elated and relieved and mentally exhausted and full of questions - what exactly did the future hold? We did not know, but we had a few ideas. Our priority now was to return to Cape Town, to be reunited with friends and family and to prepare for the next leg of the journey.

The R358 road to Pofadder (the town named after the fat, slow and deadly Puff Adder snake), the first large town on our route, was at first terribly corrugated and dusty but wound through beautiful countryside. Eventually, the dirt road gave way to perfect tar, and we wound our way past Pofadder surprised to find that the gas stations were closed in the deep sleepiness of a rural Sunday afternoon. We had dropped our guard since emerging from the Messum Crater, and we had found ourselves, time and again, running low on fuel. Rookies. We had forgotten how beautiful South Africa is and how perfect the roads are, even here in the relatively remote Northern Cape. A large bluff escorted us towards Springbok as the sun began to set, the fuel light illuminated and we realised that we would soon be driving in the dark without headlights. Occasionally a white pick-up would approach or overtake us as we calculated how far we would get, at what speed we should travel, before either the sun deserted us or our diesel evaporated completely, and it was with relief that we rolled down the perfect road into Springbok, in darkness, in neutral, on fumes. At the Engen gas station, I had the attendant fill the tank and a jerry can, just in case, as we had realised that the Defenders fuel consumption had increased significantly in the last few weeks.

Grumpy Luisa had been searching the internet for a campsite and told me that there were two options, I asked for the closest option and, after waiting for a police patrol vehicle to cruise past, we headed back the way we came, without indicators or driving lights, and turned onto a road which leads us to our camp for the night, the Springbok Caravan Park, an expensive but well-equipped campsite where we tried to organise some food, maybe a pizza delivery. Luisa was not happy with the cost of any of the options, and we made a small fire to grill a pack of sausages which we had found at the bottom of our now empty fridge. It was a pathetic homecoming meal, but we at least had reserves of booze with which to celebrate our triumphant return. The next morning we drove into the town to stock up on supplies and quaff milkshakes and cheeseburgers at the Spur Tex-Mex restaurant before heading out to the industrial area to find an auto electrician, after being referred by a flustered and very busy English sparky who had just pushed a Land Cruiser up a hill. Towns like Springbok are fascinating, the melting pot of modern South African society where tunic clad Rasta's rub shoulders with khaki-clad farmers, Charlize Theron schoolgirls, taxi drivers, tourists, every shade and shape and colour of human being. The streets are clean and busy; there are banks and a mall and clothing stores and hardware stores, toy stores, pet stores, auto parts, pharmacies and gas stations. Africa needs to emulate South African commerce and agriculture. The industrial area of Springbok serves the community near and far, and at the end of a border road, beneath a koppie, we found the auto electrician. A young Afrikaans man and an elderly Coloured gentleman set to work trying to find our elusive Gremlin, while municipal vehicles arrived and departed unloved. A few hours into the work the owner arrived, a large, potbellied and friendly Afrikaner, we chatted, and he explained that the business has a local prominent ANC member as a partner and the company, therefore, has municipal projects but has to share 50% of the profits, an all to common business model in the new South Africa. The sparkies removed parts of the dashboard and dug around the loom, removed a headlight and found that they were able to get the lights working on a new fuse but could not keep the lights working. For four hours they worked until eventually, they admitted defeat. We were not surprised that they could not fix the problem, but we were disappointed. After handing over a very reasonable R650 for labour and some fuses, we left and drove out of town convinced that we might have to strip the Land Rover to find that bastard Gremlin, we just needed somewhere to do it. I had put it out there on Social Media that we were looking for a place to stay for a couple of months and had been approached by a friend called Hein, who was leaving for a few months to go to the USA with his family and he had a house which we could rent in a small coastal town called Groot Brak Rivier, on the Garden Route a 1,000 km's away, we had a chat with Hein, and it was agreed that we would rent the house from 1st August. Well, at least we now had a semblance of a plan.

From Springbok we made our way towards the mountainous town Clanwilliam, marvelling at the beauty of the country in her mid-winter green coat. The drive was pleasant, relaxing and smooth as we retraced steps long forgotten until we rolled into Clanwilliam, a postcard-pretty town situated between the western slopes of the Cederberg mountains and the eastern bank of the Oliphants River. World-renowned citrus is grown from Clanwilliam to Ceres, along with the Cederberg mountain range and chances are exceptionally high that the perfect South African orange in your hand came from this region. We used to escape to the Jamaka campsite on the old Niewoudt farm, as often as we could when we lived in Cape Town and when we owned old Land Rovers, and it was to here, that we made our first shakedown trip with our 130 when we were planning the Cape Town to Kilimanjaro journey. In winter it is cold and cloudy, and the pass to the Grootkloof farm reminded us of driving through the Alps to Chamonix from Switzerland though, admittedly on a much smaller scale. Keelan's 20th birthday was around the corner, and we first stopped to buy him a new smartphone, Huawei and not very expensive.

The campsite was quiet as we rumbled through the valley, the dirt road used by us and the occasional low flying white pick up farmer who has long forgotten, or may never have realised, that he lives in one of the most beautiful and fertile places on earth. The Grootkloof farm was established in 1755 and has been in the same family ever since, and the owner of the farm is a tall, charismatic Art Garfunkle look-alike, called Jannie Niewoudt. Jannie welcomed us and left us in the hands of a friend, as he dealt with farmers problems and we bought firewood, oranges, mangoes, Rooibos tea and jar of honey before driving down to the campsite and settling in for a few days. A river runs through the camp and accompanied by an energetic sheepdog, who would become our friend, as we hiked around the surrounding mountains, enjoying the fresh air. It can get very, very hot in the valley, and dry, but in July it is comfortable if not a bit wet.

Perhaps the question foremost in our minds returning to South Africa was, how has the country changed? Had there been progress or was the country sliding further down the slippery slope of national despair? It did not take too long for us to realise that there were both positives and negatives, particularly after having spent some time in urban areas. Rural areas are perhaps naturally resistant to change as they are culturally conservative and there are not many opportunities for social mobilisation - farmers are generational, and they own large, expensive tracts of land and equipment and carry deep within them the inherited knowledge of agricultural productivity. Land has been an immense source of conflict in Africa in general and South Africa in particular. It does not help that the most conservative members of society are also the people who feed the nation while generally holding onto age-old concepts of master and servant. Their nemesis is a portly politician by the name of Julius Malema, who for years has been calling for the redistribution of all land while wearing a workers overall and a Breitling watch. He and his organisation, the Economic Freedom Fighters (EFF) have called for farmers to be driven from their land and at a political rally in 2016 he stated, "We are not calling for the slaughter of white people, at least for now". The man is a populist who has found support among the disenfranchised poor with promises to deliver what the ANC has been unable to. The problem is though that Robert Mugabe used a similar tactic to stay in power in the late '90s and early 2000's and destroyed the economy of his country by chasing white farmers from their productive farms, only for the current Zimbabwean regime to implore those same farmers who were robbed and beaten and expelled to return to the land they once worked and to resuscitate a rotten economy. Yes, there must be land reform, but a Zimbabwean style take over hurts everyone, particularly the poorest of the poor. The solution is most likely education and investment in the nurturing of a new generation of Black South African farmers, men and women with the knowledge and experience and capital required to establish or manage a productive agricultural enterprise. The ANC has had a quarter of a century to achieve exactly that but have squandered the opportunity to address the inequalities of the past and prepare for the future. So, tension remains, many farmers believe that there is a genocidal campaign against them, while the government responds that the rural victims of violent crime are simply part of a wider crime epidemic which claims 20,000 lives (and 40,000+ reported rapes) every year in South Africa. Generally speaking, our experiences in smaller towns and isolated villages were exactly as they had been almost a decade earlier, not much has changed, life goes on, the streets are swept and clean, the farmers drive white pick-ups and wear khaki uniforms, the workers are thin, smiling and sun-dried, the land is productive and the food delicious, sweet and of an exceptionally high quality. South Africa is the breadbasket of Africa, and that produce is finding it's way across the continent, bringing choice and nourishment to the broader public in countries where once only the wealthy could once afford a jar of jam. The agricultural sector feeds a massive manufacturing sector where raw materials are processed into packaged, processed foods and distributed widely; the irony is that our friend Julius "Juju" Malema sits at least three times a day at a table to enjoy the finest produce of the agricultural sector and three times a day denounces the people who raised that steak, pressed that wine, extracted that dairy and produced the gravy with which he smothers his locally grown potatoes. Perhaps he too suffers from cognitive dissonance? The influx of Zimbabwean (and Malawian) economic immigrants does not help the cause of the farm labourer who has to compete with people who are in many cases, better educated and motivated and organised and sober.

The towns and cities offered us another view of the new South Africa. Generally, people across colour lines seemed to speak to each other with new confidence in a shared experience. After Apartheid separated the nation and Nelson Mandela united the nation, we were, essentially, introduced to the people with whom we shared a country. Children of all races now shared the same schools, the structure of corporations gradually changed and people who never had the opportunity to visit each other's homes to share a meal, an evening or a celebration, were now able to sit together on a couch and enjoy a cold beer while the kids played video games or rode their bikes. Our home was always open, and we shared many evenings with friends of all races, Jessica's best friend was a young Zimbabwean girl, we spoke to everyone we met with the same respect, but we felt a bit ahead of our time, we were ostracised by our small, wealthy, White community (in a Plettenberg Bay "security estate") because we had Black children over for play dates and we hung out with our Indian and Coloured friends. Good riddance. Perhaps we had been too close to notice, but upon our return, after such a long absence we noticed that there was new mutual respect between most races who had common daily experiences and it was refreshing to see teenagers hang out in mixed groups, completely at ease with one another, the result of years spent together in schools where most children spend more time with strangers than they do with their own families. These young adults are the future leaders of this country, and we can only hope that the country can survive it's legacy and the current government long enough to turn the corner with the next generation at the wheel. But, unfortunately, these children are the minority in a country which is still indelibly separated by the conflict for resources which drive us apart, the resources which are plentiful but squandered by fat cats in expensive suits and public office.

Initially, upon our return, we embarked on a social experiment, we tried not to listen to the news on the radio, we did not read the newspapers, and we avoided conversations which would have presented us with one entrenched view in favour of another. And we avoided racists of all races like the plague. We were determined to interact with people on our own terms, like tourists from a strange land, we would not automatically enter into preconceived social contracts, and we were better off for it. Some people were confused - we looked South African, we spoke like South Africans (with a weird accent), but we acted so out of character that we had people ask us where we were from, Germany? Norway? New Zealand? We spoke to the cashier as we would the bank manager, we treated people with respect and we received respect, it really is that simple.

After a few months, we abandoned the hear no evil, speak no evil, see no evil social experiment and delved into the reality of South African life. The country is beautiful, one of the most blessed we have seen. The food is out of this world; there is convenience and opportunity, a wonderful climate and the possibility to live a very good life if you have the intelligence and the basic tools of education and motivation. But, there is a dark underbelly. In the first few months of our return, there seemed to be a campaign of violence against females, with one horrifying case following another - abduction, torture, murder, 100 rapes a day. There were xenophobic attacks as poor South Africans lashed out against foreign immigrants and the government was reeling from accusations of "state capture", an Indian family called the Gupta's had essentially bought control of the country from the ANC, specifically then-President Jacob Zuma and his cronies, and had strip-mined our economy, before escaping to live off the fat in Dubai. Fuckers. By the end of 2019, the national debt stood at a whopping 4 trillion Rand (about $200 billion and a drop in the ocean compared to the USA's $25 trillion debt as of May 2020), and every government department was bankrupt. The ANC fat cats and their corrupt friends were doing a great job of pretending to run the country while milking every last drop out of a withered and increasingly wild cash cow.

Driving from Cape Town to Plettenberg Bay, we noticed that there were often black scars across otherwise well-built roads and these scars seemed to coincide with the more impoverished areas. As the government looted the treasury, they neglected their base, the people to who they had promised so much over the years and that base now took to burning tyres and shutting down national roads, burning down schools and clinics and looting under the guise of "service delivery protests".

Our former temporary home-town was a victim of these protests. Plettenberg Bay is a beautiful town located in paradise, and we arrived there in September on a deeply scarred road, the N2 national road. When we came to the traffic circle, which leads to Port Elizabeth, the town itself and the industrial area where we had once relied on local businesses to provide us with all the goods and services we needed, from auto parts to alcohol, electrical supplies and auto glass, tyres, powder coating, hardware supplies and fresh fish. It had once been efficient, clean, prosperous and, well, industrious, providing employment and opportunities to many, a resource for the expansion and support of the local economy. In July 2019, a service delivery protest brought the N2 highway to a standstill as thousands marched, tyres were lit on the road surface and piled with branches and refuse. The protest lasted almost three days, and the industrial area was ransacked, almost 90 people were arrested but not before walls were broken through, and many businesses stripped of stock and assets. When we visited the town, many of the businesses were still closed, and there was apparently no intention to reopen many of them, the owners were giving up, throwing in the towel. We spoke to the owner of an auto parts store, still partially barricaded, steel sheets and bars where once there were windows. He stood with his staff and told us how rioters had used stolen vehicles to break through the walls of buildings, ransacking the bottle store first and then the surrounding businesses. He said that the police just stood at the elevated traffic circle and watched as the looters looted all that they could carry, an unofficial redistribution of wealth, perhaps they were waiting for back up. It is sad and terrible and very difficult for those who lost the entities they worked so hard to create and the employees who lost their jobs and the suppliers who lost a client and clients who lost a service and a resource.

To understand the inequality which exists in Plettenberg Bay, you need to visit the town or at least Google it, the population has doubled from 30,000 to 60,000 in the last nine years, and there is a 28% unemployment rate. There are many millionaires, multi-millionaires with homes in the beautiful coastal village which boasts hundreds of mansions with sea views, swimming pools, perfect lawns and crisp white class. There are Range Rovers and the odd Ferrari and Maserati; there are private schools and upmarket restaurants, day spas, hotels and stores. The

Woolworths supermarket overflows with upturned collar blue golf shirts and salmon pink shorts, botox and fake tits and liver spots and the smell of lobster poached and sipped down with fine white wine and a forced laugh. There are homes with three levels and two permanent occupants; there are the golf club crowd with their investments and insatiable greed and cock contests, the gossiping diamond rings, shoes worn twice and old hair made young. I know, we lived among these wretched people for a horrible while, cheek by moist jowl. There are also a lot of normal, middle-class folk in Plett, doing what they can to get by, helping out where they can, being good members of the community and living as well as possible with the challenges they face in a shrinking economy. The upper classes populate the hills, the middle classes the valleys and the poor, the outskirts.

A short drive from the pristine beaches, you will enter Kwanokutula, a township which is crammed to the gills with people trying to get by, people who have travelled far in search of a better life after their governments and presidents for life squandered natural resources, so that the elite few could live in mansions and shop in Paris and dine in New York and bath in milk. Fuckers. There were people who had travelled from the rolling hills of the Eastern Cape, from Johannesburg and the Cape; there are many more people there than there are jobs and many jobs pay less than the cost of living. How can you eat lobster every day when the person who cleans up after you and spends as much time with you as your family, earns barely enough to feed her family while living in a shack after cleaning poodle shit off a priceless rug? Too far? I can see them coming for me now, their pastel jerseys billowing from their throats like a withered superheroes cape as they march white tennis shoe feet, a polo mallet aloft, a three-iron, a hyphenated double-barrelled surname. "Traitor. *Traitor!*" Andrew Beckwith-Hughes and Stuart Crowley-Thomas, their scented pink cheeks shaking with righteous anger, "Oh, we know how to deal with people like *you*! I pay my taxes!".

The truth is elusive in a riot, but there are many who accuse the protesters around the country of being nothing more than criminals and opportunists. If I was young, bitterly poor, uneducated and continually lied to I would also be angry, I would be bitter, and I would take any chance I could, as would you. The Plettenberg Bay "protesters" wanted the head of the ANC ward councillor Xola Mantyila, who had failed to deliver on promises made. Mr Mantyila and his family were forced to evacuate their home as the mob had promised to burn it to the ground and he was reportedly confused as to why the crowd had turned against him and suggested that other members of the ANC had instigated the riots to get rid of him. The community seized the opportunity, and the industrial area was ransacked as it stood outside the town, built close to a constant source of cheap labour and a national highway. There are few positives to this story, but the upside is that the masses had turned against the true source of their despair - the ANC. The tide may be turning as the poor people of this wealthy country may eventually get the message and vote for a party which is not the cancerous, criminal ANC. That is my biggest gripe with the majority of South Africans, why the hell do they keep on voting for these thieves year after year, decade after decade?

Let's not forget that the ANC is the party of Nelson Mandela, the party which did more than any other to fight the Apartheid system and the party which was blessed to have at its head, one of the greatest statesman in history, a man adored, respected and revered internationally, a hero to every South African who does not long for the days of segregation. The ANC is not Zanu PF (Zimbabwe); there are no dark men taking critics away in the middle of the night. I am free to criticise the party; the media is relatively free, our constitution is one of the most liberal on the planet, and elections are, mostly, free and fair. The ANC is not evil, merely incompetent and corrupt.

20

Where to now?

A week became a month became six months. We reunited with our friends and family and spent a few months at Hein's house in Groot Brak Rivier where we had arrived one sunny afternoon, the next day the Land Rover would not start, she had driven all the way from Europe and refused to take another step further. Between writing the Europe Overland book and writing various articles, we stripped the Land Rover cab area and found the Gremlin! The loom which runs from the engine to the ECU had chaffed and melted atop the gearbox, and there were eleven wires which were worn through! It was decided that not only did we need to repair the Landy, we should also use the opportunity to give her a bit of a makeover; after all, she deserved it.

Luisa set about repairing the wires while at the same time we repaired rusted floors and rebuilt the rear kitchen area and cupboards and built a roof rack extension (with Hein's help), repainted the Landy, installed a Quick Pitch shower cubicle (Hein is the North America dealer for Quick Pitch) and a Howling Moon awning and linked up the spare fuel, replaced wheel bearings, installed rock sliders, Luisa and Keelan redid the pop-top canvas, cleaned and repainted the chassis and worked on a hundred other little jobs. We were invited to the Defender Trophy, which was to tour Northern South Africa into Zimbabwe and Botswana and we worked hard to get the Land Rover running right in time to drive up to Johannesburg and join the convoy. Unfortunately, we only made it 300 km inland from the coast before we realised that we still had some serious electrical issues, the fuel was leaking out of the top of the tank and the gearbox was screwed. Defeated, we returned to Hein's house and worked on removing that huge chunk of geared metal, then sending it to Johannesburg and a new friend Sean's gearbox company. We also sent the transfer box to a company in George, where a kind Afrikaans man called Dirk fixed the leak which had plagued us since 2015, at no cost, other than spare parts. Sean gave us a reasonable rate and the gearbox was returned to us after being thrown in a blender by the courier company. Together Luisa, Keelan, Hein and I installed the new box and a heavy-duty clutch from Clutchfix, and we were very relieved that again we had a second and fourth gear. A bearing had seized within the box which had destroyed the fourth selector syncro gear.

Hein had returned with his family from the USA to their rental home shortly before we removed the gearbox and we were fortunate that a former colleague of mine, Paul, had offered us his holiday home in Knysna where we could stay until it came time for his families Christmas holiday. Hein lent us a small pick-up with which we could travel to and fro until the gearbox was installed and we settled into the lovely log cabin among the trees in Knysna to ponder the future. Paul had remained a good friend over the years. He had offered me a job back in 2003, and it was working with Paul, which had taught me many lessons about success which had made it possible for us to achieve our dreams and push the boundaries of what is possible. He was and still is a good friend and a mentor, a man with massive responsibilities and a humble, down to earth nature, the kind of guy who is equally comfortable negotiating a deal in a foreign boardroom or sailing a yacht across the Indian Ocean.
We had not seen each other in years, but we had stayed in touch and will stay in touch until we are both old men reminiscing about our youth.

It was while staying at Paul's cabin that we finally settled on the next leg of our journey. We were toying with the idea of shipping the Land Rover from South Africa to Turkey and then driving across to the Pacific coast of Russia. But, why ship when you can drive? We had already driven to Kilimanjaro from Cape Town in 2010, and we would love the opportunity to drive that route again and looks for signs of progress, to see the difference, if any, that a decade has brought. Well, if we drive to Kilimanjaro then why not, Kenya, then up to Egypt, then across to Turkey via the Middle East and then to the Stan's, Mongolia (in the footsteps of the Mongols) and then across to Vladivostok? And so, it was decided, we will now attempt to drive from Cape Town to Vladivostok, one of the longest possible overland routes!

Sure, there would be a few obstacles, but nothing we had not faced before and nothing which we would not find a solution to. And then

COVID 19 blindsided the planet and put everyone's plans on hold. At first, we were paranoid but had to be realistic; we had left Paul's house in December and returned in January when his family returned to Cape Town. We did not want to overstay our welcome and left to tour, self-isolating from early March and staying initially in a camp located in a sublime area called Natures Valley until our fears came to fruition and the President announced that the country would lockdown. I found a beautiful small cottage near a farm stall and secluded in a pristine forest, where we settled in to wait out the lockdown. At the time of writing, we are still waiting for the lockdown to end, trying to predict the future, there are bushbuck in the garden, birds in the trees and the pantry is fully stocked. If South Africa remains in lockdown, we will be stuck, eating into our resources. If the surrounding countries open their borders, we can move on but may find ourselves mired in another country as the unpredictable virus mutates for an African feast of souls. With winter approaching in Southern Africa, many more people may fall ill, and the millions of poverty-stricken South Africans locked in their communities might take to the streets in revolt against the lack of food and alcohol (the sale of which was banned along with tobacco). We, like so many others, are stuck between a rock and a hard place. Before I worried about crossing Sudan and the Sinai, or Syria, or Saudi Arabia, now we worry that our lifestyles may be in jeopardy, if not our lives. Reading this you will know then more than I know now and hopefully, this ends soon and ends well for all of us. But, what can we do but keep fighting towards the future? We Will Be Free.

And so, I spend my days writing and working and planning the journey to Vladivostok. The time in isolation has had a few positives. We are finally rested; the lasted decade has exhausted our souls. We have a new love and appreciation for the freedoms we once enjoyed, without a second thought. I am calmer; I am relaxed, I am creative and more than anything else, I am looking forward to the future. We had the year before endured, one of the most difficult and dangerous routes which the world has left to offer, we had to dig deep and commit all we had to the adventure, and we came out the other side stronger, more passionate about Africa and the planet as a whole and reminded by the miracles of love kindness and friendship.

Thank you for walking this path with us.

Explorers Club

Early in 2019, I was invited by the CEO of Kensington Tours (a company with whom we have a working relationship) to become a member of The Explorers Club. Jeff- an avid explorer who had driven a Defender around the world and a fellow African, was joined by our friend Ray Hyland (the Canada chapter chair of The Explorers Club) in supporting my application.

"The Explorers Club is an international multidisciplinary professional society dedicated to the advancement of field research and the ideal that it is vital to preserve the instinct to explore. Since its inception in 1904, the Club has served as a meeting point and unifying force for explorers and scientists worldwide. Our headquarters is located at 46 East 70th Street in New York City.

Founded in New York City in 1904, The Explorers Club promotes the scientific exploration of land, sea, air, and space by supporting research and education in the physical, natural and biological sciences. The Club's members have been responsible for an illustrious series of famous firsts: First to the North Pole, first to the South Pole, first to the summit of Mount Everest, first to the deepest point in the ocean, first to the surface of the moon—all accomplished by our members". - The Explorers Club website.

I was astounded by the invitation. It is no secret that I am not an academic and I was not sure how I could justify, to myself, that I (and my family by association) deserved to belong to a club which includes luminaries such Jane Goodall, Buzz Aldrin, Teddy Roosevelt, Neil Armstrong, Thor Heyerdahl, Sir Edmund Hilary and Roald Amundsen. The invitation itself is an endorsement of our adventures, a confirmation that our journey has been exceptional, our hard work and sacrifice has been noticed. You have read We Will Be Free, you know where it all started for me, could that kid from the wrong side of the tracks ever imagine that one day he would be invited to rub shoulders with the world's greatest explorers? But, then I asked myself, how many people have achieved what we have, how many people have given up a life of comfort and stability to travel the world by land, self-financed and raising children while studying cultures and exploring the planet, living a life completely driven and focused on exploration and discovery? No, we are not academic, but we explore with honesty and with humility and our books have reached many thousands of people who, I like to believe, have a greater understanding of the planet as seen through our eyes.

I accepted the nomination and submitted an application for membership at first through the African chapter but approved through the Western Europe chapter. I am still not convinced that I belong, but I am going to do my best to one day feel like a legitimate member, deserving of inclusion in such a prestigious group while never forgetting that I will always be that kid from the wrong side of the tracks who was lucky enough to find his calling in life by digging deep.

In popular culture, The Explorers Club provided aesthetic inspiration for parts of the movie, The Life Aquatic with Steve Zissou, his famous red knit "beanie" inspired by The Explorers Club red beanie (and a few scenes were shot in the clubhouse in New York). The irony is that for many years my social media avatar was Steve Zissou wearing that red cap. Perhaps I felt like I was trying to be someone that I was not, perhaps I was making fun of myself, setting off to see the world and promising everyone who would listen that we were going to see and do spectacular things, maybe save some lives and return victorious. The humour provided a soft landing for potential failure. Well, a few weeks ago I received my very own red knit cap in the post, along with an Explorers Club journal and an Explorers Club pin to wear on my lapel. Life can be bizarre.

About the Author

Graeme Bell was born in Johannesburg, reluctantly. He considers himself a revolutionary born in the wrong era into a body out of proportion. Together with a dangerous, redheaded wife (Luisa) and deserving, ungrateful children, (Keelan and Jessica), he has spent much of his adult life chasing momentous experiences and campfire smoke across most of the "important" continents. He will regale you with tales of self-sufficient overland travel to Kilimanjaro, a circumnavigation of South America, an eventful journey from Argentina to Alaska, Europe to Asia, across the entirety of coastal Western Africa, all in a trusty Land Rover. Graeme and the family are now encouraging their self-built Defender live-in camper (and permanent home since 2012) to find a way from Cape Town to Vladivostok.

Graeme is a Member of The Explorers Club, the author of five excellent books and an Overland Journal contributor since 2015.

Connect with us

Did you enjoy this book?   If so, help others enjoy it too.

Please recommend it to friends and leave a review if possible.
Stay up to date with the Bell Family by visiting our website

www.a2aexpedition.com

Alternatively, visit our Facebook page a2a.expedition

MORE TITLES BY GRAEME BELL
We Will Be Free
Travel The Planet Overland
Overlanding the Americas "La Lucha"
Europe Overland - Seeking the Unique